FAR FROM HUMDRUM

Clemens

Sir William Charles Crocker

WILLIAM CHARLES CROCKER

FAR FROM HUMDRUM

A Lawyer's Life

THE WORLD PUBLISHING COMPANY
New York and Cleveland

Published by The World Publishing Company
2231 West 110th Street, Cleveland, Ohio 44102

Originally published by Hutchinson of London

First World Printing—1970

© William Charles Crocker 1967

Library of Congress Catalog Card Number: 70-120092

WORLD PUBLISHING
TIMES MIRROR

Printed in Great Britain

To the Insurance Community

ACKNOWLEDGEMENTS

I owe a very deep debt of gratitude to Sir Arthur Bryant who purely out of friendship has found the time and patience to advise and encourage me in the writing of this book. Among my insurance clients whose kindness to me throughout the past half century has been immeasurable I specifically thank those who so willingly waived objection to my use of material which may be thought to have come to me in my professional capacity as their legal adviser.

And I sincerely thank my Secretary, Miss Florence G. Beckley, for her years of patient research and toil and the endless typing which have gone to this book's ultimate publication.

W.C.C.

CONTENTS

1	My Father	13
2	My Father's Office	19
3	Worship Street	23
4	Articles	27
5	The Histon Case	32
6	Houndsditch Murders and Sidney Street	35
7	Lloyd's	49
8	'Thirty-Three'	55
9	The Split	62
10	1907–17	64
11	1912—to Joining Up	76
12	In the Army	87
13	After World War One	89
14	Mainly Irish	94
15	Sidney Fox	102
16	The Fire Case (one)	113
17	The Fire Case (two)	127
18	The Fire Case (three)	143
19	The Fire Case (four)	153
20	The Fire Case (five)	165
21	The Fire Case (six)	171
22	Clarkson's Will	178
23	The Most Haunted House in Britain	199
24	Budget Leakage	206

25	World War Two	214
26	The Tin Fish	221
27	Diamonds in the Desert	229
28	Amy Johnson	235
29	Pioneering in Crime	239
30	*Marie Celeste*: an exercise in detection	245
31	Curtain	257
	Index	261

ILLUSTRATIONS

Frontispiece—Sir William Charles Crocker.

'Peter the Painter'   *facing page*   48

His Death Certificate, 1916   49

Scale model of Nos. 9, 10 and 11 Exchange Buildings,
Houndsditch. *From photographs provided by Sir
Arthur Young, C.M.G., C.V.O., Commissioner of
City of London Police, and reproduced with his
kind permission*   64

The backs of Nos. 11 and 10 Exchange Buildings   64

Rex *v.* Harris. The working documents   65

'Willesden Junction'   65

Amy Johnson   236

The sketch by R. G. Eves, M.A., of Sir William
Charles Crocker   236

The *Marie Celeste* as she was found, abandoned,
*from a wood engraving by Rudolph Ruzicka.
Reproduced by permission of the Atlantic Mutual
Insurance Co. U.S.A.*   237

One

___

K INGSLEY in *Westward Ho!* quotes the old Devonshire couplet:

> 'Crocker, Cruwys and Copplestone
> When the Conqueror came were at home.'

Domesday Book lists Crockers (Norse 'Kraka'—a tenant-in-chief) as land-holders in the time of Edward the Confessor. They are recorded at Crockers' Hele on Dartmoor in 1307, but circa 1394 the head of the family, Sir John Crocker, married an heiress and thereby acquired her mansion and estate of Lyneham at Yealmpton near Plymouth. She was Agnes Churchill and from her Uncle William Churchill descended the great Duke of Marlborough and Sir Winston Churchill. Lyneham housed eleven generations of Crockers before the male line failed in 1740. Some of the younger sons struck out for themselves and did well. Sir Hugh Crocker, at one time a wealthy ship-owner, was Mayor of Exeter in 1643. His eldest son Hugh was possibly the ancestor of the Crockers who settled in New England and in 1850 spread thence to California. The Irish Crockers, the Cornish Crockers and the Quaker Crockers are all seedlings from the same Lyneham tree.

Parish registers and other records take my own family back to a John Crocker who had a lease of Swingdon, Ashwater, Devon, in 1515. His descendant, my grandfather, old Tom Crocker, Exeter born, came to London like so many of his fellow West Countrymen (Brinsmead, Broadwood and Chappell among them) to make pianofortes. His son, Thomas Edward, my father, had no desire to follow that trade. He wished to earn his living in a job which would let him use the good brain which nature had given him. The law was his choice. He joined my grandfather's solicitor as office boy, that is to say in the post which offers the best chance for those who wish to learn our profession thoroughly. By his twenty-first birthday he was a managing clerk and main prop of the small firm for which he then worked. On the death of one of the two partners the survivor, amiable but weak, brought in a new one. My father, who could not claim the right to be, and had not been, consulted about this change, disliked it. He quietly left and for a year was employed at a greatly increased salary in a practice where the clients were world famous and the principals so pompous that a clerk presuming to greet one of them with a respectful 'Good morning' would have risked instant dismissal. Neither his improved income nor the simplicity of the tasks he was asked to perform reconciled him to this frigid impersonal atmosphere. He was utterly miserable.

His former chief tried hard to tempt him back with a promise of still higher pay and full articles of clerkship. The offer of articles he regarded as no more than a compliment. Stamp duties on the deed and admission fees would have cost him £120. Short of selling up the home he could not have found a fifth of that sum. My mother, a born fighter, saw the problem differently; to her it was a challenge to be faced and beaten. She called upon her great-uncle, a wealthy stockbroker, told her story, and asked for £100 loan. He refused it, not without some pretence of indignation. Then he handed to her £100 as a gift and said it would give him the greatest pleasure to see Tom a solicitor. Thus financed, my father left his hated situation and went back to his old firm to work happily and to qualify. Already a sound lawyer, he sailed through his examinations with ease and was admitted a solicitor in 1893. Following a further re-shuffle among his principals, he left with their blessings to set up for himself in two rooms over a chemist's shop on the south side of London Bridge near the Borough Police Court.

There never was a more gentle and selfless man than my father. It is said that only twice had he ever been seen out of temper; once, for a second, when he burned his fingers handling a too-hot china plate, and once, for a few moments, when a crazy client drew a pistol on him in a Moorfield's Saloon Bar. The client fled when my father rushed him. The onlookers, who knew my father well, were dumbfounded, not because of the gun-play (which was melodramatic nonsense) but because T.E.C. had momentarily shown anger. Anyone who had seriously offered him violence might well have been 'found drowned'. For my father's early clients were genial Borough toughs who adored him. Among them life was cheap. They would readily resort to a length of lead pipe to enforce their point of view and the river Thames was conveniently near. Parts of the Borough at that period were unsafe for strangers. Policemen usually patrolled them by twos or threes. My father, in his silk hat and grey frock-coat, was received by the natives with happy grins as a welcome guest. Such a reception, he claimed, was exclusive to him and to hospital nurses in uniform.

His advocacy in court was conversational; he relied chiefly upon a reasoned but destructive criticism of the adverse evidence and made no attempt to stir magisterial emotions. The 'Beaks' liked and trusted him; his wild and wilful clients did a little better than they deserved and, when occasion arose, would send along such of their friends as needed legal help. So my father's business grew.

Soon work was flowing in from a dozen or more trade unions. Their officials were a fine lot of men, bent only on seeing that their members had a square deal. There was little 'ideology' and no self-seeking in their make-up. They were quite content to accept as pay what they would have earned at their own crafts. With the trade unions came The London United Male and Female Costermongers and Street Sellers

Benefit and Protection Society. My father regarded costers as the salt of the earth and took pride in their reference to him as 'our Mouth'.

The costers of the nineties were a tribe apart. They used a fluent aitchless speech enriched with 'rhyming slang'. They traded, from their barrows, in the simplest possible way, giving good value for money, unhampered by overheads (or tax inspectors) and getting more fun out of life than most of their shop-bound competitors. One of my earliest recollections of Father in pursuit of his calling is of seeing half a dozen costers sitting sedately on the low wall which carried the iron railings in front of our North Kensington house. They wore tight-fitting, bell-bottomed trousers and long whipcord jackets of a pattern immortalised by Phil May and now donned only by gamekeepers. To mark the serious nature of their visit, and much as one would assume a grey topper for Ascot, each had a black silk 'choker' knotted round his throat. Beneath the peak of each cap one saw the characteristic coster 'bang', the wet flat 'lick' of hair, perhaps three inches wide, sticking to the forehead, brought down to the level of the eyebrow and ending in an upward curl. A coster, in this traditional set-up, was then as unmistakably a coster as a bishop, in his shovel hat, was a bishop.

The Society's secretary, having consulted my father on the matter in hand, went out to this informal railings committee and reported that Mr. Crocker required £10 on account of costs. ('It's about the bees; the Mouth can do with ten Jimmy O's'—the bees being rhyming slang for 'bees and honey', i.e. money, and a sovereign being a 'Jimmy O'Goblin'.) I watched these men dive into their 'paying pockets' for their respective equal contributions and did not realise that this was the costers' primitive but efficient accounting system in action. The coster began his day's trading with, say, £10 in the right-hand trouser pocket and nothing in the left. Cash received from the customers went only into that empty pocket. Payments out were made only from the other one. Last thing at night, when the naphtha flares had been doused

and the 'moke' had been stabled, the coster and his 'donna'
counted out the 'bees' and struck a balance between the one
pocket and the other. Sometimes these balances were written
down in a penny notebook. More often, reliance was placed
upon that phenomenal memory which is so often found
among bright people whose formal schooling has been little
or none.

The work coming directly or indirectly from the trade
unions and societies was very varied. Folk in those days of
plenty and light taxation amassed modest fortunes. They
bought small houses, sometimes they met with personal injuries or with matrimonial trouble or got genially drunk and
landed in the dock, they made last testaments and inevitably
they died. All was grist to the lawyer's mill.

I cannot recall a time when I was too young to listen with
fascination to my father's stories of his work. They were told
with calculated understatement and in a style slyly designed
to fan my enthusiasm for a lawyer's life and to shock my
deeply religious mother.

'Had a new murder defence in today,' he would observe,
casually getting on with his meal.

'Tom,' my dear mother would gasp, 'how terrible—wh-
what happened?'

'Got tight and cut his baby's head off—could I have
another glass of ale, my dear?'

While Mother, horror-stricken, poured the ale, Father,
with no change of expression, would give me a wink and
make me feel that I was already an initiate.

During my school holidays Father let me spend as long as
I liked in his office, which had moved from Borough High
Street to the more respectable neighbourhood of Finsbury
Pavement, E.C. His Common Law clerk, Ernest Albert
Harris from Walsall, who used double negatives ('No, the
Guv'nor's not come back not yet'), and did his own typing,
would at times favour me with some account of the cases on
which he was engaged.

On one such vacation visit I attended an interview between

B

Harris and an Italian named Bresci who wished to sue the British Museum for assault and battery. He had been ejected from the Reading Room for spitting in books which preached political views contrary to his own. Harris advised him there was no case. When the Italian muttered that in his own happy country the dispute would have been settled presto with the knife, Harris said, 'We don't use no knives, not here.'

This episode, which made a deep impression upon me (I was then about fifteen), had two sequels. The first was that shortly after his abortive call Bresci sent Harris a news clipping reporting a Grimsby brawl in which fish-gutting knives had come into play. A note, to which the clipping was pinned, read: 'Thus parrots talk!!!' The envelope was addressed: 'To the clerk at the writing machine.'

The second sequel was that this obviously unbalanced malcontent went back to his homeland and assassinated Umberto I, King of Italy. I had met my first murderer.

Two

MY FATHER'S OFFICE

WHEN I bid a glad good-bye to my schooldays I went straight into my father's City practice. As late as the 1880's most solicitors' offices were still rather like those illustrated by Cruikshank. The tall, sloping desks, at which clerks sat on high stools, were only slowly giving way to flat tables and knee-hole desks with ten or more drawers in which odds and ends could be hidden and forgotten. If any two pieces of furniture in a room matched this was purely accidental. The principal's desk was often that abomination —the 'American Roll Top'. The drawing down of its flexible shutter at night, over the heaped papers within, created the illusion, until next morning, that the day's work had been done and tidied away. Current files were bundled, tied with red tape and, if not strewn over the desks or about the floor, were lodged in alphabetically marked pigeon-holes. Letters were written in copying ink. Before despatch they were placed between the damp tissue-paper leaves of a press-copy letter book. This was then screwed down hard in a strong metal letter press. The letter thus treated sometimes did and sometimes did not leave a legible copy of itself on the tissue page.

Work crept along amidst dirt and disorder, but all law clerks worthy of the name could write a beautiful engrossing hand. The engrosser's flat ivory stick which, gripped in the left fingers, travelled along half an inch below the pen nib to hold the paper firmly down, is now a byegone, a collector's piece. Filing methods had advanced little since Tudor days;

but memories were good. Each clerk and partner knew in which particular hole or corner he had put his own bundles and could make a shrewd guess where someone else's mislaid bundles might have strayed. That a lawyer should live in a dusty muddle had become a tradition. His patrons would have thought it odd, perhaps suspicious and certainly out of character, if he had conducted himself otherwise.

This was the tradition in which my father had grown up. But he was tolerant of new ideas and when my brother Archibald joined him, and I followed, he was already ripe for conversion. We two brothers had so few tastes in common that we naturally got along together well. I have never wished to be anything but a lawyer. Brother Archibald, given a second chance, would, I imagine, have chosen some branch of engineering. With great delicacy and sureness of touch he could work in any material like a trained craftsman and better than some. Technical books, over all the fields which interested him, he read with avidity and remembered with ease. Reading law he found harder going because his heart, I judge, was not in it. In the two years' start he had of me he bent towards the dreary but profitable side of our business—real estate, probate and trusts. My preference was for litigation, which meant the joy of investigation and gentlemanly warfare. But first with teenage impudence I was out to revolutionise Father's office. Archibald, with his orderly mind, was at one with me in this. If any trace of discipline had prevailed in that office, if my father had not been so delightfully easy-going, our project would have been still-born.

I could not hope to draw true portraits of the few men on his staff. Although honest, loyal and fairly efficient, they worked only when they felt in the mood. They naturally feared that the advent of the Guv'nor's two sons would disrupt the peace in which the practice until then had jogged along so comfortably. And they were right. But the only one who put up any real resistance was my early friend Ernest Albert Harris, 'the clerk at the writing machine'. Harris kept such office hours as suited him. He would stroll in to start his day at 11.30 a.m. and with intervals for liquid refreshment might leave at 8.30 p.m. I had not then learned that the ability to make wittily offensive remarks is a social handicap. When he grunted that he could never get to a theatre because he was kept so late in the City I suggested he might take in a matinée on his way down. Shafts of this kind—and how smart I thought them—goaded Harris into active rebellion.

The crisis came when I asked him to issue a writ for me. He flatly refused and told me to go issue it myself. I blush to recall that I doubled my fists and said he could either issue the writ or take a thrashing. He issued the writ. I suspect that this bellicose episode greatly amused him. He probably drank many pints with his cronies on the strength of it. I tell the story here to high-light the odd *milieu* in which my brother and I set out upon our campaign of reform.

We began with the 'Battle of the Bundles'. When a case reached its end in Father's office it was said to be 'dead'. When our pigeon-holes became overfull room for new cases was found by turning out all the 'dead' ones. These were then made up into brown paper parcels which, for lack of storage space, were heaped under a large table in the clerk's office. If perhaps years later one needed to consult the 'dead' file of *Snooks v. Snooks* one searched among the hundreds in the heap for a likely looking 'S' bundle (the year of bundling endorsed upon it was a fair but uncertain guide). In the process, and even without it (for brown paper grows weak with age), some of the bundles from time to time burst and spilled their contents. These seldom regained their proper homes. A thick deposit of dust lay over all. It would have been hard to find a less efficient storage system. But there was no space in which to house a better one.

And then my brother's practical eye lit upon the solution. Our rooms, though small, were lofty. He hung a range of racks along the length of the walls of our corridor waiting-

hall flush with the ceiling and just high enough to miss the
heads of callers. We ordered a stout book cut with a sub-
divided alphabetical thumb index. We bought thousands of
drapers' gummed labels numbered consecutively. Then night
after night, with the help of a willing office boy, we broke
open the old bundles, tagged and numbered the separate
case papers, entered them in the index under the name of
the client and put them to rest in their new home up in the
Gods. We inhaled dust by the pound. We looked like chim-
ney-sweeps. But after months of this toil we had the joy of
seeing an empty floor. Its oil-cloth was caked with the grime
of years. We crowned our labours by scrubbing it with
boiling soapy water. Having in this way made the 'dead'
files available, we brought in, unopposed, flat filing and steel
cabinets for the 'live' ones. The press-copy letter books, however, died hard. My father was so attached to them that we
had to use unfilial trickery to defeat him. Of each letter that
went out (and now they were all typed) he agreed that a
carbon copy should be kept with our working papers. But a
press copy was also to be taken in accordance with the usual
routine. And so, for a twelve-month, the two methods,
ancient and modern, ran side by side. Whenever Father
asked for a sight of the letter book during that period he was
told it was in use and was shown instead the flat file with the
carbon letter on it. He never suspected the deceit of which
he was the victim. At the year's end we confessed. He laughed
and said, 'Have it your own way.' Letter books, then and
there, passed into the limbo of byegones to join the quill pen,
the wafer, the pounce-box and other relics of antiquity.

Three

WORSHIP STREET

WE NUMBERED amongst our acquaintances a solicitor
named Abbott. Abbott was a gifted orator and by dint
of his skill in that field he built up so good a practice at
Worship Street Police Court that he was able to live a life
of solid comfort. And he dressed the part. He drove himself
to and from his office in a dog-cart drawn by a couple of
spanking horses running tandem. On his hands were lavender
kid gloves. His button-hole was never without a flower. When
he died suddenly and prematurely he left scarcely enough to
pay his debts. This was very hard on his only son, Barker
Robert Abbott, who was under articles to him but had never
tried, or been asked, to take the law seriously. Affectionate,
weak and spoiled, when the world crashed about his ears his
too long and idle apprenticeship proved fatal to any chance
he had ever had of qualifying as a solicitor. Year after year
he clung to the steadily shrinking Worship Street practice,
acting as clerk to a series of solicitor-advocates who tried in
vain to restore its former success. Poor shabby-genteel
Barker Robert, frock-coated, top-hatted, honest, amiable,
self-deprecating and slightly bibulous, must have mourned
his happy, carefree past with ever-increasing sadness as he
saw his new masters, one after the other, fail and quit. And
what a joyful day it was for him when my own father
bought that so-called practice—for £25. This sum purchased
some dilapidated furniture, one good bookcase, a *Nuttall's
Dictionary*, a large bible and the services of Barker
Robert Abbott himself, who, by long custom, was deemed

to pass with the fixtures. Business at once began to flourish.

Save in cases of cruelty to children and violence to women a policeman rarely prosecutes vindictively. His approach to the 'customer' is impersonal, and sporting, with as little malice in it as one expects in a tackle at rugby. The wife of a C.I.D. superintendent once told me of the meals her husband called upon her to provide for ex-convicts. She complained only that she never had so much as ten minutes' warning when a guest would be arriving. It did not strike her as in the least unusual that a man should celebrate his release from prison by sitting at table with the detective who had put him there. With this sort of spirit prevailing it was in the natural order of things that the 'customers' in trouble at Worship Street should ask the court officials to give them the name of a good lawyer, and get that of Abbott's boss. Barker Robert himself luxuriated in this reborn success. He grew to adore my father and would flutter around him with polite little half-finished hints. 'The magistrate is sitting at eleven this morning, sir!—only a couple of remands, sir, nothing in them—a few drunks, sir—and then our brothel, sir—say in fifteen minutes, sir—Do you think we might— ha—perhaps?—hmm [cough]?' And then with a bow he would fade away. He drank slightly more than was good for him, partly from inclination but mainly because it was then the pernicious habit for men to adjourn to public houses for the discussion of their affairs. A pickpocket, escaping gaol through the efforts of his solicitor, would have felt offended had the managing clerk refused to take a glass in celebration, perhaps in company with the court gaoler.

The Worship Street practice indulged my father's sympathy for the underdog. It faced him with problems which he had to solve instantly while 'on his feet'; it offered relief from the dull if profitable conveyancing chores which were swelling our head office income and it was (to use his own teasingly unprofessional term) 'a good cash trade'.

My father liked policemen and they liked him. The fact

that he was so often engaged in thwarting their efforts to
convict somebody did not in the least lessen their mutual
esteem. He was always an honoured guest at the Annual
Dinner of the Central Criminal Court Brotherhood. This was
a genial function which habitually attracted a distinguished
gathering from Bench and Bar. Abbott liked to go because
it fostered goodwill in the practice. One year, alas, he wished
to cry off. His clothes, he feared, were too threadbare for such
an occasion. This was only too true. But my father said,
'Nonsense, Abbott, I shall change into my tails and white
tie at the office. At the same time you can change into my
morning clothes as I take them off. We are about the same
size. What's wrong with that?' Abbott raised his hands in
horror! 'I really could not presume, sir—always too kind,
sir—the very thought—a really generous proposal, sir—so
like you, sir—but—hmm', and so on. Under strong per-
suasion Abbott assumed T.E.C.'s striped trousers and frock-
coat and joined the dinner party. What with the excellent
food, the bright lights, the soft music and the champagne,
this was indeed like old times! Abbott tilted back his chair
and dreamily slipped his fingers into his vest pockets. With
a puzzled look he extracted from them my father's gold
pencil and matchbox. The sight of these jerked him back to
reality. Hurriedly replacing the articles, he turned to Father
in deep distress, whispering, 'Most terribly sorry, sir—please
forgive me, sir—absent-minded—going through your pockets
like that—unforgivable . . . !'

Poor old Abbott was pathetic without being in the least
given to self-pity. He tried so hard to do the right thing and
so seldom succeeded. Upon the bible taken over with the
Worship Street practice thousands of oaths had been sworn.
After years of not too tender usage it had torn adrift from
its binding. In a fit of reforming zeal Abbott set about
effecting repairs. He covered the old boards with black
American cloth, and, borrowing a glue pot from one of our
cabinet-trade clients, stuck the body of the volume back into
its spine. And then to give this union every chance of per-

manence he swathed the book tightly round and round in yards of stout string. The bible remained in that swaddled state for several months. But what my father did not know was that Abbott, after his work upon the Scriptures, his zeal unspent, had looked about him for further conquests. There was plenty of American cloth left and enough boiling glue to restore a small library. He had accordingly fallen upon the office dictionary and given it the full treatment, string and all. The bible and the dictionary were of equal size and externally were now identical twins. One volume stayed with Abbott and one with Father. When the windings of string were at long last cut, my father's fervent hope was that according to the law of averages at least 50 per cent of the deponents to whom he had administered as Commissioner for Oaths had missed the *Nuttall*.

Worship Street gave Father good fees and much fun. He was loath to quit, although his promising future lay in the Finsbury Pavement office. But in due course Worship Street Police Court was shut down and its jurisdiction moved to Old Street, inconveniently far from the City. Father then decided very sadly to write *finis* to the Worship Street practice. The rooms were vacated and I was told to sell the contents. The only piece of furniture which had any air of superiority was the bookcase. An antique dealer whom I approached looked at it disparagingly, said the removal of the ugly pediment (a late addition) would cost a lot for expert restoration and the most he could offer would be £50. Hiding my astonishment, I accepted sixty. Since the price paid for the good will of the 'practice', with all the furniture thrown in, had been only £25, we all felt that the Worship Street chapter of our history closed on a happy note.

Four

WHILE Worship Street fed my taste for crime and detection, our City office was where I cut my professional teeth. There under articles we were not so much taught as left to learn our way about the many jobs a lawyer has to do. It was like struggling to keep afloat in deep water, always knowing that Father, a competent instructor, was on hand with a life-line. I have since appreciated in the light of my own experience how wide his was and how lucky my brother and I were in having such a teacher. To qualify as a solicitor I would be required to show some skill in the art of conveying real property. I therefore dabbled in the simpler conveyancing matters which came our way. But most of my time was given to claims arising from road collisions and factory accidents causing personal injuries to our trade-union members. Among the first of my discoveries was that scarcely ever can a witness, even an educated one, tell a story from beginning to end in chronological order. I found it best to let the story run its course uninterrupted and then, having recast it mentally, to dictate it in proper form to a secretary while the witness listened in to offer corrections or approval. Training of this kind was of lasting value, for getting facts down on paper is required in almost every kind of work which a solicitor touches. And we touched almost everything on the Common Law side: defamation, habeas corpus, breach of promise, broken limbs and broken marriages.

There are books which describe when and what steps have

to be, or may be, taken in the conduct of proceedings in every imaginable court. There are many which provide model forms for almost any of the transactions which a lawyer may be asked to conduct. There are, moreover, mountains of statutes and reported cases, the raw material which spawns enormous quantities of other books. These enshrine the views of learned men dedicated to the particular aspect of the law on which they write. Those views are respectfully quoted in court as conclusive until, maybe, the House of Lords, moving with the times, happens to pronounce them misconceived. Skilfully produced handbooks show would-be solicitors a path through this ever-thickening jungle of jurisprudence and promise them a 'pass' in the Intermediate and Final Law Examinations.

Mr. Wackford Squeers, of Dotheboys Hall, taught spelling by a method which, though wrongly used, was perhaps right in principle. 'W-I-N-D-E-R' (he said). 'Winder—go out and clean the winder.' The vital difference between reading about a thing and doing the thing oneself is that one easily forgets the former but the latter sticks. My brother and I, hard-working members of Father's staff, learned much of our law by handling actual cases in which that law arose. We also crammed conscientiously and began to hope that one of these days we might bluff the examiners and secure admission to the Roll. Meanwhile, for exercise, and to save the rail fare, I cycled between my North Kensington home and the City six days a week. It had not yet occurred to anyone that for five days only should we labour and on the other two we should rest.

For relaxation I read. There was some merit in buying a coveted *Everyman* for a shilling when this meant cutting lunch down to coffee and a bun. The evenings which I should have devoted to study were too often devoted to Tree's productions of Shakespeare at His Majesty's Theatre in company with my future wife, Madeline. Brother Archibald, a much steadier student than I, turned to handicraft for relief from swotting. He mocked my scholarly pursuits. When under my prodding he condescended to inspect the fine murals in the Royal Exchange his only comment was that in the King John picture the press with which the seal is being affixed to Magna Carta has a left-hand thread. I was at that time helping Father with a very heavy commercial action in which thousands of documents had to be copied. To help me in this, and my other work, Father took on a small girl straight from school. With her hair in pigtails Florence G. Beckley looked so extremely young that it seemed desirable to have her parents' assent to her proposed employment. Mrs. Beckley, duly consulted upon the subject, said, 'Florence has a mind of her own, I never interfere!' Mrs. Beckley was a good judge. She would, I believe, not have interfered had she foreseen that Florence was entering upon a service with me which would endure for sixty years.

Law students in those days came to London from all over England and Wales to the most famous of all law coaches, Gibson & Weldon. Their services were not open to me. I was not merely an articled clerk but a solicitor's clerk doing a full-time job. I could not have done it with half my days spent in a Chancery Lane classroom. I had to compromise. There was an elderly and slightly Bohemian crammer, one Montague, whose heart-breaking occupation was coaching Gibson & Weldon's 'lame ducks', men who had failed their examinations over and over again. By his own especial magic he would finally drive most of them through. He agreed to give me individual tuition at short notice whenever I could spare an hour to go to him.

Unfortunately, I have a freakish memory. It hoards any number of useless facts but jibs at retaining the uninteresting things which really matter. I could remember neither Montague's mnemonics, of which he had scores, nor their points. The remedy was to invent mnemonics of my own. The toil of doing this left in my mind, long after I had forgotten the mnemonic, the information I wished to have by heart. The only example which survives to me is 'Dirty Drive' identifying the Highway Act, 1835—important then, but now as dead as a fly in amber. I found it impossible to learn by rote 'The History of English Law' narrated so tediously in the Preface to the *Commentaries*. Warned by Montague that at least one question would spring from this dry material I tortured the whole of it into rhymed couplets. My brother knew every line of this pantomime verse and found it most useful. As for me, the labour of turning Stephen's heavy prose into jingling lines with plausibly musical endings had done the trick. My odd mind was now stocked (for the necessary few months) with everything the examiners might wish to know on this subject. All that remains to me of the masterpiece itself is the triumphant:

'Hail then the Statute blessed for evermore
12 Charles the Second, Chapter 24.'

I faintly recall that these words related to some sensational revolution which was effected under the Merry Monarch concerning land tenure and that 'Free Socage' had something to do with it.

Archibald and I worked apart both in our studies and on office matters. He shunned litigation just as I shunned conveyancing. During the whole period of our articles I can bring to mind only one suit in which we collaborated. He helped me then only because the case gave him a chance which rarely comes to a solicitor, the chance to use his manual skill.

Our clients, Siegenbergs Furnishing Stores, occupied a modern shop in King's Cross Road with a basement showroom. They found that sewage was percolating into that showroom from the ancient non-basement eating house next door. For the purposes of the action which I launched for Seigenbergs I needed a model of the respective premises. My brother made it, most expertly, like a doll's house. The shop-fronts and the floors, when removed, showed on the one hand our clients' basement in snowy plaster of Paris with trenches opened up in the floor to reveal the drains in scarlet lacquer. On the other hand one saw the soil (formerly a front garden) above which the defendants' shop stood. The 'soil' was crinkled brown paper stiffened with layers of glue. Through this ran the alleged defective drains. They were painted in a loathsome shade of greeny yellow. One could almost smell the sewer gas leaking from their joints. The defendants said that these drains, in spite of their age, were the last word in hermetical sealing. They pleaded that the liquid which admittedly invaded the plaintiffs' premises was explained by the periodical flooding of the Fleet Ditch on its way from Hampstead Ponds to the Thames at Blackfriars. It stank because the floodwater had to pass through the battleground where, in the neighbourhood of what is now King's Cross District Station, Boadicea with her Iceni had defeated the Romans. The judge raised his eyebrows and took judicial notice of the fact that Boadicea had been dead a long time. We produced a large pickle jar full of the defendants' contaminated earth and invited the judge to sniff it. He indignantly refused. Our miniature scarlet drain-pipes, flaunting their purity in contrast with the disgusting squalor of the defendants' gamboge equipment, were irresistible. Boadicea and the Romans were honourably acquitted. There was judgment for the plaintiffs, with a direction that the model-maker should be well rewarded. He was.

Five

THE HISTON CASE

WHEN I was twenty my father on the eve of his annual holiday handed over to me the defence of a wretched youth, Herbert Alexander, who was charged with the murder of his girl friend Honora Histon. Alexander, aged twenty-one, a carman, had been walking out with Honora Histon, a factory worker, almost nightly for four years. There was an unexplained two-day break in this routine from a Wednesday to a Saturday. On the Saturday evening they saw one another on opposite sides of the street where the girl lived. Alexander beckoned and Honora went across to him. After a few minutes' seemingly calm talk he drove a knife into her. The blade by an unhappy chance slipped between her ribs and punctured the pulmonary artery. She bled to death in the hansom cab in which Alexander and a bystander took her to hospital. The young man was stricken with grief.

Murder is the unlawful killing of a human being with malice aforethought. Nearly always on a murder charge there is some evidence from which the element of malice may reasonably be deduced. In this instance there was no background evidence of that kind at all. The lovers had met on the Wednesday evening, two days before the tragedy, by the door of Honora's own house and in full view of another couple, Honora's sister Julia and the lad who was courting Julia. Neither pair could have used high words unheard by the other; they were only four yards apart. It was even more unlikely that people of their class, if they had bickered at all, would have done so in politely modulated tones. I visited the scene of this meeting not in the least expecting to find anything of use to the defence. In so doing I learned a valuable lesson: that whenever the problem in hand touches the layout of a locality, or of a building or the relationship of buildings one to another, it is wise to see the site for one-self. The striking feature of Alexander's Wednesday meeting with Honora Histon was that it had taken place in a narrow tunnel-like alley, a public right-of-way, which ran between Honora's house and the next. This was no ordinary little tunnel. Its roof was smoothly rounded. Its painted walls were polished as the result of the casual rubbings they had received over the years from the arms of countless passers-by. It was a sounding-board. A word softly spoken where Honora had stood with Alexander would have been easily heard twelve feet away on the spot where Julia admitted she had stood with her own boy friend, and had heard nothing. It was therefore manifest that Alexander and Honora had not quarrelled on that occasion as some thought they must have done. The motive for which one looks in a case of murder was not to be found.

How then explain the killing? In search of that explana-tion I went alone to question our client in the gaol to which he had been remanded.

I found him to be of a low mentality and poor physique but not in the least a vicious type. My stomach turned when I saw that his trousers were stiff with the dried blood of his victim.

His story, dragged from him a few words at a time, was straightforward. It was, he said, his habit in idle moments to pull out his pocket knife and whittle anything that lay to hand, maybe a lump of wood, a pencil or his carter's whip. He had been cutting a pattern on his pencil when Honora crossed the road to him on the Saturday evening. They had no row. When she threw her arms round his neck he 'shoved 'er orf like'. He forgot he still had the knife in his hand. He never had any wish to hurt her. It was a pure accident. He had no idea what happened to the knife afterwards. An in-

C

credible yarn? Not in the least. I do not doubt that he spoke the plain truth. Early man carried on his courting with a bludgeon. At the time of which I am writing it was not unusual to see a coster mooching along with his girl a yard or so from his side. There would be some word-play, then the swain would maul and buffet the lady, who would protest with delighted squeals. It was 'mating behaviour' such as birds display; maybe it betrayed no more than the instinct of the male to assert himself.

I find it easy to believe that when Alexander hit out with the knife in his hand it was love and not malice that impelled him.

The task of converting an Old Bailey jury and Lord Alverstone, Lord Chief Justice, to that view was given to Walter Stewart, a man whose chief asset as a barrister was a command of sincere and moving eloquence.

His handling of the defence was masterly and his closing speech, ending almost in a whisper, 'Judge not that ye be not judged', had the jury in tears.

The Lord Chief Justice, convinced by Stewart's plea, summed up most mercifully and on the jury's verdict of manslaughter sentenced the prisoner to six months' hard labour.

I cite this case as an unbeatable record in legal annals not because it was the first murder defence which I managed free from parental direction but for the reason that this was the first murder trial to be heard in the newly built Old Bailey.

Six

HOUNDSDITCH MURDERS AND
SIDNEY STREET

THE Czar of all the Russias had a chef named Vassileva. The chef had a daughter named Nina. Throughout her childhood she heard from her father stories of the St. Petersburg Palace in which he worked; stories of the splendour in which the Imperial circle lived, of the endless spending, of unbelievable and shameless waste. And in contrast she saw around her the misery of the lower classes, under-privileged, under-fed, downtrodden and savagely punished if they too openly showed discontent with their lot and displeasure with their rulers.

In such a *milieu* it goes without saying that Nina was ideal fuel for the secret fires of revolution which were then being so skilfully fanned by Lenin, Trotsky, Stalin and their fellows.

At a very early age she joined one or more of the Russian underground associations whose titles were polite but whose aims were anarchy. She became so active (and probably so clumsy) that in 1906, when she was only nineteen, she was forced to flee. She came to England. Poor tragic Nicholas would have enjoyed his *borscht* the less had he known that the father of a fair anarchist on the run had a hand in the brewing of it.

At that period our ever-hospitable country welcomed streams of not-too-desirable aliens claiming asylum as victims of political and racial oppression. Most of them eked out wretched existences here barely above starvation level.

Nina settled down to work in the East End of London as

a factory girl. Her average weekly wage was 25s. She paid 4s. per week for the rent of a single room and 3d. extra for cleaning. But she did not lack intellectual companionship. Whitechapel boasted many clubs where members, some cautiously clinging to anonymity or false names, could exchange the time of day, extreme political views or, if required, sticks of dynamite. Nina favoured the Anarchist Club in Jubilee Street. There to her heart's content she could talk and dream about the millennium which was to follow the downfall of the Romanoffs. There she had the solace of hearing proscribed Russian songs sung to the balalaika's nostalgic rhythm. There she met two girls of her own age, race and political views, Luba Milstein and Sara Trassjonski.

Luba was the mistress of one 'Fritz', sharing with him a mean first-floor-back at 59 Grove Street, E. The equally mean first-floor-front was occupied by his friend, a distinguished-looking man whose true surname has never emerged. This mysterious person was an occasional visitor to the Jubilee and similar East End foreign clubs where curiosity about the identity of other visitors was discouraged. His Christian name was Peter. He was known to his friends and was to become known to the world and to history as 'Peter the Painter'. Sara Trassjonski adored him.

Nina Vassileva fell passionately in love with another member of the circle, a ruthess young anarchist of whose many aliases 'Gardstein' may be chosen as the most notorious and the easiest to pronounce. He was a soulless anti-social thug of abnormal mentality and dominating personality. In body he was an Adonis; in mind he was Vice itself.

In the autumn of 1910 a group of Russians under the leadership of this blackguard planned to break into the jeweller's shop of one Harris at 119 Houndsditch. Their intention was to cut their way into those premises through the rear wall. With that idea in mind they rented Nos. 9 and 11 Exchange Buildings, quarters which, squalid though they were, had this one supreme advantage, they backed on to the shop they meant to plunder. Indeed the backs of No. 9 Exchange Buildings and No. 119 Houndsditch were separated only by a strip of so-called yard, a mere passage just wide enough to house and give access to an outside water closet. An occupant of that convenience would sit with the left elbow touching the wall of No. 9 and the right touching the wall of No. 119.

Gardstein and Nina took up their residence at No. 11, sharing a bed on which the only cover was a tablecloth. There Nina was seen by the neighbours for three weeks on end living quite openly with her 'husband'. If she made any attempt at disguise it was that she dyed her flaxen hair a darker colour. During those three weeks innocent-looking tools such as any odd-job labourer or mechanic might use were stored in No. 9. More sinister equipment (for example an oxygen cylinder) was hidden from view in a wooden case.

One may well think that neither Nina nor her girl friends Milstein and Trassjonski (if they visited her at No. 11) saw anything to suggest that a shopbreaking enterprise was afoot. It seems improbable that Gardstein and his gang, all trained plotters, would without need have let them into so dangerous a secret.

To travel from the back of No. 11, where Nina lived, to the back of No. 9, whence the attack was to be launched, meant something like mountaineering. The intervening hovel, No. 10, presented a stiff obstacle. A high cistern was poised on top of No. 10's W.C. and so close to the wall that only a thin man could hope to squeeze through the gap. While it is likely that the men faced this awkward climb rather than draw suspicion upon No. 9 by using the front door, it is unlikely that any woman could have managed it, hampered as she would have been by the full-length skirts of that era. It may be doubted whether Gardstein let anyone except his male aids visit No. 9 at all.

On the night of December 16th, 1910, the criminals (exactly how many will never be known) set to work. They went at it so incautiously that their attack on the W.C. wall (the rear wall of 119 Houndsditch) was heard by a neighbour and the police were warned.

P.C. Piper knocked at the door of No. 11. It was opened suspiciously by Gardstein. Piper had been told that a woman was living there and, not liking Gardstein's looks, asked diplomatically: 'Is the missus in?' 'She's gone out,' was the reply, and Piper, feigning indifference, went off to fetch reinforcements.

In England the police of their own choice go unarmed. They perform their duties with good humour and impartiality. The British professional criminal, caught in the act, rarely puts up a fight. With comparable good humour he takes his occasional arrest as an occupational hazard and is not so foolish as to add years to his sentence by carrying a gun or by a futile show of violence. On this tragic night half a dozen City of London policemen, with the matter-of-fact heroism of their service, went all unwittingly to face a band of cold-blooded aliens at war with society, armed to the teeth and pitiless, looking upon all policemen as natural enemies.

Sergeants Bentley and Bryant and P.C. Martin went up to No. 11 Exchange Buildings. Sergeant Bentley knocked on the door and Gardstein opened it. Bentley asked, one imagines, what work was going on? Gardstein, leaving the door ajar, withdrew perhaps on the pretence of fetching someone who could speak better English. Other officers, Choate, Tucker, Woodhams and Strongman, waiting a few paces off, saw Bentley push the door wide open, slip into the passage and step just inside the room on his right. Almost instantly from a door at the back of that room and from someone halfway up the stairs came a stream of bullets. Bentley fell mortally wounded and in falling threw Martin to the ground, Bryant, dangerously hit, fell beside them. Gardstein, with two or more companions, rushed from the premises shooting to kill. Tucker and Woodhams were mowed down. Strongman led the dying Tucker away under a hail of fire. Choate, with many bullets in his body, a dying man, nevertheless found the strength to clasp Gardstein in his arms. One of the desperadoes, trying to finish Choate off, shot Gardstein through the back.

These events from the firing of the first cartridge to the last occupied no more than fifteen or twenty seconds.

Gardstein in the role of a drunk was dragged or carried by his two main aides, 'Fritz' and 'Josef', for over a mile to 'Fritz's' home at 59 Grove Street. There Gardstein was put in the room of 'Peter the Painter'. Only once had they aroused curiosity. Almost at the beginning of their flight they ran into a man on his way home from work. Pistols were thrust in his face and he was given the stern command, 'Don't follow'. A moment or two later he saw the bodies of the victims in the Exchange Buildings cul-de-sac and ran to the neighbouring Bishopsgate Police Station to give the alarm.

No one could wonder if this startling encounter in almost total darkness left on his mind but a blurred image of what had happened. He thought he had seen close behind the Gardstein trio a woman whose face was hidden by a fur collar blown up by the high wind of that rough winter's night. Later he purported to identify that woman as Nina Vassileva. Two Corporation roadmen on late duty saw the escaping party and said it was made up of men only, four of them.

Sara Trassjonski and Luba Milstein said they had been that evening to a cinematograph show ('the living pictures'), returning to 59 Grove Street a little before Gardstein, carried upstairs by 'Fritz' and his accomplice, was placed on 'Peter the Painter's' bed. These two men then decamped after putting an automatic Dreise pistol under the pillow so that Gardstein might fight on if the police should arrive. The two girls were left alone with the dying man. In the small hours they fetched Dr. Scanlan (acting as *locum-tenens* for an established Whitechapel practitioner). Of all the odd experiences that comes a doctor's way it would be hard to beat that which faced Dr. Scanlan on this occasion. Diagnosis was simple: the cause of the trouble, a bullet which had entered the patient's back, was protruding from the chest. Nor did prognosis offer any difficulty: it was fairly obvious that this victim of 'an accident' was nearing his end. Having done what he could, the doctor left with a promise to return later. When he called back after breakfast he found Gardstein already dead. If 'Fritz' had chosen that moment to enquire at 59 Grove Street about his injured friend it may well be thought that a bullet would have put the doctor beyond the possibility of telling the dangerous tale upon which he had chanced.

In spite of his peril, Scanlan telephoned the police. They arrived at Gardstein's bedside while the corpse was yet warm and in time to catch Sara Trassjonski and Luba Milstein in the act of burning papers and photographs. The girls were arrested. Although suspicion attached to many people, it was believed at first that the chief culprits were Gardstein, 'Fritz', 'Peter the Painter' and a woman (later identified as Nina Vassileva).

Five days after the murders the police published a '£50 Reward' poster. It carried a photograph of Gardstein (taken after death) and descriptions of the other three. But as enquiries proceeded the focus fell upon 'Fritz' and 'Josef' of the unknown surname and whose 'Josef' itself may well have been one of many aliases.

Normally these two could have laid up with any one of fifty fellow expatriates. But to shelter murderers such as these would be to risk not only prison but, what was feared even more, deportation. 'Fritz' and 'Josef' with a price on their heads were hard put to it from day to day to find a lair of any sort.

On January 2nd, 1911, they planted themselves in the first-floor front room of 100 Sidney Street, the unwanted guests of a very unwilling landlady, Mrs. Betty Gershon. They were armed to the teeth and if escape should be cut off they would have only two choices: to die fighting or to die on the scaffold. It was presumed that they would prefer to die fighting.

The police learned about the Sidney Street hide-out overnight and before 7.30 the following morning everyone except 'Fritz' and 'Josef' had been quietly evacuated from the house.

A frontal attack on the bedroom door was out of the question. The stairs leading to it were very narrow; they could be mounted only in single file. 'Fritz' and 'Josef', certainly awake by now, shooting from cover, could have wiped out the police one by one.

It was decided to use the street-door knocker. This summons was ignored. Nor did the quarry try to leave the house from the back where officers were in waiting.

Then a handful of gravel was thrown up at the first-floor window. The answer was a burst of pistol fire and Sergeant Leeson across the street fell with a ball through his lungs.

And so began the 'Battle of Sidney Street', in which a brace of Russian anarchists, not without warm sympathy from many other undesirable aliens in the East End, shot it out with the forces of law and order.

The then Home Secretary, Mr. Winston Churchill, took characteristic steps to bring this affair to a close as soon as possible. He authorised the use of troops and wisely chose shot-guns as better than rifles for the special needs of the situation. His personal attendance to watch the fight was later criticised in the Commons—but not by the police; they and the soldiers welcomed his presence.

Fire was maintained by the besieged and the besiegers spasmodically for nearly five hours. At about midday, however, silence fell and 100 Sidney Street was seen to be alight. It burned to the ground. From the charred ruins the hardly recognisable remains of what had been two men were recovered. One of them, 'Josef', had been shot through the head from behind the right ear. The other, 'Fritz', had died of suffocation.

The coroner's jury found that 'Josef' had been lawfully killed by an unknown soldier. I have always thought it more likely that 'Fritz', knowing the game was up, shot 'Josef,' intending thereafter to shoot himself, but, the house being ablaze, was asphyxiated before he could do so.

In any event the manner of their ends is of no importance. They were dead.

At first one of the corpses was thought to be that of 'Peter the Painter'. But the police felt sure he was still at large. A month after the 'Battle' they issued a '£500 Reward' poster with two alleged photographs of this man ('Peter Piatkow alias Schtern'), showing him as a good-looking type, with imperial and moustache and a distinctly French appearance. In this same poster were included descriptions of two other wanted persons: 'Joe Levi' (who was never caught) and an 'unknown' woman.

The police were already aware that this 'unknown' was Nina Vassileva. They had been shadowing her night and day since December 18th in the hope that she would lead them to 'The Painter'. Moreover, she knew that her every step was watched; that sooner or later arrest must come. Perhaps it was with relief that she found herself at last on February 15th, 1911, in the dock at the Guildhall, along with Sara Trassjonski, Luba Milstein and four other accused. Some of the latter were charged with complicity in the actual murders. The girls were charged with being accessories after the fact thereto, i.e. with 'comforting a felon' (Gardstein).

My father, always ready to drop a lucrative but dull conveyancing job for an ill-paid but exciting police-court case, accepted instructions to defend Sara and Nina. He was a first-rate judge of what was and what was not evidence. He thought there was none on which any of the girls could be properly convicted and he doubted whether there was enough to convict any of the men.

The case against Trassjonski and Milstein collapsed at the Guildhall and they were freed. They had certainly 'comforted' the dying Gardstein, but there was no proof they knew he was a murderer. In the absence of such knowledge the giving of succour was not criminal; it was praiseworthy. The Bench also released two of the male accused. The charge that the remaining three men had been parties to murder was built on nothing more than this: they were associates of the gang and two of them were said to have been seen with Gardstein just after the shootings supporting him on the walk at the end of which he died. The evidence of identification in this respect was so shaky that when the case reached the Old Bailey the judge directed the jury to reject it. The trial thereupon proceeded against these three and Nina solely on the indictment that they had conspired to break and enter the jeweller's shop with intent to commit a felony.

The evidence concerning Nina was that she had lied to her landlady about going to nurse a sick friend for a few weeks when in truth she was going to live with Gardstein in No. 11 Exchange Buildings, premises which (with No. 9) had been rented solely for the purposes of the intended raid. She had disguised herself by dying her hair. She had been 'seen' on the fatal night with the stricken Gardstein. On returning to her old apartment she had destroyed documents and had cried over Gardstein's picture in the Press, wishing that she had been killed instead of him, and had in her general behaviour shown marked signs of a fearful and guilty conscience.

One surely needs no legal training to perceive that this so-called evidence, if accepted in its entirety, showed only that Nina was Gardstein's mistress. It was without weight to show that she was aware of his criminal intentions or activities.

Had she made a clean breast of all she knew she might have escaped much of the ordeal which lay ahead of her. But Nina, obsessed by thoughts of the scant justice meted out in Russia to the politically disgruntled, and ignorant of the fairness with which all prisoners are tried in England, was resolved to deny everything alleged against her, whether it was false and damaging or harmlessly true. In taking this stand she lost the sympathy of the court. The judge summed up dead against her. She alone of the four accused was found 'Guilty' and she received a sentence of two years' imprisonment. It was, however, easy for us to persuade the Court of Criminal Appeal that this was all wrong. They agreed there was no evidence to support the conviction. It was quashed and Nina was discharged.

I remember seeing her sitting patiently in our waiting-room. She wore a voluminous dark skirt down to her ankles, a severe cotton blouse, a stiff stand-up linen collar and a flat straw 'boater'. There was nothing of the revolutionary about her, nothing to hint at the strain through which she had passed. She looked for all the world like a rather timid nursery governess seeking a post.

Sara Trassjonski was similarly a prim and demure type but highly strung. Her experiences were more than she could bear. Her brain gave way and she went into a lunatic asylum.

My father, whose fingers were all thumbs, greatly admired dexterity in others. Years after the 'Battle of Sidney Street' he stood at the window of a West End tobacconist watching a girl making cigarettes. The pile of cigarettes grew rapidly as the girl's hands moved with lightning speed. Suddenly the hands stopped. My father, in surprise, looked up at the girl's face. She was giving him a pleased smile of recognition. It was Nina Vassileva.

One name alone of all those which were coupled with the Houndsditch murders and of the Sidney Street sequel survives in public memory, that of 'Peter the Painter'.

He has become a legend and it is of interest to ask how and why. A serious student of history plodding through the evidence given before the coroner, before the magistrate and at the Old Bailey, will look in vain for anything to support the once widely held and even advertised belief that 'Peter' was an accomplice of the murderers. The trial judge thought it fair to proclaim in open court that of such evidence there was none. Nor does the record reveal anything to link 'Peter' with the renting or use of the gang's headquarters in Exchange Buildings, nor with the attempt on the jeweller's shop. One witness, and one only, a fourteen-year-old boy, spoke of having seen 'Peter the Painter' at No. 11; but this witness had to correct himself regarding parts of what he had sworn at the Guildhall and, doubtless honestly mistaken, was not called at the subsequent trial. There was in my opinion no acceptable evidence either that 'Peter' had been at his Grove Street room so late as December 16th, 1910 (the day of the crime), and none that he had been near the scene of that crime when it was committed. The case against him rested solely upon the assumption that his association with 'Fritz' and the Jubilee Club circle was a guilty one. There was never a tittle of evidence that he favoured criminal methods, violent or otherwise, that he handled firearms or was leading a dishonest life. If he had been found and charged with the others he would, like those others, I am sure have been acquitted.

Nearly thirty years after these happenings and after my father's death business took me to New York. There I met again Casimir Pilenas, a brilliant linguist who, in 1910, had been an official police-court interpreter in London. He was constantly used by the police in that capacity and had inter- preted for them when some of the Houndsditch suspects were questioned and detained. He gave evidence in this respect at the Old Bailey when Nina Vassileva and the others stood their trial.

It was clear to me that Casimir Pilenas, using his invalu- able contacts in the East End, had managed to piece to- gether, if not the whole of the Houndsditch story, at least the story to which credence was given by Whitechapel's practising anarchists and by their pale pink fellow travellers. And it was this:

The revolutionary party in Moscow needed money. Gardstein was sent here to steal it. During 1910 he had been back and forth between England and Russia several times. Moscow provided him with revolutionary literature, with works on the manufacture of explosives, with an armoury of weapons, and, last but not least, with money ($£31$ $12s.$ was telegraphed to him a month before the murders). He spied out the land and thought it would be easy to get at Mr. Harris's safe by cutting through the rear wall of the jeweller's premises from No. 9 Exchange Buildings. No. 9 was not at first available, so he took No. 11, which was. Finally he got both, but no one seems to know who the 'Joe Levi' was who did the hiring for him. Perhaps he was a dupe, for Gardstein trusted nobody outside the team who were to do the actual job and even then he disclosed no more than he must. The team, with perhaps one exception, was made up of anarchists whose motives were the same as his, to get money not for themselves but for the Cause. The possible exception was brought in of necessity; the team knew nothing about safe-breaking and had to enlist a crook expert in such matters. They let him think it was to be a routine crime carried out in the usual way, with, at worst, penal servitude as the penalty of getting caught in the act. Not for all the diamonds in South Africa would he have joined the venture had he known that his foreign pals were revolutionary fanatics, carrying loaded pistols and ready to use them. Those fanatics were Gardstein, 'Fritz', 'Josef' and 'Marx'. After the fifteen seconds' massacre the terrified safe-breaker fled and was seen no more in England. 'Fritz', 'Josef' and 'Marx' carried the dying Gardstein away. Maybe 'Fritz' or 'Josef' was disguised as a female (a woman's wig was found in the Sidney Street ruins). Although it was a wild windy night when few people were about and the streets and alleys, lit only by low gas jets, were almost pitch dark, Gardstein was a problem to his bearers. They thought of leaving him on the pavement near Commercial Road, 'but he screamed', so they made their way with him the mile or more to the nearest available refuge, 'Fritz's' rooms at 59 Grove Street.

Instead of putting him on 'Fritz's' bed, and so drawing suspicion upon that villain, they used the room of 'Peter the Painter', which was unoccupied, and there, as we know, Gardstein of the black heart and many aliases contrived to cheat the gallows.

'Peter the Painter', said Casimir Pilenas, although a

'political' refugee and correctly described as a political malcontent, was a man of culture and opposed to any form of
crime. The alliterative and romantic sobriquet 'Peter the
Painter', which appealed so strongly to the public's love of
drama, was derived from the unromantic circumstance that
Peter's modest avocation in England was that of a house
painter and decorator. Although he welcomed the chance to
speak his own tongue with compatriots and in common with
other law-abiding citizens occasionally visited the Jubilee
Street Club for that purpose, he did not seek the confidence
of the extremists there. Those extremists barely trusted one
another. They would certainly not have trusted a mere
acquaintance like 'Peter'. After the murders suspicion fell
upon 'Peter' for two reasons: firstly, because it was in his
room that the assassin Gardstein died, and, secondly, because 'Peter' disappeared, as the police were led to believe,
on the night of the crime. In fact, 'Peter', knowing nothing
of the criminal conspiracy, had weeks before made up his
mind to try his fortune in America and was already at sea
on his way there before the morning of that day had dawned.

Reminded by me that several witnesses had sworn 'Peter
the Painter' was seen in the East End on the very night of
the murders, Casimir replied: 'The evidence on that point
(and I heard the whole of it) was for the most part that of
people who were themselves suspects. Remember that "Peter"
was a newcomer to London; he had arrived from Paris only
a couple of months before. Except for Sara Trassjonski, the
sempstress, he had no close friends in London, only acquaintances. Even "Fritz" was merely a chance contact who found
him a room to live in. In that colony, many of whose members hid their real identities under false names, it was an
easy matter (intimates apart) for one person to be confused
with another. There was no doubt some such genuine confusion regarding the identity of "Peter the Painter". The
police themselves were deceived and raised a hue and cry for
the wrong Peter. And those who sought anonymity for
themselves might be expected to do all they could to en-

courage the police to follow that false scent. Nobody had reason to follow the evidence more keenly than I,' continued Casimir, 'and I say that even if the whole of it had been taken at its full face value it did not implicate Peter in the slightest degree.'

'What became of him?' I asked.

'He died out here in 1916.'

'Had you ever met him?'

'Naturally! He was my brother.'

'Peter the Painter'

This is to Certify that the following is a true and correct copy of a certificate of death filed in the Division of Vital Statistics, Pennsylvania Department of Health, as directed by Act 66 of the General Assembly, 1953, P. L. 304.

FEB 7 - 1961
(Date)

Nº 122949

C. L. Wilbar Jr.
(Secretary of Health)

COMMONWEALTH OF PENNSYLVANIA
DEPARTMENT OF HEALTH
DIVISION OF VITAL STATISTICS
CERTIFICATE OF DEATH

Primary Dist No. 1

File No. 89757-16
Registered No. 18771

1. PLACE OF DEATH
   a. County Phila.
   b. City (If outside corporate limits, write RURAL and give township) c. Length of Stay (in this place) Philadelphia —
   d. Full Name of (if not in hospital or institution, give street address or location) Hospital or Institution 151 N. 9th St.

2. USUAL RESIDENCE (Where deceased lived. If institution: residence before admission)
   a. State — b. County —
   c. City (If outside corporate limits, write RURAL and give township) or Borough —
   d. Street Address (If rural, give location) —

3. NAME OF DECEASED (Type or Print) a. (First) Peter b. (Middle) — (Last) Pilenas

4. DATE OF DEATH (Month) 8 (Day) 17 (Year) 1916

5. SEX M 6. COLOR or RACE W 7. MARRIED, NEVER MARRIED, WIDOWED, DIVORCED (Specify) Single

8. DATE OF BIRTH —

9. AGE (in yrs. last birthday) 40 If Under 1 Yr. Months | Days If Under 24 Hrs. Hours | Min.

10a. USUAL OCCUPATION (Give kind of work done during most of working life, even if retired) Salesman 10b. KIND OF BUSINESS OR INDUSTRY —

11. BIRTHPLACE (also give State or foreign country) Russia

12. CITIZEN OF WHAT COUNTRY? —

13. FATHER'S NAME Unknown

14. MOTHER'S MAIDEN NAME Unknown

15. WAS DECEASED EVER IN U.S. ARMED FORCES? (Yes, no or unknown) — 16. SOCIAL SECURITY NO. —

17. INFORMANT'S OWN SIGNATURE C. Pilenas ADDRESS New York

18. CAUSE OF DEATH Enter only one cause per line for (a), (b), and (c)

MEDICAL CERTIFICATION

INTERVAL between ONSET and DEATH

I. DISEASE OR CONDITION DIRECTLY LEADING TO DEATH* (a) Found dead. —

ANTECEDENT CAUSES

*This does not mean the mode of dying, such as heart failure, asthenia, etc. It means the disease, injury, or complication which caused death.

Morbid conditions, if any, giving rise to the above cause (a) making the underlying cause last. DUE TO (b) Body too badly decomposed —
DUE TO (c) to determine the exact —

II. OTHER SIGNIFICANT CONDITIONS Conditions contributing to the death but not related to the disease or condition causing death. Cause of death.

19a. DATE OF OPERATION — 19b. MAJOR FINDINGS OF OPERATION — 20. AUTOPSY? Yes ☐ No ☐

21a. ACCIDENT SUICIDE HOMICIDE (Specify) — 21b. PLACE OF INJURY (e.g., in or about home, farm, factory, street, office bldg., etc.) — 21c. (CITY, TOWN AND TOWNSHIP) (COUNTY) (STATE)

21d. TIME OF INJURY (Month) (Day) (Year) Hour m.E.S.T. 21e. INJURY OCCURRED While at Work ☐ Not While at Work ☐ 21f. HOW DID INJURY OCCUR? —

22. I hereby certify that a view (an inquest) was held upon the body of the above named deceased on Aug. 19 19 16. and that death occurred at .... m., E.S.T., from the causes and on the date stated above.

23a. SIGNATURE OF CORONER Wm R. Knight, Jr. / McVay 23b. ADDRESS — 23c. DATE SIGNED —

24a. BURIAL, CREMATION, REMOVAL (Specify) 24b. DATE 8-19-16 24c. NAME OF CEMETERY OR CREMATORY Northwood Cem. 24d. LOCATION (Town, township and county) (State)

DATE REC'D by LOCAL REG. Aug. 19, 1916 REGISTRAR'S SIGNATURE E. C. Lawrence Dep.

25. SIGNATURE OF FUNERAL DIRECTOR J. G. Maurer, 2009 N. Broad ADDRESS —

Certificate of Death, 1916 (see p. 48)

Seven

LLOYD'S

O NE of the first pacts known to ocean traders was that whereby the loss of a ship should not fall solely upon its owners but should be spread over all those concerned in its venture. To effect such a pact, and thus to be 'assured' that no marine peril might ruin him, a seventeenth-century sea-captain, before setting sail, would visit some rendezvous commonly used by those wishing to transact maritime business. There he would find men who, for a cash 'premium' and by 'underwriting' their names at the foot of a contract— the 'policy'—would agree to bear 'each for himself alone' a fixed percentage of any loss which might arise during the voyage. Before its destruction during the Great Fire of London, in 1666, the Royal Exchange was the most popular of these rendezvous. Thereafter came the vogue of the coffee houses—forerunners of our present clubs. Customers met there not so much to eat and drink as to gossip. The true newspaper had not yet emerged and information passed mostly by word of mouth. In 1685 one Edward Lloyd who, as a head waiter, had already learned the role of 'coffee man', opened a place of his own in Tower Street under the name of 'Lloyd's Coffee House'. This was especially patronised by gentlemen with maritime interests. To promote this connection Lloyd, whose originality and enterprise were outstanding, hired runners to haunt the docks, note ships' comings and goings, glean news from the sailors and bring all this intelligence back, post-haste, to the 'Coffee Room'. There it was read aloud by a boy called, for some long-for-

D

gotten reason, 'the Kidney'. Five years later Lloyd moved to larger premises in Lombard Street. Thence, in 1696 he began to issue printed sheets reporting ships' movements and matters of a purely marine flavour. These grew into the modern seafaring and insurance daily *Lloyd's List*, which apart from *The London Gazette* is the oldest London news-paper with an unbroken history. Edward Lloyd died in 1712. Those who succeeded him continued to foster insurance and the supply of shipping news. By the middle of the eighteenth century 'Lloyd's', still laid out as a coffee house, with each table partitioned off, breast high, in its own 'box', was recognised as the centre of the marine insurance world.

Underwriting, first transacted by merchants as a mere sideline, had become a distinct profession followed by men with no other. These, 'the regulars', were to some extent united, paying two guineas yearly for 'membership'. When they ('the regulars') were invaded by a class of customers whose underwriting of gambling policies threatened 'Lloyd's' good name, they migrated in 1769 to 'The New Lloyd's Coffee House'. This was opened for them in Pope's Head Alley by Thomas Fielding, one of their waiters. The old house languished and soon died. The 'regulars' had closed their ranks. In 1771 seventy-nine of them put up £100 each to procure a permanent building. A committee (on which the current committee of Lloyd's is modelled) chose the upper floor of the Royal Exchange. There, dropping the words 'Coffee House' from their title, Lloyd's dwelt for a century and a half. In 1871 an Act of Parliament gave them corporate status with wide powers of self-government.

Nowadays Lloyd's market is and has long since been made up of two classes of 'regulars'. On one hand are the admitted brokers who alone have the right to 'place' insur-ance in the Underwriting 'Room'. On the other are the underwriters who receive the premiums and are liable for the claims. They are grouped into 'syndicates' and one of their number, as their paid agent, conducts the actual business of underwriting for the rest. In Lloyd's language he is 'the underwriter'. Any other member of the syndicate is known as a 'name'.

The steps which bring a Lloyd's policy into being faintly echo the free and easy days of the coffee house. The risk to be insured is noted with telegraphic brevity upon a 'slip'. This is a piece of paper three and a half inches wide and eight and a half inches deep, headed at the narrow top by the style of the brokers' firm. It is 'shown' by the broker to the underwriter of his choice and is the basis of discussion between them. Once agreement has been reached and the underwriter has added the initials and figures used to identify the 'syndicate or syndicates' for which he writes the bargain is legally complete and enforceable. Where the amount at stake is small the first underwriter approached will probably take 100 per cent of it. If it is large he will 'lead' the slip by taking a percentage or 'line'. If he is well regarded in the Room as a specialist in that field other underwriters will more readily 'follow' and, in turn, accept 'lines' until the whole 100 per cent has been 'placed'. From this completed slip, nowadays, the broker prepares the policy and lodges it with Lloyd's policy-signing office to be checked and subscribed on behalf of the underwriters concerned. Where very big sums are involved (for example on a multi-million fire cover) the slip may be underwritten by practically every Lloyd's non-marine syndicate and many insurance companies. For Lloyd's brokers are not, as is often thought, tied to Lloyd's; they continually use coverage from insurance markets all over the world. And they effect, in that market, for companies and underwriters alike those 'hedging' insurance contracts which perpetuate the guiding principle of insurance which is that the risks accepted must be so widely spread as to hurt no one too deeply when losses occur.

Within living memory non-marine risks were regarded as a slightly improper intrusion upon Lloyd's true function, the insurance of risks germane to perils of the sea. But history shows that with all its feeling for the past Lloyd's has always marched with the times. Non-marine premiums flow into the

Room from every quarter of the globe at the rate of millions sterling annually. Such a vast turnover compels the use of modern business mechanisation. This overlays but will never extinguish Lloyd's cherished links with the past. Messages for brokers working in the Room are telewritten to the rostrum, whence the flesh-and-blood 'Crier' broadcasts them by microphone. Some of the reports posted on the news-board may be in typewriting ten times as large as life. But the daily shipping casualties are still entered in a heavy ledger laconically in a big round hand, with a quill pen. Lloyd's may move from coffee house to Royal Exchange, from Royal Exchange to a palace in Leadenhall Street and thence to a building, even more palatial, across the road. But in none of these changes would the Room admit under-writing tables other than those in 'boxes' closely resembling their seventeenth-century coffee-house prototypes. Nor could the Members' Restaurant ever be anything but 'The Captains' Room', remembering the days when captains met at Lloyd's to smoke a social clay, to take a drink of some-thing nautical and to chat about shipping in general and insurance in particular. And whatever may befall one may be sure the Lloyd's liveried staff, who have not the remotest duty to serve food, will always be known as 'waiters' and in their flowing scarlet robes and their gold-braided top-hats will remind the microphones and the telewriters and all the other slick gadgets of modernity that the roots of Lloyd's are deep in the mercantile spirit of Restoration days. I look back to the circumstances of my introduction to this great and august concern in 1907 and still find them, like so many of my later adventures, improbable. Carefree and twenty-one I was riding a tram along the Thames Embankment in the noon sunshine. The river boats were busy. But it was the road traffic that held my especial interest, for the years I had already spent in my father's law practice had gone largely in handling claims arising from street accidents. So it was with a professional eye that I saw a horse drawing a hansom cab shy at the tram's gong and swerve into an automobile.

At that time, 1907, motor cars and those in charge of them were held at worst in hatred or at best in contempt. I knew that none of the bystanders would speak up for the blameless chauffeur. With this in mind I alighted, gave him my card and said he might refer his master to me for the truth about the smash. This gesture wasted most of my ticket (a half-penny one). But I was content to walk the rest of the way happy in having struck a blow for justice.

Some weeks later a shy little man, A. J. Whitcombe of Lloyd's, called upon me at the office. He insured the car which the hansom had damaged. Did I agree the cabby was solely to blame? I certainly did. 'Well,' said he, 'the cabby through his insurance company denies all liability. Can I force him to foot the repair bill?'

I spoke of the heavy pro-horse bias in any Motor *v.* Horse contest; advised him to steer clear of litigation in so small a case as this (there was only £14 10s. at stake) and to aim rather at a fifty-fifty compromise. 'See if you can do it for me,' he said, gave me his file and hurried off. Was it conceivable that this modest little chap had it in his power to employ a youngster like me to act for such a world-famous insurance body as I vaguely knew Lloyd's to be? But who was I to question his authority?

Now the cabby's insurers boasted as claims manager one Grant, a dour Scot. He and I had met before. There was no tougher nut to be found in the insurance circles of those days.

I called upon him and played the only card I felt would offer any hope of success. I told him of the tram ride and its sequel. I reminded him that we should, no doubt, be against one another many times in the future. I swore that if on this new claim he would bear half the car's repair bill he might regard his outlay not only as settling a claim but as buying my goodwill for life.

Our talk developed on the lines of a Barrie play. Grant made a show of turning me down flat, appeared to weaken a little, mumbled something about 'liking to see a young man trying to get on', finally yielded ('agen ma better judgment') and no doubt laughed quietly as I left with his cheque (including fee, 10s. 6d.) in my pocket. He never had cause to regret the bargain.

To be able to send A. J. Whitcombe a 50 per cent recovery within twenty-four hours of his visit was a minor triumph. Soon I was handling his claims by the score. And, best of all, I had made my Lloyd's début. Never was a ha'penny better invested.

Eight

'THIRTY-THREE'

MY LLOYD'S work, while heavy, did not grow fast enough to swamp me. This respite—a blessing in disguise, since it left me a few hours for study—was due to the low rating which underwriters put upon the acumen of my sponsor, A. J. Whitcombe. He was a lovable eccentric from a family of parsons and doctors. What freak of fate dumped this modest, kindly but unbusinesslike little gentleman upon the insurance world I never learned. Anyone less like a pioneer it would have been difficult to imagine. And yet, to him must go the credit for producing (in December 1901) the 'A.J.W' policy under which motor insurance was for the first time subscribed at Lloyd's. No specimen of it is now to be found. It had been drafted with the help of Whitcombe's friend, Franklin Adams, a marine underwriter, and is said to have smacked of the sea, treating the insured vehicle as a ship navigating on dry land. A flat £4 was charged for the accidental-damage section and another £4 covered third-party risks up to £500. At least those were the prices paid by cautious motorists. Folk (known in 1902 as 'road hogs') who tore wildly about the country at breakneck speed (twenty-five miles per hour was not impossible) had to pay through the nose. The happy-go-lucky affairs of the A.J.W. Syndicate were conducted over a baker's shop in Pancras Lane in an atmosphere redolent of new bread. If a claim arose in unforeseen circumstances which left any doubt whether underwriters should pay or not, they paid. Before my advent A.J.W., with little or no experience to guide him, had enjoyed handling his claims unaided on a basis of trial and error. He was especially proud of one 'total loss' where neither he nor the assured had the least idea whether or not it came within the policy wording. A.J.W.'s solution was to toss the assured double or quits and win. It was known that the surveyor who went all over the British Isles for him assessing damage done in motor accidents was a Newbury blacksmith. This was judged an odd choice. It happened to be a very good one. The blacksmith had been in motoring from the start and had opened in his native town one of those motor-repair shops which attracted to them the French name 'garage'. The fact that he was brawny, bearded, cloth-capped and countryfied did not detract from his competence. Most underwriters thought that I, a young unknown, noticed only because I had witnessed a street accident, was another odd choice and to be avoided. I bear them no grudge; they long since made ample amends.

One of the Lloyd's men who might, I thought, have helped me was William Charles Campbell. Joining the important Lloyd's firm of Hartley Cooper & Co. as office boy, he had climbed rapidly and was now their claims manager. As such he continually passed cases to solicitors in a way to make one's mouth water. Extremely intelligent and methodical, he had adopted a set of rules to guide him through life. One of them was that he would never invite reproach by using his business influence to favour a relative. This ban, alas, applied to me because I had married his first cousin. His judgment was so highly regarded at Lloyd's that my prac-tice there would have shot ahead had it become known that Hartley Cooper were instructing me in their non-marine work. The chance of cousin Willie ever relaxing his 'no nepotism' principle seemed very remote. In my heart I felt this went too far; that for reasons which I could not precisely define I had a right to his support. Before long, and not without a touch of comedy, his hand was forced.

Out of a flat calm a sudden gust of wind tore loose an awning on the private yacht of one of Hartley Cooper's best clients. The loose canvas slapped the backside of a bending sailor hard enough to topple him over the rail on to the deck below. Misunderstandings arose regarding the compensation due to the injured man. His employer on a Saturday morning demanded Hartley Cooper's immediate attention. Telephoning the offices of three solicitors whom he habitually used, Campbell learned they were all away (probably golfing). In desperation he rang me. Would I go at once to the Isle of Wight to smooth out the difficulty? By making the journey, solving the problem (an easy one) and leaving the assured happy I won cousin Willie's gratitude. His sense of fair play led him to add me permanently to his list of legal advisers.

Francis Robert Bussell was a man so fine and rare that one could not bring him to life in cold print. His most marked trait was a modesty deep beyond belief. Shy, retiring, affectionate, full of quiet fun, doing much good by stealth and selfless as a saint, he thought his great success at Lloyd's was due solely to luck. All that he owed to luck was that with an underwriter for father he was destined to follow suit. His flair and his pluck made up the rest. If he had been told the truth, that he was Lloyd's most popular member, he would have wondered with discomfort how anyone could talk such drivel. Campbell and he had grown up side by side at Hartley Cooper's. By 1908, when I first met F.R.B., he was already underwriting for the Hartley Cooper names in their non-marine syndicate. As one of my earliest clients he was of great help to me both directly and indirectly. He was known as a good man to follow and my stock rose when I was seen at work for his box.

The 1908 Lloyd's non-marine market was a mere baby. He and I were among those who nursed it through its teething troubles. Enterprising brokers, exploring new insurance fields, would try out novel risks on F.R.B., who was always ready to quote a rate. Once I asked him how he knew what premium to charge on risks of a type which had never been written before? He replied that he would let me into a trade secret: 'When I have no idea what the rate should be I charge 7½ per cent—it always works out right!' This was a typical F.R.B. leg-pull. In fact, he relied upon his instructed judgment and feel for insurance problems. Taking chances as he did in hazardous ventures he made a good profit for his names steadily year by year. A witty American has said Lloyd's thrive by maintaining that 'the client is always wrong'. The client fears he may break his leg or lose his house by fire or his gems by theft or libel someone or have twins or, being a surgeon, take out the wrong kidney, or, being an architect, build on the wrong site or, being an inn-keeper, poison a guest or burn his baggage. The underwriters bet him he is wrong and meet the loss if, after all, he turns out to be right. It was common practice for the Bussell box to stipulate when accepting an unusual risk that I should draft the policy wording. Often F.R.B. over a morning coffee would chat with me about such risks and ask, tongue in cheek, if I thought he should write them? But I was not cut out to be an underwriter. To my mind the perils were always giants and the premiums pigmies. Gradually I found my true role. It was not to say that I thought a risk a good or a bad one. If I knew of any facts relevant to it I gave them. If any law was involved I said what I judged it to be. And I tried to express in three lines of terse prose a contract of insurance for which a Chancery draughtsman would have taken a quire of foolscap. 'The intention is what counts,' said F.R.B., 'drop the legal jargon.' As between gentlemen this was sound doc-trine. An honest little jeweller with an F.R.B. policy had his stock looted from his lock-up shop while he was at home for lunch. The policy was worded to cover 'Burglary' and nothing more. Since burglary is the crime of breaking and entering a *dwelling house* in the *night-time* with intent to commit a felony I advised that underwriters were not liable. My letter, full of good law, came back to me endorsed: 'I have rarely read such nonsense. Pay. F.R.B.' He later chided me for not knowing that 'burglary' must be read in the light of intention, i.e. sensibly. I took many a fall like this before

I learned to say, 'On a strict view of the facts the position is so and so but underwriters may perhaps feel, etc.' Even this approach with its hint of morality might bring a jesting reply, i.e. 'How much will it cost me to be honest?' I was not seldom the victim of this gentle teasing. The bait might be a toothsome legal morsel. 'I am asked' (said F.R.B.) 'to pay a total loss of £50,000 if a plaintiff loses a law-suit. His mother had a fear she might be buried alive. He was to inherit her fortune only if he had her throat cut after death. He did not carry out that direction but nevertheless asks the judge to construe the old girl's will in his favour. What about it?' 'Impossible,' said I, 'the Probate Court does not remake wills—it is concerned only to give effect to the wishes of the deceased'—and much more in the same style. F.R.B. heard me out and gravely shook his head. 'No, no, William, while all that is no doubt first-class stuff the point on which you should pounce is—*why* did the son not sever his mater's jugular?' 'Well, why?' I asked. 'She was lost at sea and her body was never recovered.' This was no doubt one of his 7½ per cent cases and an 'arrival' at that. But he wrote litigation risks rarely and with reluctance; his respect for our judicial system being, I regret to say, limited. To insure against a reversal in the House of Lords his rate, if the proposer had won without any dissenting judgment in all the courts below, was 25 per cent. But after a few disastrous experiences he held that such business even at so high a premium was less reliable than a flutter on the Derby.

* * * *

Working under two such men as Bussell and Campbell was invaluable experience. It let me see how the insurance world revolves, in what relationship the public stand to the brokers, the brokers to underwriters and the underwriters to one another and (under reinsurance treaties) to insurance companies universally. I learned what ethical standards, customs and traditions have to be respected. I saw that in these circles I must rely upon common sense and preach law sparingly. Happily the Room has a rule, convenient and rarely broken, that no matter how many syndicates may subscribe one policy it is left to the top syndicate, when a loss occurs, to appoint a lawyer or assessor to handle it and the remaining syndicates automatically adopt him. Thanks to this I became known to all the syndicates then taking lines on non-marine risks, even to those legendary figures Cuthbert E. Heath (the inaugurator of the Lloyd's non-marine market) and George Simmons (who was the first man at Lloyd's to devote himself exclusively to non-marine underwriting). Few budding lawyers can have had a rosier future. Even when my luck seemed to fail it was only for a moment. Campbell, one of my main props, left Hartley Cooper to join Heath's. Thanks mainly to F.R.B.'s influence the Hartley Cooper claims trickled in to me as before.

Meanwhile, Campbell in the course of his new duties helped Lloyd's auditors in closing the affairs of a defunct syndicate which had written reinsurances on practically every taxi-cab in Paris. He had small experience of motor claims. I had a lot. He had no French whatever. I spoke French of the *'Ou se trouve le Louvre?'* variety and in the country of the blind the man with one eye is king. He sought my aid and we went to France together. I looked into some thousands of outstanding taxi-smash claims and told Campbell what, in the end, I thought it might cost to settle them. He then clinched a deal whereby for a payment which I regarded as beyond all reason the reinsured company agreed to cancel the Lloyd's covers. Time was to show this as a feat which saved underwriters a fortune. The reinsured company made the worst bargain in its history. For Campbell, with a touch of ancestral second sight, saw, as the men on the spot did not, that damages for personal injuries were about to enter upon an upward spiral with the sky as the limit. I collected a fair fee, and, what was even better, Heath's work began to drift my way.

On our return from Paris, Campbell advised that my

father should be persuaded to move his practice into the offices which the defunct insurance firm had occupied. These were within a pistol-shot of the Royal Exchange and with my utter belief in Lloyd's as my destiny I would have given my eyeteeth to be practising as close to them as that. But our Finsbury Pavement landlords, to whom we were bound for a long term of years, if willing to release us at all would want compensation in cash and much more of that than we could afford. I had almost despaired of finding a solution to the problem when the problem solved itself. The landlords, in urgent need of extra space for their clerical staff, came to us, cap in hand, to know whether we would give up our rooms and if so what compensation we would expect? In the result, with something more than all our expenses paid, we moved to 33 St. Swithins Lane and so broke into that exclusive City insurance circle of which Lloyd's was both the topographical and historical centre.

*   *   *   *

Fate, I thought, frowned on me when cousin Willie left Heath's to join another important house, Matthews Wrightson. But it was no frown; it was a smile. He became their non-marine underwriter. What with one thing and another my income trebled.

Nine

THE SPLIT

THE work from Lloyd's now flooded in and I was hard put to get through it efficiently. Loss of efficiency would mean loss of the work itself. I had to risk scamping either the work or the study for my Law Final, which was close ahead.

In this dilemma I took the grave decision, theoretically inexcusable, to nurse Lloyd's and to let my Final slide for the time being. Nearly all my law reading, from then on, was done in spasms during train journeys, usually *en route* to investigate motor smashes, or at home between midnight and dawn. And when in July 1912 I became one of His Majesty's Solicitors of the Supreme Court of Judicature I had the cheek to believe that the £1,000 per annum then in sight from Lloyd's (much more than enough to keep me and my wife and infant daughter in comfort) was only a start.

It had long been plain that the practice which my father had built up and the new one which I was developing could not march together. Our old clients were mostly folk claiming damages for personal injuries. My insurance clients were those at whom such claims were levelled. We were trying to run with the hare and hunt with the hounds. I proposed that we should take the defendants' side and let our plaintiffs' work fade away. Father did not share my view that this sacrifice (for sacrifice he thought it) would be worth while. He spoke of dropping the 'substance to grasp at the shadow'. To this problem we found a happy answer: my brother. Archibald and Father in partnership would foster the substance. I would launch out on my own and chase the alleged shadow. It was agreed that my younger brother Walter should, if he wished, come under my wing on leaving the City of London School where he was then in his last year.

At the start of this century every solicitor to be in the mode had to show at his street door a name-plate of brass. And if the name through years of polishing had vanished, so much the more professional. He used letter paper with his address printed in the top right-hand corner. I kicked against these drab conventions. For my name-plate I went to an Arts Guild, who cut me one in cuprous bronze. The lettering in cream enamel was in the style of that found on ancient Roman monuments. My letter-heading was *en suite* and the address was centred. I was derided for my bad taste. I have seen, not without satisfaction, that many of my fellow lawyers now tread the path I trod. My desk and chairs, severe, sturdy mahogany (still in use), were the best I could buy and better than I could afford.

What I hated most about the City in those days was its air-borne dirt. Every chimney added its pounds of grime to the thousands of tons which daily fouled London's square mile. I had to take my share with the rest. But I could and did plan an office easy to clean. My walls, enamelled white, were scrubbed down for me once a quarter under contract. My mother said my room looked more like a clinic than the seat of a young man hoping to make his mark in the world. Her brother Jack, acting the fool, sat in my armchair, threw back his head, opened wide his mouth, pointed to an upper tooth and gurgled, 'I think it's this one.' All these gibes I took in my stride and on July 12th, 1912, still another law practice, 'WILLIAM CHARLES CROCKER', with two rooms on the third floor of '33', with small credit in the bank and one small girl ('Beck') as staff, burst upon the legal firmament brightly shining.

Ten

I T IS not easy, sixty years later, to recall the traffic conditions which, in giving me my first Lloyd's case, launched what became my own specialised practice.

In 1894 a National Race for 'mechanically propelled vehicles' had been won at 11½ m.p.h. Such vehicles (an unimaginative government called them 'light locomotives') were hobbled by stupid 'safeguards'. Two able-bodied men had to be aboard. A red danger signal had to be borne far in advance by a third. Five miles per hour was 'furious driving'. *The Autocar* (the pioneer of motoring periodicals) printed an entire issue in red ink when the Light Locomotives and Highways Order 1896 loosened some of these shackles. The signal carrier went. And the speed limit was raised to a daring 12 m.p.h.

Although by 1903 the legal maximum had jumped to 20 m.p.h., old-fashioned horse-minded people still thought, in 1907, that no motorist with any consideration for his own neck or for other road-users would dream of travelling at so crazy a speed. Small wonder, then, that Whitcombe, when writing me about a new case on December 5th, 1907, remarked gloomily, 'The only thing against us is the fact that our assured was going *15 miles an hour.*'

Five years later, in 1912, when I began my own practice, public detestation of the steadily growing motor traffic was little abated. Our judges, unconsciously biased, saw the motor as a fad, not as something which had come to stay. A quick compromise in collision cases paid better than a

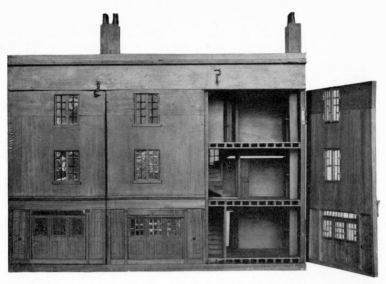

Scale model of 9, 10 and 11 Exchange Buildings, Houndsditch, preserved in City of London Police Black Museum, Bishopsgate

This photograph of the police model shows the backs of Nos. 11 and 10 Exchange Buildings and the cistern above the w.c. of No. 10 (see pp. 37–8)

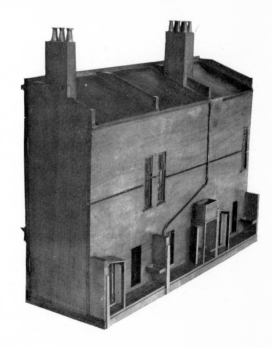

Rex *v*. Harris. The working documents (see p. 159)

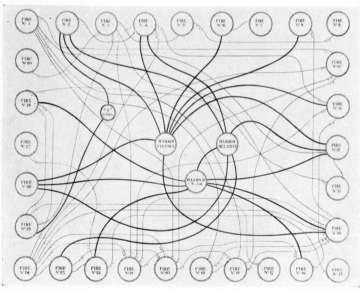

'Willesden Junction' (see pp. 153–4)

fight to the finish in court. The dice were loaded against the
automobile.

Many of the claims made against motorists insured at
Lloyd's were for injuries to horses in towns and to cattle and
sheep in the country. The owners of these beasts were not
infrequently rascals. The swindles they attempted were new
to me. With an ever-growing interest in detection—whetted
as it was by the shady insurance claims which passed through
my hands—any novel form of fraud cóming into the office
was more than welcome. I pass over those cases in which a
genuine casualty was followed by a claim inflated to the
point of dishonesty. One is asked to accept exaggeration of
this kind as no more than a polite gambit in the business of
bargaining. I have in mind cases in which alerted by some
peculiar feature or lucky chance I was able to unearth facts
enough to bowl the claims clean over and to leave the
claimants more than content to escape with their liberty.

For success as a detective, according to Scotland Yard
(where they have the best in the world), one needs only luck
and persistence—in the ratio of 98 per cent persistence to
2 per cent luck. This 2 per cent was evident when an insurance friend let me see a list of claims all relating to slight
collisions in which hand-barrows carrying cheap dinner-
services were concerned. Although the so-called street-
traders in charge of the respective barrows were supposedly
strangers to one another, expert examination (enlisted, unfortunately, rather late in the series) had shown that the
same crate of china had figured in several and probably in all
of the 'accidents'. The names of the participants lodged in
my memory. A year or so afterwards one of these names
cropped up, borne by the apparently innocent victim of an
accident for which my assured, a tramway company, were,
on the face of things, clearly liable. Perhaps this new 'accident' was the old china-crate swindle in a more ambitious
form? It was (as I proved to my own satisfaction) the most
recent of half a dozen by which the gang had already profited.
Their *modus operandi* was simple. In certain areas where the

E

cobblestone road-bed had sunk, one could find stretches of tram track so defective that it was pretended cats could crawl under the metals. The gang, choosing such a section in a quiet neighbourhood, would wait until the coast was clear and then stage their show. The next tram to arrive would find the way blocked by a collapsed pony-cart. One of its wheels lay on the ground, having been 'wrenched off by the projecting tram-line'. The pony 'which had been down' was out of its harness. The pony's owner, a most reasonable man, would assure the tram-driver that so far as could be seen 'the 'oss 'ad come to no 'arm'. A few days later, however, it would be reported that the animal had died as a result of its injuries and a preposterous claim for damages would follow. I do not know how many times this comedy, or rather tragedy, was played. I encountered it only once. My veterinary surgeon, J. W. Baxter, carried out an autopsy. He found that the animal's death was due to its gut having been twisted by a lubricated hand inserted per *anum*. Baxter, a horse-lover and born sleuth, was not only an ex-prize-fighter—he looked it. The precise nature of his threats to the brutal claimant are not repeatable. But the claim was not pursued.

He used the same technique in another of my cases, one which related to the very logical legal doctrine that a person must so enjoy his own property as not to injure that of anyone else. Some sheep were said to have died through eating clippings from a neighbour's yew tree. I was, so to speak, on the side of the yew tree, which was indeed poisonous and had certainly been recently trimmed. Baxter carried out a post mortem and reported that the sheep had died as alleged. 'What is a fair price to pay?' I asked. 'You pay nothing,' said he; 'the yew which I found in the sheep's stomachs had been deliberately fed to them; it had passed through a chaff-cutter.'

With him to help me I navigated animal claims by the hundred. Without him I was lost. If he had only been along when the Gravesend elephant died I would not have met my

zoological Waterloo. Whitcombe had been induced to insure
this animal solely because it plied for hire in a local fair-
ground in which he himself had often played as a child.
When the elephant died (as it did soon after the policy was
issued) Whitcombe became irrationally suspicious. Pro-
crastinating, as always, he took no action until the carcass,
to put it mildly, was 'high'. And then without consulting me
he ordered an autopsy by a vet of his own choice, an eminent
and fashionable gentleman who had rarely handled anything
much larger than a toy terrier. It is to the credit of this dog
fancier that, without a gas-mask, he went close enough to
see that 'Jumbo' had a club foot. Since the law imposes upon
a person seeking insurance an obligation to disclose to the
underwriter, in the utmost good faith, every fact material to
the risk, failure to discharge that obligation renders his
policy voidable. A.J.W. argued that the existence of the club
foot was a 'material fact' which should have been brought to
his notice. He refused to pay. Mr. Justice Darling tried the
resulting action and a good time was had by everyone except
me. The learned judge was a notorious jester. His *Vanity
Fair* cartoon depicted him watching bells being sewn on his
Black Cap. My elephant case was a welcome diversion. He
and defending counsel fed funny lines to one another. 'Club
foot!' said his lordship. 'Byron had a club foot. And did he
not swim the Hellespont?' Judgment for the elephant!

By this case I scored my first press notice. It appeared,
not inappropriately, in *Punch*.

*   *   *   *

The big insurance companies—'the Tariff offices'—are all
tied to a fixed scale of premiums and may not undercut one
another.

Mr. J. B. Kyffin, a draper member of the Hackney Borough
Council, took a poor view of this arrangement. He argued
that the non-hazardous property risks which municipalities
are obliged to cover merited much more favourable terms

than the Tariff allowed. Few underwriters, he thought, being free to make their own rates, would charge a high one for subscribing a fire policy on the local water-works. A man of iron will and powerful personality, Kyffin rallied a few other enthusiasts and brought into being, in 1903, Municipal Mutual Insurance Ltd. This embodied the simple idea that municipalities should no longer pay out for their very choice risks premiums either loaded with a profit margin or inflated by association with less profitable business. Instead they should insure among themselves co-operatively and so take full advantage of the situation which they felt entitled to enjoy in an insurance sense. When the company first began to operate, its resources were slender and the risks it wrote were almost wholly reinsured at Lloyd's with F. R. Bussell and others. Occasionally people sustained personal injuries on property covered under a third-party policy issued by Municipal Mutual Insurance. I would then receive instructions to deal with the resulting claims actually for underwriters but nominally as though I was acting directly for the company. This happy state of affairs brought me into continual contact with the fiery J. B. Kyffin. Many of the claims were small. I was given *carte blanche* to handle these as I deemed best. I would snap quick settlements and postpone the reports until I could find time to get down to them.

J. B. Kyffin enjoyed discussing the heavier claims, but membership of his company increased enormously and he had a mass of problems other than claims to keep him busy. I was left more and more to get along without his intervention. Suddenly this calm was broken. The telephone rang and an irate J.B.K. wished to know why I had done nothing with two cases sent to me fourteen days earlier? When I replied that both had been settled by me a week ago and would soon be reported for underwriters to pass as usual he barked, 'They've nothing to do with Lloyd's—we now carry these risks without reinsurance. I am coming along to see you at once!' My heart sank. This was calamity! In assuming authority to dispose of these two cases without so much as

'by your leave' I had done the unforgivable. My very first
insurance company clients were coming along in the person
of their formidable managing director to retrieve their files
and bid me an ironic farewell. When J.B.K. arrived, looking
less grim than I had dared to hope, I humbly apologised for
my misunderstanding. In mitigation I explained my reasons
for rushing settlements in the cases concerned—they related
to children injured in municipal playgrounds—and respectfully suggested that I had not paid too much. The art of
negotiation was more easily exercised in those days when
golden sovereigns ringing with seductive music were still in
circulation. To my profound relief J.B.K.'s reaction was a
genial 'Good work! That's the ticket! Get rid of 'em quick.'
And diving into his Gladstone bag he dragged out and gave
me two further claims files, the forerunners of the thousands
with which Municipal Mutual Insurance were destined to
nourish my practice during the succeeding half-century or
more.

*   *   *   *

To keep step with the steadily expanding Lloyd's non-
marine market, new policy wordings and endorsements were
required. The task of drafting these historic documents often
fell to me with a dry hint that I could forget the lawyers'
phraseology and use English so plain that even the assured
might understand it. The difficulty of such work was shown
in the birth of the Film Producer's Indemnity Policy. This
indemnified a film producer against the loss he sustains if
the shooting of a picture has to be abandoned or is delayed
through a star being disabled by sickness or accident.
Pregnancy was to be regarded as neither. My instructions
were to find delicate terms by which to make this clear. I
had to admit defeat. Full credit goes to the underwriters
themselves for having evolved the ingenious clause, still in
current use—'Warranted free of claim for any indisposition
not common to both sexes'.

*   *   *   *

When a claim arises under a fire or burglary policy (and under many other types of non-marine covers) the insurers, except in the smallest and simplest cases, engage independent insurance loss adjusters to act for them and after appropriate enquiries to recommend on what terms the claim should be settled. The true function of these adjusters is to hold the scales fairly between the insurers and the assured. In the vast majority of claims their duties call upon them to do no more than assess the extent of the loss, the right of the assured to be indemnified being clear on the face of it. Sometimes, however, and just as clearly, the claim is seen to be bad—for example when made under the wrong policy. In other cases and in circumstances capable of almost infinite variation doubts arise and have to be resolved before it can be said that the insurers are liable at all. Perhaps the assured may be thought to have procured the policy by misrepresentation or by concealing facts material for the underwriters to know, for example, that his assumed and distinguished surname hides the identity of a rogue with a criminal record. Or the claim itself may appear to be bogus. Circumstances overlooked by the lady who alleges her pearls were taken by burglars may demonstrate upon close examination that there were neither burglars nor pearls. Claims for loss of merchandise by fire may hint that quantities or values or both have been falsified. Or the books and documents put forward to prove the loss may do just the contrary by revealing themselves as clumsy forgeries. My adjuster friends would talk to me about their doubtful cases informally across the morning-coffee table and before the claimants knew that any suspicions had been aroused. Together we would devise tests in the hope of satisfying ourselves whether or not the claims were honest. In this unofficial way I saw hundreds of cases which ordinarily would not have come before me at all. Insurance transactions tainted with bad faith are microscopically insignificant compared with the huge bulk of business which is placed on the London Insurance Market. Of those doubtful matters which I debated with adjusters and of those on which my advice was directly sought by insurers few led to repudiation of liability; fewer still led to litigation. But they afforded ample exercise in the art of compromise which expresses chances in terms of pounds, shillings and pence.

It may be thought that the adjusters and I, both handling claims for the insurance community, were in competition with one another. To a limited extent this was so, but it created no friction. A natural frontier divided our respective territories. Adjusters are not trained lawyers and have no ambition to act as such. I am not a trained adjuster and never had any ambition to try my lack of skill at the sort of things which make up an adjuster's daily round: the measurement and costing of damage done to buildings by fire, the preservation and disposal of goods damaged by smoke or water, the diplomacy needed to reconcile the at times warring views of parties with a stake in these operations and the rendering of the countless other services which go to smooth the path between the raising of a claim and its acceptable settlement. The matters falling on my side of the frontier were those in which legal considerations were paramount and questions of material damage were only incidental. The claims in which that position was reversed fell to the adjuster's domain.

Motor policies provided claims in each class. If an insured car is destroyed or damaged in circumstances casting no blame on anyone all that has to be decided is what sum the assured should recover. This is clearly a matter for the loss adjuster. If, however, the assured seeks indemnity under his policy in respect of claims made against him by the victims of a motor smash the retention of a solicitor is not only expedient but practically inescapable for the reason that claims of this kind bristle with law. They normally raise two issues—'Who was to blame?' and 'What damages would a court be likely to award?' There is rarely unanimity among individuals who see a road collision and wish nothing more than to tell the truth about it. Some blame A, some blame

B, and some divide the fault equally. As for the drivers themselves, each, as a rule, honestly believes that the other was entirely responsible. This phenomenon led a cynical judge to say that in most of the motor cases he had tried, the cars at the moment of impact had each been stationary on its proper side of the road. Often the case which looked strong on paper would fall to pieces in court even when, as sometimes happened, both plaintiff and defendant were motorists and anti-motoring prejudice was neutralised.

Litigation has always been a highly speculative undertaking. I still avoided it whenever I could get a fair compromise. And when a fight was unavoidable I had to guess how the witnesses would shape in the box. The cocksure witness always made a bad impression. But when juries were all male a nervous lady witness was usually a winner. Obviously dreading her ordeal, she pierced the hearts of the jurors. If she tripped up in cross-examination and made some damning admission they would assume she intended the contrary and that the cross-examiner was a cad for confusing her. Sympathy of another kind, that felt for maimed bodies and pain and suffering, is one of the elements to be weighed when damages are claimed for personal injuries (P.I.). Nothing is more difficult in this class of work than to estimate what damages are likely to be awarded and accordingly how much it is worth paying for a settlement. By keeping in close touch with current 'P.I.' trials, by noting what sums were being recovered for what injuries and which judge had presided (some were notoriously generous, a few, like Darling, J., were 'defendant's men') I felt able to advise with reasonable confidence, in an admittedly unsteady market, what any specific P.I. claim was worth. One could, however, never tell what weight a jury might attach to their secret belief that the plaintiff himself had been partly to blame for the accident. I say 'secret belief' because in strict law, as the judge would tell them, the claim of a plaintiff was utterly defeated if he was found guilty of any, even the slightest, degree of negligence, contributing to the accident

out of which the claim arose. Juries quite rightly refused to
apply this rule in all its severity. Instead, tongue in cheek,
they would hold the slightly blameworthy plaintiff faultless
and to do substantial justice would knock a percentage off
the damages they would have awarded had he in fact been
wholly innocent.[1]

As motor traffic grew, so lawyers reaped a richer and ever
richer harvest from road-collision cases—probably the most
prolific crop of all. But gradually the accident offices and
Lloyd's awoke to the fact that the crippling cost of fighting
one another, a cost borne by motorists in the form of increased premiums, could be cut to the bone by recourse to
'knock for knock' and 'pooling' tactics. This meant, under
the first heading, that the repair bills of colliding vehicles
would be paid by their respective insurers, neither of whom
would seek recovery from the other no matter where the
blame might seem to lie. Under the second heading such
insurers, again ignoring questions of blame, would provide
equally the funds needed to satisfy a compromise settlement
or judgment regarding personal injury claims. I drafted
many of these agreements, feeling as I did so that I was
committing professional hara-kiri. But ample work always
remained for me, investigating, negotiating and, when
forced, fighting. Moreover, my Lloyd's clients began using
me to deal with claims where legal training was valuable but
by no means essential. Most of these were employers' liability
claims, i.e. those arising under policies covering employers
against their liability to pay compensation or damages to
employees injured at work. Neither their number nor the
modest fees they brought gave any hint that in the near
future they would threaten to lift me out of the law and
plant me in commerce for life.

1. The law was changed by the Law Reform (Contributory Negligence)
Act 1945 which requires the court to reduce the damages 'to such extent
as the Court thinks just and equitable having regard to the claimant's share
in the responsibility for the damages'.

. My role in this field was similar to that performed by the claims department of an insurance company. The adjuster in me was uppermost; the lawyer dormant, awakening only in the small proportion of cases where the injured workman's right to compensation was in question. Malingering was not unknown and efforts to unmask it led me still further along the paths of amateur detection. Looking back I realise that almost every claim—whether fire, burglary, motor or employers' liability—coming into my office called for some degree of enquiry. This not only whetted my detective appetite but to my great ultimate benefit brought me into touch with men to whom I should be opposed over and over again. The victim of a street accident regaining consciousness in a hospital might well find a gentlemanly agent at the bedside waiting with a tempting offer to recover damages on a flat 10 per cent commission basis. And the citizen whose premises caught fire might equally well find an even more gentlemanly agent on the site, while the flames were still roaring, offering to conduct the claim against the insurers with a skill which would soften the calamity and perhaps lend it some of the aspects of a blessing. It is only fair to say that those who succumbed to the blandishments of either agent, at the fire or in the hospital ward, rarely had cause to say that their claims received anything less than the most expert handling or that the agents' percentages deducted from the sums recovered were not fully earned.

Two brothers named MacCullum, with a highly trained and highly paid staff of touts, built up an organisation and a reputation which gave them (in the face of stiff competition) almost a monopoly in representing personal injury claimants among the under-privileged who hardly knew what a solicitor was and could not have afforded to instruct one if they did. Once the patient had signed the retainer he or she was handed over to a firm of solicitors (there were half a dozen of them) whose experience in this class of work promised that the damages obtained would be such as to secure the best conceivable result for the MacCullums (under any of their several aliases) and of course for the client. I was soon on first-name terms with the unqualified managing clerks who, in that epoch, practically ran these firms. And since it was clear that in the years which lay ahead some of their cases against me would be strong and some not so strong we tacitly agreed that a fair spirit of give and take should prevail over all. This paid dividends.

The 'MacCullums' in the fire field (but in no way connected with them) were Harris & Co. They were old-established assessors who invariably acted for policy-holders and had numbered among their clients banks, colleges and some of the biggest industrial concerns in the country. Fire claims, in their adjustment, are like personal injury claims; they offer opportunities for the widest and quite honest divergence of views when neither quantities nor values can be extracted with arithmetical accuracy after stock or contents and the books recording them have been wholly consumed or charred beyond recognition. Honest claims were of small interest to me. A couple of fires and a convenient bankruptcy were known to have put more than one scamp well on the road to wealth and to an honoured place in society. My interest was for the most part limited to those claims in which there was a smell of fraud but proof of it was hard to come by. In the search for that kind of proof I was giving myself a liberal education and automatically pigeon-holing for future use all sorts of seemingly insignificant facts which, in the aggregate and ultimately, were to spell the downfall of some very misguided and unhappy people.

Eleven

1912—TO JOINING UP

I AM not a thrifty man. Saving for saving's sake never gave me any satisfaction. It was, however, only by cutting overheads and by ploughing income back into the business that I could build up capital enough to feed my growing practice. And for more than a year after my admission the office staff consisted solely of the diminutive but indefatigable 'Beck'. Although my health stood up well under the strain of excessive work, snatched meals and no exercise, common sense suggested that I might organise my life to greater advantage. The time I spent in travelling around England to deal with motor cases could, I thought, be better employed in the City keeping touch with my clients at '33' or at The Bijou over morning coffee. To do this I entered into a form of limited partnership with two youngish but experienced solicitors—Vernon Spencer Wood in Manchester and John Sinton in Newcastle upon Tyne. My London office was to become theirs and do their London work while their respective offices were to become mine and deal with my provincial work. Nevertheless, the load left was more than '33' could carry without extra help. I had hoped that brother Walter, due to leave school at the end of 1912, would then join me and ease the strain. But I had first to win him from a belief that he was destined to be a motor engineer. Direct opposition would have been idle. I sank so low as to use cunning. While he would, I said, be wise to follow his bent and adopt an engineering career, before doing so he should have a year's general business training in a solicitor's office (to wit mine). He stepped into the trap and learning later that he was a hard man to bluff, I suspect he did so with his eyes wide open. Perhaps the crucial date when he decided to throw in his lot with mine to my everlasting satisfaction may be assigned to Lent 1913.

Having to visit Paris on business I asked him to go with me just for the ride. The real purpose of the invitation was, of course, to let him realise how pleasant a solicitor's life could be. We arrived on the evening of the Mardi Gras, February 4th, 1913. The boulevards were gay with bunting and thronged with Parisians and Parisiennes (especially Parisiennes) *en carnival*. Half-masks were worn with fancy dress and funny noses. Strangers battled one another with bladders and paper streamers. Bands played. The people danced and sang songs whose ribaldry, no doubt, mercifully, made sense only to the *cognoscenti*. I thought this Bacchanalia could do no harm to a man of my mature age—twenty-seven. On the other hand to expose to its influence a boy like Walter, scarcely free from scholastic discipline, might undermine his morals for ever. Accordingly, hypocrite that I was, I prescribed early bed for both of us. We put our shoes outside our bedroom doors and retired with mutual 'Good nights'. Half an hour later when the coast was clear and wearing a second pair of shoes I made a silent get-away down the back stairs.

* * * *

Fifty years later I told Walter about this shabby trick and belatedly apologised. He replied, 'Don't give it another thought, I also had a spare pair of shoes. What a lark it would have been had we smacked into one another in the Boule' Mich'! I have already said he was never an easy man to bluff.

* * * *

Walter came on to my staff at Midsummer 1913. It was further strengthened in the Fall of that year by the advent of two new and, as time was to show, very important members. One was Violet Roberts, who came over to me from my father's office where she had already worked on my type of case. The other was a rosy-faced, curly-haired office boy alive with rude health and common sense. His father, addicted to brevity, had given all his children names of three letters. My lad had been christened 'Bob' and kept that name up to the day years later when my gift of articles of clerkship to him (on his way to partnership) awoke the thought that the monosyllable 'Bob' might be replaced by something with a more professional ring. Accordingly he became by deed poll not merely Robert Whiting but for good measure 'Robert Clive Whiting', thus doing honour to Clive Road, the thoroughfare in which he resided.

*   *   *   *

Lloyd's continued to foster novel types of insurance. A new and profitable chapter was opened for me when Keith Marshall, an enterprising underwriter, introduced the 'K' series of policies. The 'K' stood for 'Keith' and is still used, although he himself died in 1920. The market called the series 'Death and spare parts'. They granted benefits on an agreed scale if the assured should be killed or lose a limb or an eye by accident or be totally incapacitated through accident or sickness. The claims made were rarely controversial and did not strictly demand the services of a solicitor. But someone had to deal with them. It was often my good fortune to be chosen as that someone. Here was a new and steady source of income, humdrum on the whole but now and then capable of producing an odd experience.

Many people live secret lives. When for reasons known only to themselves (maybe love unrequited or requited) they wish to disappear and start life anew, they sometimes stage a 'drowning'. A not unusual set-up is a sad little heap of

clothes on a sea-shore, often with a suicide note, but no
corpse floats in to confirm the rash act. The 'corpse' in one
of these farces was a young man who had effected a 'K' policy
in favour of his wife. If there is good reason to suppose that
a person, having vanished, has died, the Probate Court will
grant leave to presume death. In dealing with this claim my
attitude was that I would most gladly hand over the insurance money if the wife could obtain such a grant and so rank
officially as a widow. The grant was never sought. It was my
guess, one which perhaps the poor lady shared, that in all
probability her husband had sustained no worse calamity
than collision with a blonde.

                *   *   *   *

My professional life so full of fun and promise was clouded
over, as so many were to be, when war came in August 1914.
Most of us welcomed the comforting prediction that it would
end in six months. Young men rushed to join up lest they
should miss the chance. Brother Walter, to my dismay, was
among the first to go. Within a month he marched off
wearing the blue uniform of Kitchener's Army, straight into
a canvas camp where heavy rain, ankle-deep mud, the
pouring dark and lost heads spelled chaos. With neither
food, lights nor bedding his seven tent mates resigned themselves to a night of misery. 'There has clearly been some
mistake,' said Walter. 'Let us correct it.' With his pocket torch
he found a stores marquee and creeping in unobserved broached
a few crates. He was able to collect 'ground sheets, rubber,
other ranks for the use of, 24' and three dozen blankets to
match. His discreet fatigue party hauled home the loot and
left him to carry out a much more delicate operation, that
of purloining one of the cold joints hanging behind the H.Q.
mess kitchen. And so eight happy warriors full of good meat
and sinful pride slept the sleep of the pure in heart. And in
the morning Walter, suspect but unreprimanded, was promoted lance corporal. Moreover, he was promoted in my

estimation as a prospective partner. The *nous* to grasp a problem whole and to evolve its best answer, the nerve and skill to act thereon and win, the readiness to cock a snook at Law when Justice beckons, and last, but certainly not least, the sense which ensures for himself a cut from the joint by way of fee, these are the qualities which a solicitor needs most and Walter had shown that he had them all.

*　　*　　*　　*

I wish to write only about my life as a lawyer, not to add to the mass of war stories already told. Unfortunately the war to end all wars (1914–18) and that which followed it, twenty-one years later, affected my legal career so deeply that I cannot tell my tale without touching upon both of them.

The war's first effect upon my practice was to load me with new employers' liability claims. Factories with only a few score hands before August 1914 now employed hundreds or thousands. Most of these plants were on war work. Disabling accidents—multiplied by inexperience, fatigue and contempt for familiar machines—were inevitable. My Lloyd's clients when insuring such concerns endorsed the policies with a notice that all claims must be reported direct to me. To handle these claims efficiently I devised an office system which earned for itself at Lloyd's a flattering title 'The Sausage Machine'. It had to collect details of each accident, the data from which weekly compensation could be calculated and keep me in close touch with the patient's progress until the incapacity ended. For the assured's sake and my own the system was as automatic as routine could make it and aimed at reducing clerical labour to a minimum. It used a series of printed postcards each dealing with some commonly recurring situation on which I either needed or had to give a report. They were time and postage savers and turned what would ordinarily have been a daily flood of letters to a mere trickle. The assured, many of whom were short of office staff (as I was), found the easy-running 'Sausage Machine' an unqualified boon. To fellow solicitors who damned my postcards as unprofessional and icono-clastic I could make the excuse then current for any departure from the normal, 'There's a war on!'

Violet Roberts took charge of all this 'E.L.' work and became so expert that she sought my help only in very serious or complicated cases. Hers was a good example of a woman in wartime doing what under peace would have been a man's job.

*   *   *   *

Early in the morning of December 16th, 1914, German battle cruisers opened fire upon the Hartlepools, Scarborough and Whitby. In this 'hit-and-run' raid nearly 500 civilians were killed or wounded. The great shells caused heavy damage to small houses. The Cabinet thought it politically expedient that those who had suffered in the attack should be compensated. My good friends Messrs. Toplis & Harding were instructed as government assessors for this purpose. The adjustment of claims for material loss was straight-forward and proceeded on ordinary fire-insurance lines. The claims in respect of death and personal injuries presented a problem. By what standard were they to be measured? I vividly recall the thrill with which I received an invitation to help find an answer to that question. A modified version of my well-tried employers' liability 'Sausage Machine' worked at full speed and collected the facts upon which, whatever yardstick might be employed, compensation in each case must depend. It was a grand experience to meet the tough Yorkshire 'tykes' who were wholly unmoved by the 'frightfulness' which was meant to cow them. Their talks with me were terse and often grim. An old lady telling of her husband's end said, 'They scraped 'im off t' wall!'

I set out several alternative scales from which the govern-ment might choose to measure the proposed awards. Among

F

them was one (it happened to be the cheapest) which the minister-in-charge, Mr. David Lloyd-George, saw fit to adopt. This assumed that the claims arose from injuries to workpeople and were adjustable under the provisions of the Workmen's Compensation Act. I did not criticise him for his parsimony: economy in wartime must begin somewhere. But all my figures had been carefully adjusted so that no one recipient could fairly say that he or she had been less favoured than another. What annoyed me was that the Cabinet quadrupled the compensation I had recommended for one Mistress Marjorie Makepeace, a cockle-gatherer, and for no better reason than that her name and occupation were 'so delightfully Shakespearean'! This threw a monkey wrench into my nicely balanced machinery and doubtless led to the sort of jealous comparisons I had been at such pains to avoid. Nevertheless, my irritation gave way to astonishment that a cabinet minister, a world leader immersed in titanic problems, could take time off to influence the fortunes of so remote and humble a fellow creature.

* * * *

By January 1916 three and a half million patriotic volunteers, the cream of the nation, were under arms. Many of them would have done more towards winning the war had they carried on with their peacetime work. The realisation of this, the dreadful casualty lists and the sight of fit young men still living safely in 'civvy street' taught the public that things could be handled more wisely. The result was conscription. No longer were citizens taken into the Forces indiscriminately. The situation of each man was weighed and from time to time reviewed. If on balance it was judged the national effort would lose rather than gain if he were put into uniform, his call-up was 'deferred'.

Solicitors are essential units in the machinery of government. The administration of justice, the conduct of com-

merce and industry and the vital affairs of private individuals
are all dependent in one way or another upon the members
of my profession. The Lord Chancellor, as the Head of the
Justiciary, was accordingly reluctant to allow solicitors to
be conscripted wholesale. He asked the Law Society to prepare a nominal roll of all the remaining conscriptable
solicitors so that they could be 'released' for war service in
rotation whenever the need for recruits should be deemed to
override other considerations of State economy. I was duly
entered upon the roll and in spite of my commitments—a
wife and two children and a single-man practice—it seemed
probable that if the level of war wastage should not fall even
I would ultimately be 'released' to don khaki. Meanwhile, I
donned the blue uniform of a City of London Special Constable. In that force I was given the task of sifting and
debunking peculiarly stupid 'spy mania' stories: no war
escapes them. Enemy agents were said to be sending light
signals from the top floors of City offices, to whom or why no
one could imagine. The 'signals' which with binoculars and
much clambering among the chimney-stacks I traced to
their source all had this in common: that while they wore a
'dot and dash' pattern they were never in Morse or any other
recognisable code. And they were all due to a pencil of light
from an ill-fitting black-out curtain being irregularly inter-
rupted between its source and the beholder's eye by some
moving object, the flapping of a loose rope in one instance,
the activities of a caretaker at the sink washing up the
canteen china in another. These adventures added little to
my sleuthing repertoire, but they emphasised how people
living under nervous tension will blindly accept, as Gospel
truth, stories which under the cold eye of reason would stand
out as plain absurdities.

*   *   *   *

The most common purpose of a fraudulent fire is to turn
bad stock into good money. In wartime merchantable stocks

are hard to come by. Under the threat of inflation it is wiser to hold saleable things than to hold vulnerable currency. This may explain why few doubtful warehouse fires came my way during the war years. But 'How oft the sight of means to do ill deeds makes ill deeds done!' A Mr. X whose fire history was so calamitous that he was no longer insurable saw a golden chance in the then popular 'War Risks Policies'. These anyone could buy for a few shillings and no questions asked. He bought one. It may be thought that he was then placed like the gentleman whose 'all-risks' policy included 'flood' and had to ask a more experienced operator, 'How do you do flood?' How was Mr. X to 'do' enemy action? This seemed easy; from the ruins of an already-bombed site he retrieved the metal parts which the incendiary bombs then in use always left behind after they had burned themselves out. He took a ladder from his garden and planted these remains in his loft. It was a fine May evening when next the maroons went off to give warning of a coming Zeppelin attack. A little artistic work on the part of Mr. X soon set his place satisfactorily alight. One tries to look into these matters with an open mind, prepared with reserve to believe that lightning may strike twice in the same place. That one of the few bombs which fell in that period should fire the house of a man most of whose previous homes had gone up in flames was a coincidence calculated to strain even the most accommodating credulity. I took the bits of the bomb from Mr. X's attic to the government explosives expert and asked if they meant anything to him. He answered, 'They do indeed,' and laughed heartily. Poor Mr. X in his ignorance had used too much bomb; roughly, a bomb and a half.

This case has several special memories for me. It was the first in which I acted for a police force on the prosecution of an insurance swindler. It was the only case in which I ever heard a juryman score a crushing point which everyone else had missed. The trial took place in the autumn of 1915. The prisoner was asked to explain why his ladder was not hanging in its usual place on his garden wall after the fire? He replied, 'My children took it to reach some high branches when blackberrying.' *'What?'* came with guffaw from the jury-box, 'in *May*!' A golden rule for the cross-examiner is 'Don't put a question unless you know what the answer should be.' One of my several uniformed witnesses had sworn he was watching the sky when the fire started and no Zeppelin was in the locality. Counsel asked him sarcastically, 'Do you spend much time star-gazing?' and drew the deadly answer, 'Naturally, sir, in civilian life I am an astronomer.'

*　　*　　*　　*

Among the many aircraft factories which expanded enormously under the impetus of World War I was that in which the giant Handley-Page bombers were produced. This expansion proved an embarrassment to Frederick Handley-Page, the founder and presiding genius of that establishment. He was at that time dedicated as an aviation engineer to problems of invention and design. But his very success drove him more and more into what he judged a less essential role, that of a big-business executive. He spoke of this when we lunched together. From his pocket he took a small steel model of a new bomb-release mechanism. He patted it and said, 'This is my line. The time I spend directing the commany, talking to prospective purchasers and going abroad to discuss orders is in my view time used uneconomically.' I made sympathetic noises. He continued, 'Some people enjoy that sort of work—keeping the customers happy—shooting trouble—getting an organisation ticking over smoothly. You could do it on your head—just as you do our accident claims. Will you take it on and leave me to make some more and better planes?' I drew a deep breath and hinted that a knack for handling employers' liability claims might not indicate my ability to act as stand-in for an aviation tycoon. These modest doubts were swept aside and the bargain was struck. But red tape killed it. The War Department, lacking the

elasticity of that ministry which had bent its august mind
to the welfare of a humble cockle-gatherer, could find no way
to delete my name from the Law Society's list of solicitors
who would be called to the Colours if and when the country
should need them badly enough. My gratitude to the War
Department for their 'No' is immeasurable. Had they said
'Yes' I might have slipped out of the Law and into industry
for good, missing all the spice and variety which in my belief
our profession alone has to offer. It was a narrow escape.

*   *   *   *

That we should win the war in the end was beyond
doubt. But how or when no one could say. By the beginning of 1917 we all saw that sooner or later nearly every
fit male would be called up. A young litigation clerk, A. J.
Clements (whom I had engaged in 1913), and Bob Whiting
had long since gone. Could my practice be kept alive while
I was away pretending to be a soldier? My good luck held. I
explained my plight to a very patriotic, intelligent and
charming solicitor neighbour, Edward Mackie. He had a
cardiac murmur so strong that even under powerful drugs it
had beaten all his efforts to bluff past the army, navy and
air force medicos. He at once offered to spend the few months
or less of liberty which might remain to me in meeting my
clients, in studying my rather odd practice and in planning
to carry it on when the call should come for me to bid it at
best 'au revoir' and at worst 'good-bye'. I suggested an immediate partnership. This he refused: 'We will go into that
very happily when you no longer have a pistol at your head
—après la guerre!' He proved as good as his word. And
thanks to him when I marched off to war in the early days
of June 1917 (rather less than five years after my admission
to the Roll of Solicitors) it was with a comparatively light
heart.

Twelve

IN THE ARMY

THE Artists Rifles camp was at Gidea Park, near Romford, in Essex. There, after many days of woeful exercise, my soft civilian muscles gained the proper martial hardness. I hated the iron discipline and yearned for the joys of 33 St. Swithin's Lane. But many of the Britons from all over the world who joined the regiment to train as officers were worried by matrimonial, business and family problems. In giving such of these as sought it a little free advice I felt that I had not yet wholly lost touch with the Law.

I was, in due course, commissioned a second lieutenant and sent to the Dorset Regiment in Londonderry. This put an extra load on my conscience. Edward Mackie was running his own Ealing practice and mine also. The Misses Beckley and Roberts, when a new case came into the office, would dig out a file to show how I had dealt with a similar one before. Both Bussell and Campbell stood by to explain insurance technique. And I had been able to help him by frequent talks over the phone and by rare face-to-face talks at Gidea Park when crises arose. Now these were to cease; he was to be marooned while I sailed for Northern Ireland, a lush and friendly country where there were fewer signs of war to be seen than Salisbury Plain could show on a pre-war Saturday afternoon. After a few months of not unpleasant regimental routine my past overtook me. I was appointed Brigade Intelligence Officer, with a free hand to interpret my duties as I thought fit. Justifying my existence by making tasty little reports on items of a security nature, I went where I liked when I liked and I resumed my mufti. Mackie was able to visit me in Ireland only once. We had a four days' orgy of consultations. He hoped that I should stay where I was and never face any worse peril than that which the ample Irish diet was offering to my figure. This was not to be. The War Department suddenly whipped me away from a particularly amusing investigation upon which I was secretly engaged and ordered me to join our regular battalion, the 1st Dorsets, somewhere in France.

* * * *

I believe it is the done thing for an officer to 'say a few words to the men' before leading them into battle, on the lines of 'We few, we happy few, we band of brothers'. I faced this blush-making situation only once when my depleted platoon (about ten all told) was to force its way across the Canal de La Sambre. Before our barrage began I told them that if they would stick close to me during the advance they would all be safe because the ruined barn in which we had passed the night had been marked by the enemy before their withdrawal with my own 'lucky' number '33'. Not one of them was scratched.

* * * *

A week later the Armistice was signed. And a few months after that our H.Q., moved almost to tears by my plea that '33' was being torn down in a big rebuilding scheme and none but I could hope to find alternative accommodation for my practice, gave me compassionate leave. I went home resolved that the army should never see me again.

Thirteen

AFTER WORLD WAR ONE

AFTER a long spell of 'indefinite' leave I was at last able, legally, to shed my uniform for good. The new offices which I now took above a haberdasher's shop in Gresham Street were a shade larger than my old ones at '33'. They suited me if only as a stop-gap. No one could foresee whether or not the war would be followed by slump or boom. I played for either, with a slight bias in favour of boom, providing enough space for some extra clerks and hoping that I might need them.

*   *   *   *

Among my treasures I keep a Restaurant Frascati menu, dated May 31st, 1919. It is headed:

'33'

A Staff Dinner to Celebrate
A Re-union After the War

On the back are seven signatures—namely, mine, those of 'Beck', Vi Roberts and Mackie (the trio who had so staunchly held the fort) and of brother Walter, Bobbie Whiting and Clements. The magic '33' had become a staff joke. But if we laughed at it we did so with a note of respect. I felt that its ties with the good luck which had so often blessed me and my team deserved recognition. Accordingly each of the seven diners received as a memento of the evening a small gold charm—the magic number in a plain circle. These charms, today prized as emblems of seniority, no longer swing precariously on bracelet or watch-chain. They repose in jewel-boxes. It was an historic dinner. We bade farewell to arms and drank to the future. Edward Mackie was to join me in partnership at once and we were all set to go. Unhappily Mackie *père*, to my sorrow, had other ideas and eventually the versatile and dexterous Edward, forsaking the law, stepped into his father's shoes as head of a flourishing electrical and mechanical engineering concern.

* * * *

My post-war practice prospered as never before. This was largely due to the slump which hit so many folk less lucky than I. Certain mercantile stocks—war surplus, for example —became redundant. It seemed that they were no sooner insured (or over-insured) than they burst mysteriously—one might have thought even spontaneously—into flame. Other people, not necessarily merchants, feeling the pinch of peace and seeking to turn a dishonest penny, looked guiltily at any suitable policy they had by them or could procure and tried their 'prentice hands at simple little frauds. These did not often succeed, but the examination of them gave me both pleasure and profit. Among the men whom I added to my staff at that time to help master the influx of new work were two who merit special mention. 'Sammy' Loe came to me as an unqualified managing clerk. A sound all-round practical lawyer with a special talent for conveyancing and company work, he had been keen enough and able enough to help coach a succession of clerks articled to his former employers and to shepherd them through their Law Society examinations. In the genial atmosphere of my establishment he ripened and was soon giving me more assistance than I could have expected from many a fully qualified man. He took over a load of general, that is to say non-insurance, matters, the natural accretions in every lawyer's practice, and left me free to pursue my own chosen path among insurance claimants. He was so clearly cut out to be a solicitor that I at once gave him his articles.

The second newcomer, W. J. Emmens, I had long known as claims agent for the National Omnibus Company. They carried their own risks uninsured up to a fairly high figure and covered the excess through clients of mine at Lloyd's. I had often read his claims files, models of neatness and precision, showing how exhaustively every aspect of a road accident could be laid bare by an expert such as he, endowed with ample detective skill, industry and personality. A short stocky Cockney with a blue jowl and a winning smile, he revelled in the human contacts with which his job provided him. When the National buses left London to operate only in the provinces those human contacts went with them. Overnight he became an office executive, a mere writer and reader of letters, handling nearly all the claims by remote control. In this situation Emmens, as I learned by the happiest chance, was miserable. He called on me at my request. It was a Friday. I asked him if he would care to run my motor department. He beamed and said, 'Yers, Guv'ner!' 'What salary do you want?' 'Pound a day!' 'When can you start?' 'Monday!' My relationship with National had always been a friendly one. I did not wish to give offence by taking so valuable a man from them without reasonable notice. I said as much to 'W.J.' (as he became). 'Leave it to me, Guv'ner, I'll keep 'em sweet,' he replied, and was gone. A pound a day to me was a lot of money in 1921. I wondered where I should find it. I need not have worried. When 'W.J.' reported for duty on the Monday morning he gave me a charming letter from his employers praising Emmens in the highest terms, and thanking me for so readily agreeing to allow him, in his new post, to continue the management of the National London claims. 'I thought you wouldn't mind, Guv'ner, I didn't want to leave my old boss in a hole and we can charge him enough in "our" fees to pay *my* salary anyway.'

*   *   *   *

One of the men to whom I was continually opposed was William Cooper Hobbs. Nominally managing clerk but *de facto* partner in a solicitor's firm, he received an endless stream of 'running-down cases' through the 'ambulance chasing' organisation which I have already mentioned. Hobbs was a cunning and wholly unscrupulous scoundrel with notoriety and penal servitude as his ultimate destiny. But for unfathomable reasons of his own he usually gave me a more or less square deal and for the sake of my clients I wished to retain this measure of his goodwill. Most members of the accident insurance fraternity knew that once when Hobbs himself was slightly hurt in a collision between two National 'buses he demanded preposterous damages and bolstered up his claim by taking to his bed and staying there. Emmens, then with the National, did not encourage people to swindle his employers. Moreover, he regarded any attempt thereat as a personal affront. In some way which he never disclosed to me, but no doubt giving a false name and assuming a fictitious character ('Enery Chapman from the oil shop in the 'Igh Street, Cromer', was one of his favourite roles), he made up to Hobbs's housemaid, took her for walks and bought her good meals. For a long time in her running commentary upon the Hobbs' ménage as seen from below stairs she imparted nothing of which W.J. could make any use at all. 'But one night' (he told me) 'she happened to speak of the one spark of warmth in Hobbs's flinty heart— it was for a young female relative living in the provinces. I got the name and address and I had an idea. A pal of mine went to the post office nearest this girl's home and he sent a telegram to Hobbs reading: "Millie seriously ill asking for you." Old Hobbs fell for it! We photographed him fairly sprinting along the road. At Marylebone Station I bumped against him, not looking where I was going like, and put on a terrific act of being surprised when I recognised him. "Why, Mr. Hobbs," I said, "I really am glad to see you so much better. I feared you could not leave your bed!" But Hobbs knew he'd been had. He wasn't half wild! "You damn' rascal!" he shouted and shook his fist at me. "Now! now! Mr. H.," I said, "you mustn't mind my little jokes. And don't worry about Millie, she's as well as you are!" ' The evidence provided by the photographs of Hobbs *en route* to the station satisfied the jury that Hobbs was an impostor. The damages awarded were less than the amount paid into court by the defendants and this in turn was less than the costs of the action for which Hobbs was held liable. I thought it unlikely in the circumstances that Hobbs would look upon Emmens with anything short of loathing. But I was wrong. When I challenged him on the subject he professed unbounded admiration for the cleverness with which W.J. had caught him. He congratulated me on having acquired 'the best claims man in England'. I suppose in his cold money-grubbing way he calculated it would pay better in the long run to keep on the safe side of so wily an opponent. He was certainly not moved by any sporting instinct. Such a weakness was entirely foreign to his mean nature. The only touch of human kindness that he was ever known to display, so far as I ever heard, was towards Millie and ironically enough it betrayed him.

*   *   *   *

In 1923 I moved my practice with its steadily growing staff to a pleasant building at 21 Bucklersbury. Fired by optimism, I negotiated for the right to cut a communicating door from '21' into the adjacent Mansion House Chambers (which had hundreds of offices) if at any time my business should demand even more elbow room than the five floors which '21' itself already provided. Gresham Street had served its purpose as a stop-gap for only four, but four very happy, years, years which were enriched by three matters regarded, at least by me, as important chapters in my career.

Fourteen

MAINLY IRISH

A SMALL group of ex-officers with their war gratuities, little or no trading experience and the help of an artful lady, opened up as manufacturers and vendors of hairdressers' sundries. They operated in a cheap half-basement where, one month after their annual stocktaking had given a value of £533, a fire broke out. As the result of a claim presented through Messrs. Harris & Company for over six times that amount I was asked to investigate. The assured's chairman told me the jump in figures was due to the fact that goods worth over £2,500 had arrived after the stocktaking. Unfortunately, these newly arrived and costly goods were just those to suffer most in the flames. They were made up (as to £1,700) of synthetic perfumes in glass bottles of various sizes and (as to £800) of a fawn-coloured powder containing '1½ drachms of uranium'. This remarkable powder, 'the active ingredient in a proposed anti-rheumatic massage cream', had, it was said, been bought in Nice by the artful lady and smuggled home in four one-pound packages. I like such tall stories; the taller they are, the more easily they topple. The younger members of the outfit looked scared. I thought that if scared a bit more they might break down and confess. Inviting all the ex-officers and the artful lady to meet me by appointment in the fire-swept basement, I turned up with a band of poker-faced helpers. My own role was to ask each of the conspirators disquieting questions about the fictitious stock. That of 'Sammy' Loe was to take all this down in shorthand. Behind us waged a war of nerves. My architect and his aide, measuring the room and its shelving, shouted dimensions to one another and every now and then whipped out a ratcheted surveying tape which clicked like a machine-gun. My chemist (from British Drug Houses) clattered away with a crook-handle walking-stick among the heaps of broken bottles. My photographer startled everyone by letting off his magnesium flashlight when it was least expected. The artful lady may have guessed that this hubbub was largely bogus. She did not turn a hair. But the youngest ex-officer, on whose collapse I had counted, unable to put a match to his cigarette for trembling, could hardly wait to get me alone to shed his guilty knowledge. Meanwhile the chemist showed me the ease with which one may examine a mound of glass fragments and tell how many and what kinds of bottles those fragments represented. He merely matched up the bottoms and necks, which rarely break! And of those allegedly late arrivals, the Winchester and Corbyn quarts with their synthetic perfumes, there was no trace at all.

The truth of the tall 'uranium' tale proved to be this. The artful lady's stepfather was an honourable Frenchman, Monsieur X, living on the Riviera. During a visit from his stepdaughter he had given her as a souvenir some 'uranium' which he had acquired as a natural curiosity.

It was not in powder form but resembled a little bit of rusty iron and was contained in a small glass tube. He thought perhaps the young lady might wish to turn it into cash. When later she asked him for an invoice he complied, assuming it was wanted as a sort of pedigree. I let him see the original invoice and he agreed that with one important exception the writing was his. The important exception was a scribbled '43,200 Fcs'. I repudiated liability under the policy and the claim was dropped. This not strikingly remarkable case dwells in my memory as of historical significance. The reason is that one of those who watched my theatrical show in the assureds' basement was their tall, well-groomed and quick-thinking assessor, Mr. Leopold

Harris. I had never seen him in the flesh before. If in later years he was to make grave errors of judgment he made none in this particular matter. So soon as he realised that the claim was dishonest he wrote withdrawing from it. I respected him for that.

*　　　　*　　　　*　　　　*

Not least among the three Gresham Street cases which I look upon as milestones in my career was one bearing the title 'IRISH, R. & C.C.' If political upheavals are likely to cause death or destruction, in no matter what quarter of the globe, Lloyd's, the world's most sinister sounding-board, will receive very early warning of them. Prospective victims of those upheavals will run to Lloyd's for insurance coverage. Accordingly, 'The Troubles' which ravaged Ireland in the years 1919–21 were foreshadowed by a heavy demand for Lloyd's special 'Riots and Civil Commotion' policies. ('R. & C.C.' for short.) These insure property against loss or damage '. . . directly caused by persons taking part in riots . . . or civil commotions . . .' The Irish Republican Army (the I.R.A.) were so keen to get credit for the havoc they wrought that when a claim arose the facts were seldom in dispute and underwriter's liability to pay was clear. Now and again mansions would be fired by a secret intruder working off a private grudge. Some of these cases came to me when the assured, having let his ordinary fire insurance lapse, argued that his 'R. & C.C.' policy attached. But he was out of luck, for riot is a highly technical offence requiring five essential elements: (1) not less than three persons must be engaged in it and have (2) a common purpose and (3) proceed to execute it (4) with intent to help one another by force if necessary against any opposition and (5) use force or violence 'so as to alarm at least one person of reasonable firmness and courage'. 'Civil Commotion' was even wider of the mark. It is 'An insurrection of the people for general purposes not necessarily amounting to a rebellion'. Claims for losses which could not be laid to riot or civil commotion as so defined afforded no problem. A much more serious one concerned the burning of Cork. The I.R.A. said the British Army had deliberately fired the city as an act of reprisal. This the British have never admitted. Its importance to Lloyd's lay in the fact that the 'R. & C.C.' form excludes liability for loss through ... *wilful destruction by or under the order of the government. . . .*' Underwriters, jealous of their good name, wished to pay the Cork claims without delay. They also wished to preserve any rights they might have against the governmental authorities. Here was a dilemma. What was to be done?

*   *   *   *

'Timmie' Marshall, one of the underwriters deeply interested in this situation, had a gun in Graham Harding's shooting syndicate of which I was a member. Between beats and over lunch he would unofficially invite my views. By virtue of the Malicious Injuries Act of Ireland, liability for damage done by rioters was placed squarely upon the police rates. Insurers who had settled such claims were in law subrogated to their assured's rights under the Act and under any other provision available to make good the loss. In other words, inheriting or standing in the assured's shoes in respect of such privileges underwriters, theoretically, could hope to recover from one authority or another every penny of what they had paid out under their policies. The operative word is 'theoretically'. Those in tune with the Irish mood scorned the idea that huge rates would be levied on the public to make such a recovery possible. And yet it seemed unfair that underwriters should bear the Cork losses for which most of us believed they were not liable at all. In the end I hit upon a course which I thought might make it harder for the government, when 'The Troubles' should be over, to treat the Malicious Injuries Act as a dead letter. My device, a forlorn hope, was this: When a claim had been adjusted, the

G

assured on receiving payment signed a one-page agreement across a sixpenny stamp. It recited that there was a question as to whether or not underwriters were liable and pending determination of that question underwriters were making an advance *by way of loan*. This was to be repaid ... *'exclusively out of monies received by the Assured ... by way of compensation for the said damage ... from the County Council British Government military or other authorities. ...'* The chances of recovering anything from these sources were at that time thought to be valueless. I had already so reported to Marshall. When therefore he asked me to do the whole of the work involved in pursuing the subrogation claims on a collection-fee basis—say for 10 per cent of anything I might recover—I told him that I could not afford to agree. He replied that on the contrary I could not afford to refuse, that if I were wise I would take the gamble for the sake of prestige and goodwill. And so with great reluctance on my part the bargain was struck.

* * * *

The I.R.A. road transport was largely made up of cars (Rolls-Royce and such for choice) stolen from the unsympathetic landed gentry. When these cars developed faults, e.g. punctured tyres, it was more bother to repair them than to seize others in replacement. I learned that a great many of these 'unserviceable' but still valuable cars which had been insured under R. & C.C. policies were parked in a remote and disused stone quarry. Could the I.R.A. be persuaded to release them to my clients, the subrogated underwriters to whom the cars now belonged? I went to Dublin to find out. When Dail Eireann ratified the treaty which had been signed with Great Britain the I.R.A. split into two. One part supported the treaty and called itself the Free State Army ('Free Staters'). The other opposed the treaty, retained the I.R.A. title and were known to the pro-treaty party as 'Irregulars'. On the night of April 13th, 1922, I.R.A. units under General Rory O'Connor occupied the Four Courts plumb in the middle of Dublin City. The building bristled with barbed wire and gun barrels. A clash of arms seemed imminent. But there were no signs of Free State forces, no look of alarm on the faces of passers-by and the trams were running as usual. And so it had been for two months. I asked a senior officer of Constabulary would he object if I should visit the I.R.A. commandant at the Four Courts? 'Not at all,' he replied. 'May I then say I have police permission?' I asked. 'You'll be shot up the backside if you do!' was his grim answer. Thus encouraged, I decided to go ahead. A friendly intermediary, who knew O'Connor well, thought he could pass me into the 'fortress', but hoped this might be avoided. 'By a happy chance,' he said, 'tomorrow, Saturday, is the Races and Rory and his boys should be there. We always have a truce for the big meetings! You must come along.' At the Curragh I saw Spike Island win the Irish Derby but I saw nothing of the Four Courts commandant. Nor could I spare time to dawdle on in Dublin until he should be willing to receive me. If I had waited I would have waited in vain. Three days later the provisional government decided the cold war should end. At dawn on June 28th the attack began and on July 1st the garrison surrendered, leaving the Four Courts little better than a blackened ruin.

*　　　*　　　*　　　*

When the Irish Free State came into being under the leadership of Michael Collins 'The Troubles' were thought to be over. A committee, of which Lord Parmoor was the chairman, was set up to ascertain 'what compensation ought in reason and fairness to be awarded' for the damage done in Ireland between January 21st, 1919, and July 11th, 1920. I offer no excuse for having contrived that the first claim to come before the committee was for one of the big Cork fires. I saw the angry flush on Lord Parmoor's face when in answer to his question, 'Were you not insured?' the Cork claimant from the witness-box handed across my 'sixpenny' agreement recording the 'loan'. 'This is a mere device!' said his lordship, thereby betraying his intention to pass for compensation no claim which had been already paid under an insurance policy. In the light of the committee's terms of reference it was doubtful whether the 'mere device' could be circumvented by anything short of a new Act of Parliament. On hearing that almost all the claims on Lloyd's 'R. & C.C.' policies were the subject of similar loan agreements, Lord Parmoor adjourned for a short time to think things over. When the sitting was resumed the chairman, now suave, if still a little pink, uttered some of the sweetest words I have ever heard. They were to the effect that if Mr. Crocker, for the insurers, and Mr. Otto Niemeyer, for the Eire and British governments, would put their heads together he felt that, as reasonable business men, they could reach a fair compromise. Trying not to look too pleased, I nodded assent—and shook hands with myself under the table.

*   *   *   *

The haggle which ensued—with the mystery of Cork as my trump card—netted a salvage recovery of £233,000 odd. It reached me in the form of a paymaster's order on the Irish Provisional (and possibly ephemeral!) Government. I endorsed it, banked it and, feeling like a millionaire on the strength of my £23,000 fee, set out with my family for a long-delayed holiday in Switzerland. But my anxieties were not yet over. Michael Collins was assassinated before the paymaster's order had finished its passage through the clearing house. And in our Paris hotel brother Walter turned up with the order in his hand. It had been returned marked not 'R/D' but 'endorsment unacceptable'. Was the Provisional Government tottering? Was this a trick to delay payment? Or did my execrable signature justify the paymaster's rejection of it? I re-endorsed the order in half a dozen varying forms, using everything from copper-plate to block capitals and travelled on with fingers crossed towards the peace of Zermatt. Walter, meanwhile, at a loose end in Paris until his night boat-train should leave, asked himself where he could best enjoy a little relaxation. He decided upon the *Bal Tabarin*, thinking that never again would he have the chance to go dancing with nearly a quarter of a million in his breast pocket. I am glad I did not hear about this hair-raising dare until the money was at last safely in the hands of my bankers.

*   *   *   *

The sequel to this story is of more moment than the story itself. Three years of overwork had sapped my strength. I reached Zermatt a frail and easy prey for any germ on the look-out for a snug home. Typhoid moved in and I ended the summer of 1922 fighting for my life.

During my long absence from the office, at least once each week, Vernon Spencer Wood motored through the night from his Buxton home to Bucklersbury to help young brother Walter keep the practice running. He fell in love with the work and with the South of England. Under this urge, coupled with mine, the London and Manchester firms were amalgamated. The London end of the partnership was run by V.S.W., Walter and me. We were joined in the course of time by members of the staff (who under articles which we gave them had qualified as solicitors) and by a few others among whom, to the happiness of all, were ultimately numbered V.S.W.'s only son and my own.

Fifteen

SIDNEY FOX

A<small>T MORNING</small> coffee on October 29th, 1929, Vernon
Wood handed to me a thin sheaf of papers which had
just come from our clients, the Cornhill Insurance Company.
In his rich Lancastrian accent (always richer under any
emotional strain) he asked, 'What do we do with this lot,
Will?'

The facts recorded in the documents were simple. Less
than a week earlier, on October 23rd, a bedroom in the Hotel
Metropole at Margate went on fire. An old lady, Mrs. Rosaline Fox, when carried from the room was found to be dead.
The chief witness at the inquest was the victim's son, Sidney,
a well-mannered and handsome man of thirty. His very
moving story was this. On the night of the tragedy he had
left his mother reading the evening paper by her gas fire
and had gone to bed in the adjoining room. Barely an hour
later, at about 11.30 p.m., he was aroused by what he thought
was the rattling of his window. On rising to deal with this
minor nuisance he smelled burning, and opening the communicating door he found his mother's room alight. He tried
to reach her, he said, but was beaten back by dense smoke.
He rushed downstairs for help, and one of the guests, with a
handkerchief over his mouth, crawled through the blinding
smoke into the room until he came upon the legs of Mrs. Fox
hanging over the side of her bed. She was on her back. He
succeeded in dragging her to the corridor before he lost
consciousness. A doctor, C. C. Austen, was on the scene
almost at once. Having examined the woman, he satisfied

himself that she was dead 'as the result of suffocation from inhaling fumes and shock'. The news was broken to the son. To help him bear up, and enjoy a night's sleep, he was given a hypodermic injection of a powerful soporific.

The inquest, for the convenience of the key witnesses (commercial travellers who wished to be on their way), was held next morning, within a few hours of the death. The coroner, accepting the medical evidence (he had no cause not to) and dispensing with an autopsy, returned a verdict of 'misadventure'. If the doctor and the coroner before reaching their conclusions had seen the documents which my partner and I were now digesting they would have believed, as I did, that here was either an astounding coincidence or one of the rarest crimes known to British criminal experience—matricide. Sidney Fox, as those documents showed, had effected upon his mother's life a series of short-period insurances with the Cornhill under policies such as are often issued through travel agencies. The sum payable in the event of accidental death was to be £2,000. The first policy covered a period of fourteen days, but this had been extended on eight successive occasions. Subject only to a break of ten days the insurance had been kept in force from August 10th to October 23rd, 1929. In accordance with Cornhill routine, policies of this nature expire at noon on the last day of the cover. The first eight of the Rosaline Fox policies had so expired. The last cover (one for three days only) at Sidney Fox's specific request (and how sinister it now seemed!) had been timed to expire at midnight.

My opinion, which I have never had cause to modify, was that Fox, bent upon his crime, had kept the policies open by extensions, a few days at a time, until he could screw up courage enough to carry it out. It was no doubt in desperation that he ultimately committed the murder, for the final policy had not many minutes to run when his old mother breathed her last. By her will she left him all she had. The Margate solicitor acting for him was asking our clients for the £2,000 payable under the insurance. One does not lightly assume that a mother's sudden death points to matricide. Perhaps I was over-hasty in exclaiming across the coffee table, 'My God, this is murder!' But if the story told by the Cornhill file did not in itself justify that exclamation it did at least cry aloud for speedy investigation.

Where was I to begin? Sidney Fox had said that he and his mother were making for their newly bought home, End View, at Lyndhurst, Hampshire. A telephone call to a Lyndhurst friend told me that there was no such address. Among our staff investigators at that time were Harry Goodrich (ex-C.I.D.) and W. J. Emmens, with the innocent blue eyes and the incomparable flair for detection. They set out at once. Soon it transpired that Fox had insured his mother not only with the Cornhill but also with the Ocean Accident Corporation for an extra £1,000. The shrewd and experienced claims inspector of that company, Mr. R. E. Hawkins, made a few local inquiries and, concluding that the 'water was muddy', handed his company's interests to me for attention. In cases of murder one looks for a motive. In this particular crime there was motive and to spare. More murderers than have been caught have killed for much less than £3,000 a head; and inquiries revealed that to Sidney Fox, £3,000 meant great wealth. Before the coroner he had described his mother as 'of independent means'. This statement, like most made by this man, was intended to deceive, but it was not wholly false. Mrs. Fox had 'independent means' in the shape of a pension of 10s. a week granted to her for the loss of a soldier son killed in France. Although he had never been submitted to the inconvenience of service overseas, Sidney Fox himself drew a 'war' pension of 8s. per week. This joint weekly income had proved inadequate to support mother and son in the style of living to which they aspired. For weeks before the Margate adventure they had lived by bilking hotel after hotel. Inquiries made by Goodrich showed they had been victimising innkeepers six months earlier when the son, pretending to have lost his wallet, had borrowed, with sublime effrontery, from the Coventry police

10s. with which to get home and had omitted to repay it. The publicity given to Mrs. Fox's death roused these various creditors to action. The luck which had produced what all murderers must hope to hear, a 'death by misadventure' verdict in the coroner's court, was turning against him. That Sidney and Rosaline Fox were little better than paupers became evident when Emmens questioned a Metropole chamber-maid. Neither mother nor son had sleeping attire, neither had a toothbrush, nor any other hygienic equipment. The young man had only the suit he stood up in. The old lady had two stockinette dresses which she wore one over the other. Their luggage, according to the son, 'had all gone on'. It says much for his carefully developed 'Oxford' accent and for his remarkable histrionic talent that while reduced to this miserable state he and his mother were able to pose successfully as an affluent couple and to live comfortably on credit in one of Margate's best hotels without any show of embarrassment. Their method had been to drift, usually by 'bus, from one country town to another. Their luggage, if any, would be carried in a paper parcel. On arrival at an hostelry that attracted them the son would settle his mother comfortably in the hall and then, smiling charmingly, would ask the reception clerk to reserve two rooms. He would add in his cultured voice, 'I must just put my car away—I'll sign the register when I come back.' He would disappear for a short time to deal with his non-existent car and would then return, his credit thus well established. He 'would not bother to bring in the bags'; their stay was to be 'only a short one'.

Sidney Fox after his mother's death had gone to Norwich. Harry Goodrich's assignment was to run him to earth there and to take from him a signed story with sufficient details to justify his claim against our clients. This written story would have been full of interest and lies. It must, I think, be the common experience (it has certainly been mine) that a crook, whether an old lag or a mere beginner, invariably esteems himself highly as a spinner of a plausible yarn. He not only tells unavoidable lies but also adds many unnecessary ones, apparently for the sheer joy of exercising his craft. As a rule it is easy to disprove the irrelevant falsities—which the crook ignorantly imagines will never be checked—and so to cast doubt upon all his other allegations. This simplicity among villains has helped me in many a difficult case but it was not to avail me with Fox.

The Margate police had, naturally enough, accepted Fox and his mother at their face value. Any doubts they might otherwise have had were lulled by the confident but faulty medical evidence on which the coroner had acted. Once suspicion was aroused, however, they moved swiftly, too swiftly to suit my own plans! In supplying the Chief Constable of Margate, Mr. C. J. Haycock, with a photostat copy of our damning Cornhill and Ocean insurance files I told him I meant to get from Fox a full statement in writing. But the police realised that he had a passport and might flee. When Goodrich called at the Royal Hotel, Norwich, during the morning of November 2nd, 1929 (eight days after the inquest), he learned that Mr. Fox, although still in residence there, had gone out 'to make some purchases'. He had not returned by 1.45 p.m. and since it was unthinkable that a guest at that high-class establishment should be disturbed during his luncheon hour, an appointment was made for Goodrich to return at 2.45 p.m. Mr. Fox, whose apprehensions may have affected his appetite, perhaps lunched lightly, if at all, elsewhere. He went back to the Royal Hotel only to be snatched away by the Norwich police almost from under Goodrich's nose, to face charges of obtaining credit by fraud. We thus lost the chance of securing what would, I feel sure, have been a document of deep dramatic interest and one in which a superb liar would have made a supreme effort to escape the hangman's noose.

Once Fox was in custody his fingerprints were taken and he was found to have a criminal record. This showed that he had turned a strong homosexual urge to financial advantage, among men similarly afflicted, and had also practised forgery, embezzlement, plain theft and various forms of fraud. Although he had been sent to prison on four occasions, he had never been charged with any crime involving violence. The most striking characteristic of the habitual criminal is his inability to change from his regular line of crime to another of a different type. Since for that reason one does not expect an ordinary swindler to threaten life, the police would not have suspected the peaceful Sidney Fox of murder had they not become aware of a nearly successful attempt he had formerly made to gas a wealthy woman whose misguided lust for him had led her to insure her life and make a will in his favour. As soon as Fox was safely in custody Chief Constable Haycock asked for the help of Scotland Yard. Chief Inspector Walter Hambrook was put on to the case. Like most of the really good detectives with whom I have worked there was nothing about him to suggest even remotely any connection with police activities. He was on the small side, mild-mannered, quietly spoken and a lover of good literature. His overcoat pocket invariably held not the paraphernalia of his calling but a volume from the Battersea Public Library with a 'bus ticket as a bookmark. I knew him as a profoundly experienced, astute and indefatigable officer. His appearance on the scene meant that Fox's days were numbered.

The Margate undertaker who buried Mrs. Fox (of course on credit; he was never paid) did his work with reverent care. The body was packed tightly in its coffin with sawdust and the lid was sealed with putty. When, therefore, an exhumation was carried out sixteen days after the death the corpse was dry and in an exceptionally favourable condition for examination by that prince of pathologists, the late Sir Bernard Spilsbury.

Sidney Fox had been held in custody on the accusations of fraud from November 4th, 1929, to January 9th, 1930. He was then charged with murder. His trial before Mr. Justice Rowlatt and a jury (with only one woman member) began at Lewes Assizes on March 12th, 1930, and lasted nine days. I sat within six feet of the prisoner and watched his handsome face intently. He had, I thought, decided to play the part of a wronged young man whose outward calm should indicate the inward calm of a clear conscience. It was a difficult role and he overacted it. An innocent man facing the possibility of capital punishment naturally shows patent signs of tension and horror as the circumstantial evidence in all its gruesome detail closes upon him. Fox betrayed superficially no more emotion than the court usher. I am convinced that this air, almost of indifference, made a very bad impression on the jury. One had to be close to him, as I was, to detect the throbbing pulse at his temple and to realise that for all his studied detachment the blood was racing through his guilty heart. Once Fox had been arrested my own duties were officially limited to preparing for the police the formal but deadly insurance testimony. But unofficially I was privileged to see stage by lethal stage the case for the prosecution brought to perfection.

Mrs. Fox had been easily killed. Under the steady pressure of her son's hands on her throat she died very quickly. There were no signs of external bruising. Corpses do not bruise. And Mrs. Fox was a corpse before the pressure was relaxed. One hesitates to record the additional and obvious fact (so often overlooked by criminals) that neither do corpses breathe. Alive and breathing in a room on fire a body draws smoke and soot into the air passages and lungs. A dead body does not. The absence of soot in Rosaline Fox's air passages showed that she was dead before the fire was started. Moreover, a smouldering fire such as that to which she had been subjected produces the poisonous gas, carbon monoxide. The blood of anyone who has inhaled carbon monoxide undergoes a marked change of colour, which, ironically, produces the cherry-red complexion and lips of healthy youth. Spectroscopical analysis of Mrs. Fox's blood showed it to be as free from carbon monoxide as her air passages were from soot. These circumstances were embarrassments for Fox, but how could he have avoided them? To collect under the accident policies he had to stage a death that looked sufficiently accidental to deceive the authorities. There had to be a fire and if he gave a thought to the possibility of an autopsy, and what it would reveal, he had to gamble on none being demanded. He would have been justified in regarding his chances in that direction as a bit better than evens for this reason: three days before the murder, with the anxiety to be expected of an affectionate and dutiful son, he had asked a doctor, recommended by the hotel staff, to examine his mother, who, he said, had fainted. The doctor who called on that occasion was cheerfully intoxicated, and on leaving his new patient had crooked a finger on either side of his forehead and said playfully, 'Bogey-bogey,' by way of farewell. It was fair to assume that so blithe a practitioner would not be too exigent about the manifestly accidental death which was shortly to take place. Nor was he; for when he came to the hotel on the night of the fire and saw a fireman or a policeman (he did not afterwards recall which) applying artificial respiration he bade them 'stop that damn' nonsense' and said the woman was dead. To that extent only his diagnosis was right. He drew an unscientific conclusion from a casual glance and in waiving a post-morten examination he came within an ace of giving Sidney Fox success.

Fox's luck, which had produced the 'death from misadventure' verdict, proved fickle. We all have in our throats just above the sound-box a circular bone called the hyoid. In aged people it is so brittle and fragile that with rare exceptions it breaks under the hands of a strangler. Sir Bernard Spilsbury found Rosaline Fox's hyoid bone intact. This was clearly one point in favour of her son and it looked as if his good luck was holding. On the other hand, Sir Bernard, whose trained and powerful eyes saw things which others could see only with the aid of a microscope, spotted a couple of bruises, one inside the old lady's windpipe and the other on her tongue. The former from Sidney Fox's point of view was bad enough: it was a sign of strangulation. But the tongue bruise meant that the victim (whose gums were toothless and smooth) had been throttled while wearing her dentures. This bruise could have been caused in no other way; and since the woman's dentures were found in the washstand basin after the fire it was an inescapable deduction that Fox had put them there after they had fallen from his murdered mother's mouth. Mr. James D. Cassels, K.C. (as he then was), in defence of the prisoner fought valiantly and did all that could possibly be done to exploit the evidence of his expert pathologists who sought in vain to throw doubt upon that of Sir Bernard. But it was no use. The jury's verdict was a foregone conclusion. Fox was condemned to death and hanged.

*   *   *   *

It was always my belief—strange as it may seem—that Sidney Fox had a deep affection for his mother. Good-looking in her youth and middle age, she had enjoyed to the full what is commonly called a 'gay time'. Old age, failing health and abject poverty put an end to all that and left her nothing worth living for. It may well be that her son, keenly appreciating the tragedy of this decline, thought a quick death would be better for her than endurance of the miseries ahead. Having reached that conclusion he may have argued that the old lady would have wished her death to enrich him. Hence the insurances. This speculation may appear to be illogical, but when some years later I had the chance of putting the theory to the learned King's Counsels who had prosecuted and defended Fox at his trial, neither found it wholly untenable. The criminal who regards his own crimes as quite inexcusable is indeed a rarity. Even had the prosecution of Fox failed, his policies would have proved worthless. They were issued on a warranty that Rosaline Fox was in good health. She was in fact a paralytic, and only able to walk with great difficulty. Sidney Fox's own silent agreement with the jury's verdict is, I suggest, implicit in the fact that he did not appeal.

During the afternoon of Friday, March 21st, 1930, and perhaps an hour after Fox had been sentenced to death, a pleasant young reporter called upon me. He asked if I would very kindly explain to him, in simple terms, the nature of the Rosaline Fox travel policies about which rather technical evidence had been given at the trial. I was happy to oblige. After noting the points which seemed to interest him he put his pocket-book away and engaged me in polite and general conversation. Did I run into much fraud? What was the commonest type of insurance swindle? Were they fun to tackle? Never for one moment did it occur to me that the replies I gave had any 'news value' or that this quietly genial fellow was concerned less with what he had written down than with the raw material which he was carrying away in his head. . . . Next day, motoring through Epsom on my way home after hunting with the Mid-Surrey Drag, I caught sight of an *Evening News* contents bill. It screamed in enormous type:

'THE MAN WHO UNMASKED FOX'

My heart sank, but I felt a compulsion to learn the worst at once. I defy anyone, dressed in full and colourful hunting kit, to enter a small stationer's shop and look nonchalant when buying a paper whose special 'feature' relates to the unmasking of Foxes. I bought the paper with stealth and crept back into the car to examine it. Splashed across the front page was an article lauding me to the skies for my share in Sidney's downfall, and inviting all the world to admire me for sundry other alleged feats of detection. To a film star publicity of this kind would have been invaluable. To me it was an ominous black cloud. On the one hand it might be read as self-sought advertising of which the Law Society Council could take a very bleak view. On the other, my underwriter clients in need of legal advice might well shy at the idea of getting it from one who was apparently not so much a lawyer as a cut between Sherlock Holmes and Sexton Blake. I need not have worried about the Council. Indeed, on their invitation within a couple of years I was elected to membership of that august body. As for Lloyd's, where hearts are ever young and gay, I had to suffer no more than elaborate leg-pulling. On my approach, grey-haired under-writers would either slink furtively away in stage-villain style or stand with crossed wrists ready for the handcuffs and say, 'It's a fair cop!' And they continued to send me their work in ever-increasing volume.

Sixteen

THE FIRE CASE (ÓNE)

I SPENT half of 1931 and the whole of 1932 deep in just such a plot as Edgar Wallace might have used had he found the truth of it not too tall for fiction. The prologue had been spoken by one George Simpkins Mathews, a shrewd middle-aged Cockney who dropped in upon me out of the blue. Both he and his friend Cornock were slightly acquainted with a Mr. Harry Christopher Priest, a Tottenham printer, who, from time to time, had done printing jobs for each of them. With no closer contact than this and no reason to assume that Cornock was other than what in fact he happened to be, a man of unblemished character, Harry, gay, bibulous and the very soul of indiscretion, put up to him a staggering proposition. This was that Cornock should join the long-established, wealthy and highly skilled fire-raising organisation of which Harry was a member and open up in some suitable trade—that is, one with a readily combustible stock. He would then let the gang's expert fire-lighter take such steps as would enable the participants to collect a small fortune from the insurers.

Mr. Mathews, on hearing this story from Cornock, felt there might be enough truth in it to merit enquiry by the insurance community. But to whom could he safely turn to get such an enquiry going? Priest had boasted that the gang were in league with Scotland Yard, the fire brigade, insurance company officials and adjusters of insurance losses and, backed by such allies, ran not the least risk in pursuing their nefarious courses. Mathews thought it would be wise to act

H

as though even this sensational boast might not be wholly false. He had formerly been for some years on the staff of Lloyd's Registry and had there heard of my work as an investigator of insurance frauds. Weighing the pros and cons Mathews decided that I was the person most likely to obtain the results on which his heart was set—prison for the culprits and a reasonable reward in hard cash for himself.

*   *   *   *

I listened patiently to all he had to say. In reply I told him that as a rule I had no use for fire-bug rumours; that every fire claim on which he could throw doubt I could match with scores from my own records. Nevertheless I said I would be willing to gamble a little time and thought on testing this particular rumour if he would act with me as I should direct. He agreed, and what I planned was this: he must cultivate Priest and pose as a man of spotless reputation, who would not dream of embracing a criminal career unless its safety and advantages could be illustrated for him by identifiable examples of swindles, successfully operated by Priest and by his associates in the past, and, above all, by advance notice of an 'accidental' fire to be lit in the near future. Once satisfied by Priest in these respects, and in order to worm himself still further into the confidence of that gullible little fathead, Mathews would offer to open a toy factory in partnership with Cornock who had experience of that trade. I thought that a stock of toy boats—wooden ones—would sound attractive.

*   *   *   *

It may be asked why Priest, even in his cups, should have talked so freely about his crimes to men with whom he had little more than a nodding acquaintance. My guess was that he and his friends had run out of dummies with clean insurance histories and in whose names, therefore, 'good' policies could be obtained. A person whose several enterprises in the past were known to have proved singularly inflammable would find it hard to procure insurance at any price. Priest, with three or four fires behind him, was of no more use. He may well have feared that his fellow criminals, typically dishonourable and ungrateful, were on the point of giving him his *congé*. By introducing Cornock and Mathews, with their spotless records, he might, if they proved trustworthy in his sense of that word, still keep his place in the team.

Mathews played his part well. Priest saw him by turns sceptical, scared, jeering and yet too greedy to relinquish what was held out to him as an easy fortune. To calm Mathews' pretended fears Priest gave examples of four fine coups which had been brought off recently under the inspired leadership of 'The Prince', the gang's master-mind. One was in Manchester ('a sixty thousand pounder') and three London affairs were staged respectively in Golden Square, Goswell Road and Staining Lane. Mathews listened to all this with a quizzical grin. What, he hinted, was to prevent Priest from pointing to any convenient ruin left by a perfectly innocent fire and saying, 'This was one of ours'? Priest sensed this doubt and, to kill it, told Mathews where the next fire was to occur.

On May 20th, 1931, Mathews brought me the catch. The scene of the next fire would be a Poland Street shop selling 'medals, bowls, bric-à-brac and antiques'. It was to be lit within a fortnight. I looked ahead and saw an Old Bailey trial with Priest in the dock. His counsel would ridicule my evidence that his client knew the fire had been planned. To forestall such an attack I prepared a typed digest of Mathews' story and sent it by registered post to myself at my banker's to be held unopened until further orders. This created an unimpeachable dated record by reference to which, in case of need, my foreknowledge of the Poland Street swindle could be demonstrated. In due season this device justified itself.

*   *   *   *

By 9 p.m. on June 1st, 1931, 25 Poland Street was ablaze. The shop-keeper, Felix Bergolz, had a Lloyd's policy covering his stock: Venetian glass, bric-à-brac and antiques. The claim was for nearly £6,000. It chanced that underwriters, although not in the secret, instructed me to act for them. This was helpful. It gave me a plausible excuse to dig wide and deep without arousing the conspirators' suspicions.They thought I was merely displaying the obnoxious nosiness which I had so often shown towards claims presented through L. H. Harris & Company. Priest boasting about the Poland Street enterprise told Mathews he had fired the place himself. This, much later, I found was a lie. With no admitted share in the Bergolz business Priest nevertheless knew a good deal about it. He knew, for example, that the claim was supported by a sheaf of forged invoices for fancy Venetian glass. He predicted that Lloyd's would settle the claim within three weeks. He was too sanguine; the claim, when I repudiated it as fraudulent, was dropped.

*   *   *   *

Chatting with Mathews over pots of ale in The Highbury Tavern, Priest had mentioned another of his current ventures, a dress-making factory which he was running jointly with the Franco-Italian Silk Co. at Belfast Road, Stoke Newington. Enquiries, which could not be traced back to me, confirmed the existence of such a factory but it was idle. They also revealed that the Franco-Italian Silk Co., alias Camillo Vittorio Luigi Capsoni, had drawn large sums from insurers after a destructive fire on May 29th, 1930, at the company's headquarters, 185 Oxford Street. One could without cynicism apprehend that Belfast Road would soon be the scene of another one. I traced 'cause unknown' fires in Goswell Road and Staining Lane, probably those which Priest had cited in his early talks with Mathews. These might well have been organised, as Priest said, by the gang of which his chief 'The Prince' was the head. I believed that such a gang—although of unknown size—was at work. Could it be exposed and eliminated? I thought this possible. But I knew full well that the gap between suspicion and convincing proof in this type of fraud is often so wide that the bridging of it—if it can be bridged at all—entails an incalculable expenditure of time, toil and—last, but not least —money.

The matter clearly called for consideration by the insurance community in general. How might I make an undercover approach to that amorphous community? Its members, the individual syndicates at Lloyd's and the Tariff and non-Tariff offices are continually engaged in competition with one another. They have no central bureau or controller empowered to deal with problems of common concern. I had, however, learned that a few men were then sitting as a joint committee to iron out certain difficulties affecting both Lloyd's and the companies. The companies' representative on that committee, Mr. W. W. Otter-Barry, was known to me only by repute as the wise and highly regarded general manager of the Sun Insurance Office—the oldest fire office in existence. But Lloyd's representative was my good friend and client Robert Walker Roylance, with whom I was on first-name terms. On July 14th, 1931, I gave him the barest outline of my story and pointed out that to convict the few people responsible for the Poland Street fraud would be an anticlimax if in truth it was but one of many such arsonical fires. I advised that the only fair promise of landing the entire gang would lie in an investigation to be carried out so secretly that no hint of it would reach the ears of any corrupt official on whom the gang boasted, perhaps falsely, they could rely for timely warning of threatened danger. It was eventually agreed that, with the knowledge of no more than three or four very senior men, the insurance world would provide me with funds on which I could draw for out-of-pocket expenses and would, still in the deepest secrecy, procure for me such insurance files as I might need from time to time. And I was to have a free hand to pursue my enquiries.

The Roylance-Otter-Barry combination was a strong one. They put up a fund of £3,000 (far more than I thought I should require) and left me to carry on as I might think best. It is said that this joint venture led to a much more friendly association between the companies and Lloyd's. It pleases me to think that my work for both fostered that improved relationship.

*   *   *   *

How big was the gang? In the hope that Priest's movements might lead me to other members of it and maybe to fires or contemplated fires of which, as yet, I knew nothing, I had him 'shadowed' day after day. The shadowing was done by one of my staff investigators, the late Harry Neighbour (ex-C.I.D.), who possessed the necessary skill for such a difficult task. The car he used for it belonged to and was driven by my daughter Barbara. They were, of course, both wholly reliable. Nevertheless, on principle, I gave neither of them the least idea that my interest in Priest went beyond one swindle in which it was hinted he had played a part. They understood only that his activities might confirm my suspicions and therefore I wished to know how and with whom he was passing his time.

Priest was the most blissfully trusting little man one could imagine. Never for a moment did it occur to him that he was being trailed. He went gaily on his not-too-industrious way, apparently without a care in the world. Real detectives have told me again and again that only a very small percentage of their enquiries are productive. Our shadowing of Priest produced precisely nothing. Did he use aliases when engaged in some of the fires about which he bragged so cockily? I thought a good portrait of him might come in useful. When Priest left his printing works one day he was startled to see a camera levelled straight at him. With a look of surprise he stopped dead. 'Would you mind moving on, guv'ner,' said my photographer mildly. 'They want a picture of the empty street.' Priest then realised that the 'they' were a couple of young men measuring the roadway presumably in connection with an accident case. For a moment Priest thought his own picture was being taken. It was an excellent portrait and well worth the trouble.

*   *   *   *

Never from first to last did I unearth the remotest suspicion of corruption attaching to anyone employed on the staff of a fire office or at Lloyd's. I feared only indiscretion. If it should become widely known that I was calling for insurance files on claims long since settled, the curious, having been entertained by some of my earlier cases, might ask, 'What is Crocker up to now?' Rumours, thus innocently started, might alert the intelligence system said to be serving my prey. To ward against this any material I wished to draw from the fire offices came not through the usual channels; it was collected for me by Mr. Otter-Barry personally at top level through the general managers of the offices concerned.

*   *   *   *

What a stupid liar Priest proved to be! His brother (he had said) was 'dummy' not only for the Goswell Road fire but also in the name of 'Priestly' for the Belfast Road effort, then, so to speak, in rehearsal for its flaming end. In fact that nominee, a guileless and guiltless ex-musician, enjoyed quite legitimately the delightful surname of Bottom. Nor had Priest's brother the least connection with the Goswell Road fire in which the claimants were Christopher Brothers, i.e. Priest himself and one Alan Riley, trading in partnership. What was the point of all this lying? And who was Alan Riley? A new recruit to the gang, a founder member, an obliging dummy or just a dupe? The fire which resulted in Christopher Brothers' stock of art prints, Christmas cards and the like being damaged by water had been lit not in their own rooms but in those above occupied by honest tenants. This ingenious scheme presented the swindlers as the innocent victims of a bit of carelessness upstairs!

Messrs. Robins, Davies & Co., the astute assessors acting for the insurers, found among the Christopher Brothers' stock some packages with double wrappers. The external wrappers had escaped damage but the internal ones had not. Leopold Harris, acting for the claimants, was asked to explain this unusual phenomenon. He produced an invoice to show that some of the goods had come from a fire in Plough Court, E.C., *via* his own brother-in-law, Harry Gould, a well-known salvage buyer. The outer wrapping could have served no other purpose than to hide the fact that the packages contained 'old soldiers' which had been under fire before. This was not in itself proof of criminality. It might have been nothing worse than window-dressing. But it was significant that this soiled, trashy stock had figured in the claim as new.

*   *   *   *

The office files which I drew from the insurers of Christopher Brothers and of Bergolz illustrate as well as any how a close study of such files opened up new paths of enquiry and added to what I already knew of the gang's technique. Although one occasionally runs across a versatile exception such as Sidney Fox, criminals in general, having once adopted the type of crime which is to bring in the big money, repeat it again and again, with only such changes of method as special requirements may force upon them. Accordingly, if as Priest had blurted out in his cups, businesses had been started solely to be burned, I might expect to find, once I had traced them, firstly that their stocks (perhaps ex-Gould) were rubbish dressed up to look like honest merchandise and secondly that the respective fires had not necessarily originated in the premises occupied by the assured.

I never doubted that the mysterious master-mind to

whom Priest referred as 'The Prince' was Leopold Harris.

Sometimes friends had told me in shocked whispers of occasions when Harris had gained the scene of a London fire ahead of the fire brigade! This, it was said, could point only to one conclusion: that Harris knew beforehand the very minute at which the fire was to break out. This I thought was nonsense. With such guilty knowledge he would keep well out of the way. It seemed more probable, as much later proved to be the fact, that by some means, then unknown, fire warnings were reaching fire brigade headquarters and Leopold Harris almost simultaneously. He only arrived at the fire first if his Rolls, which always waited at his office door, had a mile or so less to travel than the fire engines.

In the days before Priest's advent no one in insurance circles had the least idea that Leopold Harris might be implicated in an arson conspiracy. I was unwilling to believe, in spite of Priest's story, that, however low Harris's standards of commercial morality might have fallen, he would think it worth while risking his peace of mind, even his liberty, just for the sake of adding a few dangerous thousands to the steady and substantial income he was drawing, with his brothers, from the prosperous, legitimate and old-established assessing concern which had become Harris & Co. (Assessors) Ltd. But the Christopher Brothers affair made me think again.

*   *   *   *

A fire criminally raised in a building and causing damage to nothing but its contents does not involve the crime of arson. To constitute that crime there must be some damage, no matter how little, to the building itself. In looking for proof that the actual premises, 334 Goswell Road, had been damaged by the Christopher Brothers' fire I traced the insurance effected by the reputable landlord. I then drew the fire office's loss papers. Among them I was elated to find a most illuminating document. It was a claim form asking for payment in respect of fire damage to the *structure* of 334 Goswell Road and embodying a declaration of the claimant reading: 'I am the sole owner of the before mentioned property—no other person is interested therein except Barclay's Bank as mortgagees.' The 'claimant' who signed the declaration was none other than Leopold Harris. He had acquired the building—and of course all its keys—a week before the fire.

*   *   *   *

Messrs. Robins Davies, highly suspicious of the double-wrapped salvage paper from the Plough Court fire, approached Mr. A. J. Loughborough Ball, the well-known adjuster who had dealt with that fire for the insurers. They asked him to inspect that salvage and say whether or not it had been still further damaged through its exposure to the Goswell Road fire. Mr. Ball declined the invitation, 'considering that he would be unable to identify any of the property so long [i.e. twelve months] afterwards'. This unhelpful response was regarded as odd, but, at the time, not in any way sinister.

*   *   *   *

The new paths of enquiry which radiated from the insurance files, now coming into my hands, were long and tortuous. I was a spy and had to move by stealth lest my quarry should scent danger and take evasive action. This made for slow progress. Often I would find myself in a cul-de-sac where some worthy citizen bearing the surname of a man known to me as a rascal had sustained a perfectly genuine loss. Sometimes the path would peter out in what looked like no-man's-land and leave me with nothing more than a scrap or two of apparently irrelevant information. But the scraps might in the end turn out to be useful pieces of the jigsaw. I added them to the heap in the hope that one

day they might fall into place and help me to complete the
puzzle picture. Research on Alan Riley, for example, revealed nothing of immediate value. A blameless victim of
the Lancashire cotton-trade slump, he had turned to a new
line of business in Chorlton-cum-Medlock, where he sold
household supplies. In his home town he was, and with
justice, well regarded. Many months later I was to learn that
the innocent Alan had been duped into lending his name to
the Christopher Brothers partnership as cover for his own
superficially honest brother Leonard, of whom I had never
heard. This helped my jigsaw along. Leonard Riley was the
Secretary-Director of Messrs. Art Publishers (Accrington)
Ltd., a concern which had experienced fires in 1927, 1928
and 1929 and in each had used Leopold Harris as assessor.

*   *   *   *

The Staining Lane fire over which Priest had gloated so
unwisely when talking to Mathews in The Highbury Tavern
was traced. It had broken out on December 11th, 1930, in
a building leased to one William Herivel, a gentleman long
since respectably established in the silk trade but now apparently dabbling in arson as a sideline. Priest, well known
to Herivel, but posing as a stranger, was allowed to rent
some rooms on the upper floors. There he pretended to carry
on the business of H. Priest & Co., Mackintosh Manufacturers. It did not matter in the least that he knew nothing
about making mackintoshes, since his really lucrative
business—about which he knew a good deal—was the
making of satisfactory fires. When the time was ripe he made
one most adequately in his upstairs rooms—reflecting the
Goswell Road technique—and recovered £7,250 from his
misguided insurers. A young Niagara was required to extinguish the peculiarly fierce flames resulting from Priest's
handiwork and Mr. Herivel's stock suffered water damage—
to the tune of £3,664. Or so said Mr. A. J. Loughborough
Ball, who assessed both losses for the fire offices in agreement

with Mr. Leopold Harris representing the claimants. Doubts began to creep into my mind as I noted how often, and how speedily, these two men representing opposite interests came to terms on claims which, one would have thought, had called for long and careful scrutiny. Was it anything more than coincidence that before this last fire Herivel switched his insurance to an office which commonly used Loughborough Ball as assessor, and that Priest had chosen an office which would be more likely to use Ball than anyone else? Ball was the assessor upon whose report Priest's mysterious Italian associate Capsoni, alias Franco Italian Silk Co., had collected, *via* Leopold Harris, £22,000 for the Oxford Street fire. Ultimately I had to ask myself, 'Does this distinguished Mr. Ball deserve his solid reputation or is he a lazy bluffer too easily bamboozled by the blandishments of Leopold Harris—or is he a flat crook?'

*   *   *   *

Over the months my jigsaw pieces poured in upon me in a steady stream. I could already fit some of them together. And I felt sure that ultimately, no matter how many might be missing or prove useless, there would remain enough to produce a picture of guilt sufficiently damning to put before a judge and jury. Many, perhaps most, of the steps I took brought either no benefit at all or none that was at once apparent. The story of the conspiracy did not steadily unfold itself as one would have the right to expect in a well-written 'Who-dun-it?' It emerged jerkily with no respect for chronology or continuity. I was badly in need of some luck to help me fill in the blanks.

*   *   *   *

When a certain warehouse near London went up in flames large quantities of goods were said to have been reduced to ashes. The claimants put forward their original stock sheets in order to prove how many of each kind of article had vanished. These stock sheets were kept in triplicate. It was discovered that the true quantities so recorded had been inflated after the fire.

A forger to be successful must avoid many pitfalls. In this instance it doubtless seemed easy enough to turn, say, '11' items into '111' merely by adding a pen stroke fore or aft. No great skill is required to copy anybody's figure 'one'. But the honest stock-keepers compiling these particular records made them out in handwriting. And to get the two duplicates they used double-sided carbon tissue, which incidentally left on the back of each stock sheet, in 'looking-glass' writing, a copy of what they had written on the front. The forger forgot about this and left the backs untouched. So the face of the sheet bore the faked number while the back still carried the true one to deny it. This claim, defeated by a mirror, was I regret to say allowed to lapse without recourse to any form of legal action. It stands out in my memory not because my part in it was amusing and profitable but because it produced that essential slice of luck for the want of which my search for confirmation of Priest's story had come almost to a halt.

*   *   *   *

That luck turned up in the form of a young and prepossessing Scotswoman with a tale to tell. Among those involved in the fraudulent claim which I have just described was one Louis Jarvis (*née* Jacobs) of whom I had never heard. The young lady knew more about him than was good for his peace of mind. The sorry truth was that both he and she had been members of 'The Prince's' gang. But now she wished to make amends. Until she could satisfy herself that I was trustworthy and not, as she had been told by Leopold Harris, one of his close friends, she met me as 'Mrs. Brown'. Happily, like many women she was logical. So soon as she saw my face she realised that my virtue must border on the saintly, for I was the living image of the old family doctor who had brought her into the world. She therefore decided she could safely run the risk of giving me her full confidence, and began by disclosing what I had pretended not to know, that she was in fact the wife of Camillo Capsoni.

Once she began to speak of her own guilt I warned her of the danger she ran. No one, I said, could guarantee her immunity from prosecution. I could only promise that if the gang should be prosecuted I would do my best to see that she and her husband, if he was willing to help, would be called as witnesses for the Crown. Mrs. Capsoni was content with this and broke off our conversation in order to fetch Capsoni along from a nearby tea-shop where he was awaiting her.

Their talk among the teacups must have been brief and to the point, for the lady knew her own mind, and her husband, docile where she was concerned, bent to her judgment. Within ten minutes they were back in my room agreed that, come what might, the confession should be a joint one. And what a confession it was!

Seventeen

THE FIRE CASE (TWO)

THE Capsonis' story, with what I knew already and would build up by many months of subsequent enquiries, seemed to be this. In the spring of 1926 Capsoni—'Cappa' to his friends—an agent for Continental silk factories, was distressed to learn that the premises of his customer, Mr. Louis Jarvis, at 14 Margaret Street, London, W., had been on fire. Mr. Jarvis himself did not seem in the least put out; on the contrary he met Cappa's condolences with a broad grin. He had every reason to be cheerful. His fire claim had brought him in £21,500, of which less than £3,000 had gone out to his secret allies, the brothers Leopold and David Harris. Capsoni, a volatile, romantic Hollywood type with broad shoulders and narrow hips and features reflecting his changing moods, took a keen interest in Mr. Jarvis's happy attitude. He gathered that if one knew the right people, if, in particular, the insurance company's adjuster (Mr. A. J. Loughborough Ball in this instance) was incurious and tolerant, a skilfully planned fire, looking like a disaster, could prove a very profitable investment. It was not long before Cappa, his business ruined by the McKenna duties on imported silk and critically hard-up, agreed to share in Jarvis's next swindle.

Fabriques de Soieries Ltd., with premises at 196 Deansgate, Manchester, was registered on June 22nd, 1927, with three directors, i.e. Jarvis (in his original name, Jacobs), Capsoni and Mrs. Capsoni. Its capital was never more than £300, but it acquired bankrupt stock and 'old soldiers' enough to make an impressive display and effected insurances at the fantasti-

cally exaggerated figure of £60,000. To buy even junk in large
quantities and to run even a dummy concern means money.
This was secretly provided by Leopold and David Harris.

An able incendiary (or 'torch' as he is called in America)
would never dream of raising a fire by means of any apparatus
with indestructible parts likely to survive the flames and give
the game away. Capsoni was shown by Jarvis an ingenious
method free from such a hazard. At 6.15 p.m. on November
7th, 1927, when Fabriques de Soieries was less than six months
old, he put his instructions to good or, perhaps one should say,
bad use. On the showroom floor he placed two highly inflammable photographic developing trays sitting one within the
other. Nipped between them so that it stood almost vertical
was a length of wax taper timed, by experiment, to burn for
fifteen minutes. Crêpe de Chine and similarly combustible
flimsies were draped about the room to carry the hot flames
from the trays to the general mass of contemptible but potentially valuable rubbish masquerading as saleable merchandise.
He lit the taper and was in his lodgings with Ada some miles
away long before the alarm was sounded. The fire brigade
were so swiftly on the scene and so efficient when they reached
it that this criminal enterprise might well have ended in
failure. The damage done, except by water, was small.
Fortune, however, was on the side of the conspirators. The
adjuster for the insurance companies proved so co-operative
that he did not so much as ask to see the invoices which Jarvis
and Capsoni had toiled a whole night through to forge.
He readily agreed the loss with Leopold Harris (representing
the claimants) at £29,000. Leo took £8,000 of it and Jarvis
£12,000. David Harris and Capsoni got only £1,000 each. It
must be admitted that Capsoni had put up no finance for this
venture and that, so long as Fabriques de Soieries lasted, he
and Mrs. Capsoni had drawn a modest weekly wage for doing
practically nothing.

Cappa, well educated and a superb penman, had employed
his leisure on an album in which he tastefully mounted a
snippet from every roll of silk the company had stocked.

Against each he wrote a faithful record of the origin and actual cost. Jarvis, with a keen eye for beauty, could not bear to see the album go when the rest of the Company's records were sent away for destruction. It survived in his custody and was, in due time, to afford me evidence worth many times the negligible thousand pounds which its author drew as the price of his fall from grace.

*   *   *   *

Ten months after this Manchester success plans were laid for another one in Leeds. A retail shop was opened there in the name of Continental Showrooms. Capsoni went to Italy, his native land, and bought with cash put up by Leopold Harris and Harry Gould enough cheap but expensive-looking articles to serve as the sort of stock a firm so styled would be likely to carry. But stock was of less importance than insurance. Mrs. Capsoni in her enthusiasm went all out and obtained policies totalling £15,000.

They did not last long. Those responsible for their issue had second thoughts and cancelled them. A more modest but still grossly excessive insurance was then procured covering £6,300. At a date which fitted into the social engagements of all concerned, February 18th, 1929, Messrs Leopold Harris and Harry Gould travelled to Leeds. When it was dark, and timing his movements most carefully, Capsoni did what was required of him with trays and taper. Inside a few minutes he was on a train for Harrogate to join his beloved wife, already installed in a fashionable hotel, ostensibly to exhibit a choice selection of her Continental bibelots to the visiting gentry, but actually to establish a reliable alibi.

Leopold Harris did not find the resulting claim an easy one to handle. Mr. Thomas Waddington for the fire offices met it with something approaching derision. He was tough 'Yorkshire' and one of the ablest adjusters then living. He denied that there was anything like enough debris to account for that part of the stock alleged to have been totally destroyed. 'This'

I

(said the outraged Leopold) 'is an accusation of fraud. I shall report you to our clients' head office!' But he did nothing of the sort. He had seen the red light and was glad of the chance to settle the £6,300 claim for £3,350, of which he took only £1,500 for himself. One might reasonably write this particular plot off as a failure.

Among the salvage left in Capsoni's hands was a quantity of Venetian glass which he had bought from Bon Compagnie of Milan. For all its delicacy it seemed indestructible. The time was to come when no member of the gang could hear the name Bon Compagnie without shuddering.

* * * *

After the Leeds fiasco the gang ran two schemes simul- taneously, one in Manchester, the other in London. They were almost comically mismanaged. For example the premises chosen for the London venture, just off Regent Street, were boastfully fireproof and so constructed that a taper burning in them after dark could and probably would have been seen by people using the common stairway. And Bernard Bowman, the crook whom Leopold had put in charge of the Manchester concern, Alfred Alton Ltd. (a dress and mantle warehouse), had chosen as manager John Smith, a scrupulously honest man, whose knowledge of that trade was unrivalled.

In October 1929 several interesting things happened. Capsoni, who, with his wife, had been registered as owning Capsoni & Co., Wholesale Silk Merchants (the actual owners, Leopold and Harry Gould, retaining their usual anonymity) moved from the 'unsuitable' Regent Street address to accom- modation more in keeping with their true aims at 185 Oxford Street. He changed the firm's name to one with which I was already familiar, Franco-Italian Silk Co. The stock, although in the main 'old soldiers', rolls of material re-wrapped after the scorched or smoked edges had been cut off, was massive and represented an actual expenditure of roughly £3,000. An insurance of £20,000 was therefore, by the gang's standards, not out of the way, while a £10,000 'loss of profits' policy was well within what their experience had taught them to regard as about right.

This figure of £10,000 was queried by a more than ordinarily cautious insurance official. But a dignified note from Capsoni saying that such a figure would bear little relation to the potential loss should the current turnover be maintained put all uneasiness at rest. It was an impudently truthful statement, for the turnover was nil.

Capsoni, although a lion for courage, began to wonder whether his luck as a fire-raiser would hold. He took extra precautions. He gave orders for a quite unnecessary wooden partition to be erected across one of the showrooms. His sole purpose was to have 'work in progress' as a plausible theory to explain the forthcoming accidental and otherwise inexplicable fire. And after arranging the stock in a manner best calculated to tempt the flames he thought it wise to leave the actual use of the trays and taper in the capable hands of his wife.

His trust was justified. At 6 p.m. on May 29th, 1930, the place went up and burned briskly. Cappa, on his way back from an alibi in Birmingham, felt that he could not have done the job better himself. The lady after relaxing in a local cinema for a few hours went quietly to her flat a mile away. There she received the whispered congratulations of Mr. Leopold Harris who was awaiting her in company with a policeman. She identified herself as Mrs. Capsoni, heard with convincing symptoms of shock the news of the fire and allowed Leopold posing as a stranger to introduce himself as a well-known fire-loss adjuster willing to present her claim in the most advantageous way. At that moment Capsoni arrived.

Now Herivel (of Staining Lane! How glad I was to see this jigsaw piece again!) had played a minor part in this Franco-Italian swindle. Leopold had brought him in for a while during the earlier stages (at £2 per week) to keep a wary eye on finance. Cappa bitterly resented the implied slur and Herivel had been withdrawn. Nevertheless this episode left Leopold, who did not relish having his own plans thwarted, over-ready to condemn any which Cappa himself happened to favour. What Cappa favoured above all was a spot of emotional acting. In his role as the honest merchant just hearing of his ruin by fire he grew better and better with each repetition. Real tears would pour down his cheeks. Leopold could not bear the sight of them. Cappa in the sheer joy of histrionic achievement carried on with his act even after the sympathetic P.C. had gone and all excuse for it had ceased. This was more than Leopold could stand. 'Cut out the comedy,' he shouted, 'and get down to business.' Cappa, choking back a few final and artistic sobs, obliged by signing the form appointing Leopold his assessor.

From then on all was plain sailing. The fire offices chosen to insure the bogus concern did what it was always hoped and expected would be done. They followed their well-known practice of appointing Mr. A. J. Loughborough Ball to represent them. His price for betraying them on this occasion was £400 (in £1 notes). He obligingly concluded that although the cause of the outbreak must be classified as 'unknown', it was probably due to some carelessness on the part of workmen who were carrying out alterations to the assured's premises at the material time. He did not pry into the sources whence the assured's stock came. Nor did he ask to see their books. There were none. He passed the claim at a little less than £22,000.

*   *   *   *

Things were not going too well for Bert Bowman in Manchester. Alfred Alton Ltd. was doing little genuine business and nothing like enough to give Mr. John Smith, the manager, that degree of profit commission which he could reasonably expect from so capacious an establishment. He showed dismay when told to get a £4,000 insurance on the stock then worth, as he pointed out, no more than £250. He suspected lunacy and said so when the policy was increased to £10,000 a few weeks later. And he clamoured for saleable merchandise. But

when so-called merchandise arrived, and in such quantities
that an adjoining room had to be rented for its accommodation, he was more dismayed than ever. It was, he said,
rubbish, and out-of-season rubbish at that, furs and suchlike
with August approaching! The danger of having an honest
man about the place became obvious and acute. Mr. Smith
might at any moment put two and two together and realise
that the true purpose of his managing director was not trade
but arson. Accordingly, and in spite of his protests, John
Smith was sent away for a premature summer holiday.

The coast was now clear for a fire and Cappa was to light it.
He not only detested but despised Bowman, whom Leopold
had forced upon him as financial watch-dog in London before
Herivel had taken over that duty. He was one of the very last
persons he would have picked as partner in a fire-raising
exploit. Indeed during a preliminary survey of the Alfred
Alton premises, Cappa saw that the stock was heaped about
the place without any real thought for that supply of air
without which combustion cannot be supported. And many
of the garments were on *metal* hangers! With all his skill and
experience he would have found it well-nigh impossible to
burn up more than a tithe of the stuff which had been so
painstakingly amassed. Capsoni directed what steps must be
taken to correct these faults if his incendiary efforts were to
meet with any measure of success. And yet when he reached
Manchester to operate as planned, on July 23rd, 1929, it was
only to encounter still another of Bert's idiotic blunders. There
was but one key to the communicating door of the newly rented
stock-room, crammed with junk all set ready for the flames.
This meant that Cappa, expecting a duplicate, had to work
with the original key and incur the unnecessary risk of being
seen and identified when passing it back, after the fire, into
the hands of its only legitimate custodian, the insufferable
Bert. It was maddening.

Nevertheless he went ahead. Nonchalantly strolling back to
the scene of his latest triumph, while the firemen were still at
work, and mingling as one of the crowd enjoying this most

popular of all free shows, he felt a hand squeeze his arm affectionately. It was 'Prince' Leo.

*   *   *   *

True to form, and as though bent on building up evidence for future use against himself, Bert wrote John Smith to prolong his holiday, but made no mention of the fire which had put Messrs. Alfred Alton Ltd. out of business for the time being and perhaps for ever. Leopold Harris gave a fur coat to Ernest Satterthwaite, the assessor who acted for the insurers and very easily agreed the loss with him at £8,700. That coat proved to be a tragic gift. Years later when I sent to ask Satterthwaite about it he made no denial. But within a few hours he died (as the coroner said 'accidentally') from his car's exhaust fumes.

*   *   *   *

The sharing of the Alton spoils was complicated. A first cut of roughly £6,000 went to the benefit of Leopold in that it wiped out the Alfred Alton bank overdraft which he had guaranteed. Next, less understandably, he took £1,300 for furs which purported to have been sold to Altons, not by him but by one H. Gilbert. Lastly he encashed a cheque for £1,500 drawn by Gould in payment for the Alton salvage (Bert obliging with the necessary endorsement). Capsoni did not expect to participate in the profits from the fire. He looked upon himself as an independent expert called in to render one specific service at an agreed fee, i.e. to set the place alight, and was content.

When Alfred Alton Ltd. was being wound up, the liquidator embarrassed Leopold Harris and Harry Gould by demanding from them formal statements to explain their transactions with the company. To escape this dangerous inquisition Leo found it wise to provide through a 'dummy' money enough to pay out the genuine trade creditors at 15s. in the pound. I mention this because it disclosed still another member of the gang: the 'dummy', one Simon Wolfe. I was to become better acquainted with him. He it was who told me in due course that the Gilbert furs were not sold to Alton's but merely hired to them for the fire like stage 'props' at a charge of £200. Only three skins had suffered at all.

*   *   *   *

For me it was fun at its best to hear the Bergolz fire story from Capsoni's own lips. In October 1930 his wedding anniversary was approaching. He was in search of some small gift by which he could let his wife see that he still remembered this red-letter day. Chance led him to the Bergolz bric-à-brac shop in Poland Street. There he bought some suitable *objet d'art* and conceived an idea. Why not let Bergolz sell that indestructible Bon Compagnie glass? It was just the sort of stuff which would sit tastefully among the existing stock. Few could resist the Capsoni sales technique. In due course, not only was this salvage glass on show in Poland Street but, with cash in aid from the ever-helpful Leopold, more of the same sort came in from Italy.

But it did not sell. Bergolz begged that it might be taken away. For Cappa to have the old glass back on his hands would be gall enough. To carry the new as well would be more than he could bear. The time had clearly come for a good fire. It was far from easy to get Bergolz into line. Capsoni's charm, however, turned the trick and with the twenty years of clean trading and insurance history behind Bergolz, policies for £7,000 were procured in his name without trouble.

In the spring of 1931 Capsoni met Priest for the first time. Leopold effected the introduction with one of his rare touches of humour. 'Show Capsoni your card, Harry,' said he. Priest, always gay, whipped out a well-worn portrait of himself taken in the uniform of a fireman complete with shining helmet. Cappa, although slightly startled by this light, even clownish approach to what he thought they should all look upon as a serious subject, responded with the expected laugh. But he felt disturbed. The aim of this meeting, ostensibly a social one, was in fact to bring Cappa and Harry together with an eye to their doing incendiary business on a partnership basis. It resulted directly in their joint venture, the Crown Mills, Belfast Road dress factory, the registration file of which had first told me of Capsoni's existence.

*　　*　　*　　*

By searching official records, and by the use of less orthodox methods, I had compiled a modest dossier upon this Italian silk merchant. After twenty minutes at my first meeting with Mrs. Capsoni I judged that she was no spy sent by Leopold, as she might have been, to pump me under the pretext of imparting information, but a very worried woman who had been drawn, out of love for her man, into a life of crime and now meant to quit it. I was not so sure of Capsoni himself. He had more to lose, and might, I thought, be tempted to trim the truth in telling me his story. Time was to prove that in this I did him less than justice. He believed he came into my life as a stranger and that I would know nothing more about his past than he might care to reveal. It shook him to find that when he hesitated for a name or a date I could often supply it from memory. He had no means of judging how far my knowledge went. Maybe this helped to keep him on the straight path of candour.

*　　*　　*　　*

I was now hot upon the trail and had the help of my Manchester office. It was found that in the Fall of 1929 Herivel and a Mrs. Cross (as nominee for her undischarged bankrupt husband James) had incorporated Acevose Silks Ltd. So soon as the December fire in Staining Lane was well out of the way Acevose Silks (secretly financed by Leopold Harris) had taken the second floor of 27 York Street, Manchester. Its stock, mostly 'old soldiers' from Staining Lane, was insured for £35,000. A £15,000 policy for consequential loss was added.

The floor below was occupied by a new firm of silk merchants with the Anglo-Saxon name of Richard Glen & Co. In due course I was to learn its history from Simon Wolfe. His father-in-law, Harold Gilbert, and Leopold Harris were its joint anonymous founders. David Harris provided £1,000 of the capital. The nominal owner, a dummy of dummies, was Simon's brother Ernest, a fishmonger. He had been accepted as a tenant on the strength of glowing references from two apparently independent firms, both of which belonged to Harold Gilbert. His total ignorance of the silk trade was of no moment. His sole duty was to set fire to the stock—all salvage rubbish—when told to do so.

There was no bungling this time. The fire, lit on September 9th, 1931, was fierce enough to go right up through the ceiling and cause damage justifying heavy claims in both establishments. Acevose Silks (on the stock loss) were lucky in meeting a helpful assessor, Leopold's pal Mr. Satterthwaite (of the fur coat), and recovered £26,400. But on the 'consequential' loss they had the misfortune to face very different assessors, Messrs. William Owen, who repudiated the claim as a swindle and paid nothing. Still worse, my old friends Toplis & Harding were given the job of assessing the Richard Glen claim and being in close touch with me at that time bluntly refused to pass it. It was not pressed. Mr. Ernest Wolfe drifted back for a time into the 'ancient and fishlike smell' of Billingsgate Market. Messrs. Richard Glen, having failed in every sense of the word, put up their shutters for good. But Leopold was not despondent. Looking upon Acevose Silks and Richard Glen as what they were in fact, two parts of one swindle, his own share in a very tortuous split-up was not to be sneezed at. He took about £9,300 without counting his firm's 'assessing' fee, £750. Moreover, he had other irons a-heating and almost ready for use.

*   *   *   *

At this stage Harry Priest reappeared. He was at work once more with Leonard Riley, his *de facto* partner in the Christopher Brothers fraud of 1929. They were registered as holding most of the shares in Metro Radio Ltd., a company formed early in 1931. It was secretly owned by Leopold and meant to end in a profitable blaze. But if some real trade could be done meanwhile, so much the better. A camouflage of honesty would help if in due course the bogus claim should be checked by a too intolerant and suspicious assessor. With this in mind Leopold installed as managing director an experienced radio dealer, Victor Ewart Cope. They had met one another a year earlier when Cope's own shop (in his wife's name) had gone on fire. It may be said that in the matter of fires and fire claims the two men thought as one. Metro Radio Ltd. occupied a gaunt one-storey factory (175 feet deep and 60 feet wide) in a lonely part of Wembley, Middlesex. Its floor had a small store and offices at the front and a roomy manufacturing area beyond. Across the width of this ran an agreeably inflammable wooden partition fitted with open storage shelves or racks. The insurances repeated the history of Continental Showrooms, Leeds. Cope, like Mrs. Capsoni, was too ambitious. He procured a £50,000 fire policy and one of £20,000 for consequential loss. But the insurers, a little later and for reasons unexplained, cried off. Others were then persuaded to insure the stock for £10,000 and the attempt to obtain a loss of profits indemnity was dropped. With this Metro Radio would have to do as best they could. The genuine business which they did demanded a genuine staff. This, of course, multiplied the chances of the fraud being detected.

But the risk had to be taken. At one peak period the works manager, John Duke, had as many as sixty hands (mostly boys and girls) assembling wireless sets from parts. Albert Jones, an ex-naval telegraphist, was taken on as a tester. George Freeman, the storekeeper, was another perfectly straight, and therefore dangerous, man. It must have been alarming for the conspirators to see so many honest people about the place.

Preparations for the coming fire were made with little variation from the now familiar pattern. Some of them were so apparent as to render suspicion almost inevitable. There was, for example, a want of material for the hands to use, the staff shrank, work tailed off and the company's operations became (as Jones was to put it) 'very lackadaisical'. 'Old soldiers' arrived. Among these were hundreds of portable gramophone cases. They were brought along by a 'Mr. Williams'. Anyone could see they had been scorched. Many of them were beyond repair and ended in the boiler-house furnace. 'Mr. Williams' was, in fact, Bernard Marks, an electrician who for the time being was trading as a tobacconist at 37 Barbican in premises owned by Leopold Harris and Harry Gould. Several car-loads of saleable goods were taken away (that is to say, 'rescued') from the factory by one Dorbin, with whom Cope and his family were sharing a Thames-side bungalow. Less saleable goods were shifted from the comparative security of the store-room and set in the open racks against the wooden partition like faggots in a grate ready to be lit.

It was time for the alibi. Mr. Cope went off to Baden-Baden. But fate now took a hand. 'Mr. Williams', using a key which Cope had given him, entered the factory one evening expecting to have the place to himself. He was dismayed to run into Jones, who had stayed behind (with the manager's know-ledge) to work on a little invention of his own. It may well be that 'Mr. Williams' ' lame tale that he had called to look at some of his recent deliveries, about which complaints had been raised, was not readily swallowed by the blunt Jones. 'Mr. Williams' was told to come back in the morning. He did not accept this invitation. But Cope came all the way back from Germany in a raging temper and complained to Duke that he had been obliged to return because Jones 'had been left in the factory that night'. Excitedly he demanded Jones's dismissal. Duke, puzzled by this inexplicable anger, ignored the order and after Cope had consulted Leo about the contre-temps the topic was not again mentioned.

Fate, however, was still in a whimsical mood. Freeman, the storekeeper, kept chickens. He was allowed to save a sackful of old packing straw with which he meant to line their run. He dumped the sack out of the way at the far end of the building. A few weeks later when he went to retrieve it the sack had gone. He searched and at last to his astonishment found it stowed away under the open shelves by the wooden partition. He left it there. This was on October 2nd, 1931. That night Metro Radio went up in flames. I have often said that no fiction writer would dare to invent for his stories stupidities such as those which rogues in real life habitually commit.

Cope's incredible stupidity on this occasion was that he put that sack of fuel in position while in full view of an electrician who was working on top of a ladder nearby. This witness saw Cope's lips move as though addressing him, perhaps to explain his odd behaviour. If so the explanation was not heard and so far as I know has never been passed on to anyone.

*   *   *   *

The Metro Radio fire (lit only twenty-four hours after the Acevose-Glen blaze) must be counted another of Leo's failures. The stock loss alleged was £11,000. Honest men familiar with that stock put its worth at no more than a tenth of that sum. The adjusters had the debris sifted. The indestructible parts found were far short of those which would have been left by the numbers of articles said to have been destroyed. The claim, repudiated, was never pressed.

The luck of the gang was at a low ebb. But Leopold Harris and Harry Gould had the resilience of rubber balls. They shrugged off their recent flops with smiles of confidence and bounced back into action. Their highly desirable premises, 37 Barbican, were all set for another spell of arson under what they felt sure was expert management. On the ground floor Bernard Marks (the electrician knowing nothing about any other trade) purported to run a tobacconist's shop. It was registered (in his wife's name) as The United Cigar & Tobacco Co. Its true owners were Leopold and Harry, who provided respectively the working capital and the stock, i.e. salvage

pipes and other suitable 'old soldiers'. Among the firm's few
genuine customers were two cigar-smoking gentlemen, Messrs.
A. J. Loughborough Ball and William Herivel. The stock was
insured for £6,900, a consequential loss policy for £3,500 was
obtained and invoices were forged against the day when the
need would arise to justify figures in that region. One of Marks's
old friends, Walter Ernest Westwood, a naive type, hard-up
and easily led, had jumped at the chance of occupying the
basement. There financed, as he thought, by Marks, but in fact
by Leopold Harris (who was unknown to him), he blossomed
out as a radio and gramophone dealer in his own name. He
pottered about the place happily day by day amidst a grim
collection of almost unsaleable junk and seems to have done
just as he was bid.

The Westwood insurance was for only £3,250, a figure
reflecting a new touch of caution and a readiness to rest content with small profits and quick returns. History is strewn
with stories of trivial oversights and of unforeseen or un-
predictable events which have brought criminals to justice.
Leopold Harris and Harry Gould were now beset by just such
misfortunes. When Westwood's fire was at last lit—on
December 17th, 1931—with ample fuel and a fine up-draught
beneath the staircase leading from his basement to Marks's
floor above, the resulting heat was terrific. It was indeed so
great than an old leaden main on the adjacent wall was melted
and poured volumes of water over the flames with a pressure
and accuracy which professional firemen might well have
envied. What with the fire damage and the soaking it received,
first from that tragic pipe and then from the hoses of the
brigade, Westwood's stock looked like a total loss. Two items
in his claim are worthy of note. For salvage which in fact came
to him from Gould at £300 he asked double. For some radio
sets which came from an auction of bankrupt stock at a cost
of £47 he asked £800. There is no cause to doubt that he and
his fellow conspirators were handsomely rewarded in the final
settlement effected at £2,533. On the other hand the negotiation of Marks's claim called for all Leopold's gifts of imagina-

tion and advocacy. A good deal of damage had been done by smoke. But owing to the lamentable speed with which the well-laid Westwood fire had been dowsed, no flames reached the upstairs stock and it could not be said that even so much as one single item had been destroyed. This ruled out any inflation of quantities. All that remained was to inflate values and here the forged invoices were of the greatest help. The best that Leopold could do was to agree the stock loss at £2,300 and to hope for better luck on the consequential loss claim. He was doomed to disappointment. My tough little accountant sleuth, Joseph Augustus Cook, worried it as a terrier worries a rat. The claim collapsed. Not a penny was paid. Leopold had drawn another blank.

Eighteen

THE FIRE CASE (THREE)

For Leopold Harris and Harry Gould the opening months
of 1931 were full of action. During this period the Marks
Westwood, Glen-Acevose and Metro Radio enterprises had all
set out upon their crooked journeys. To that trio a fourth was
now added. Mantgown Ltd., a ready-made dress concern, took
premises at 6 Church Street, Manchester. These were passed
by Leo as 'suitable'. They were crammed with re-wrapped
textiles, 'old soldiers' (some of them from Acevose), outmoded
silks from a bankrupt Italian house and the like. In case they
might be needed false invoices were provided. Insurers were
induced to cover £25,000 on merchandise and £10,000 for
consequential loss. The fire was lit on April 25th, 1932. An
optimistic claim was presented but circumstances enabled me
to subject it to the scrutiny of trade experts and of my skilful
Joseph Augustus Cook. The salvage in itself proved fraud. I
secretly bought it through a nominee and held it for use in the
prosecution which I felt sure I should be able to launch before
long. And then Mantgown Ltd., to the dismay of its pro-
prietors, was told that the claim was repudiated. Nothing was
paid.

*   *   *   *

The last fire in the series was, in my view, the most daring
and stupid of them all. It was the fourth to hit Art Publishers
(Accrington) Ltd., who printed Christmas cards and calendars
and had been doing so on a big scale since 1912. In 1927 they
were visited by a purely accidental fire—and by Leopold

Harris. In acting as assessor for the claimants Leopold was soon on intimate terms with their secretary-director, the innocent stooge Alan Riley's brother Leonard. Leonard Riley controlled Art Publishers (Accrington) Ltd. to an extent out of all proportion to the number of shares he held in it, only 600 out of the 10,000 issued. So soon as that first claim was settled the insurances were increased. The policy on stock and machinery was lifted from a justified £12,000 to an outrageous £30,000. The consequential loss cover, which had stood at £4,000 for many years, was replaced by Lloyd's policy for £15,000.

In September 1928 the company met with further loss through a fire which started in adjacent premises. Leopold Harris negotiated a settlement over the two new policies at £67,000. Of this he took 1,000 guineas. His brother David had £400. The insurances were then raised once more: to £40,000 on stock, etc., and £20,000 'consequential'. There was nothing in the company's current or prospective trading to warrant the enormous premium outlay those insurances entailed. But what had looked like wild extravagance paid handsome dividends. On March 20th, 1929, a fierce fire broke out in the assured's stock-room on the ground floor. Leonard Riley argued nonsensically, and in spite of all the evidence to the contrary, that it began in neighbouring premises occupied by a Mr. Kay. On this occasion Leopold learned, perhaps without surprise, that the assessor acting for the insurers was his old and reliable friend Satterthwaite. The stock loss was agreed quite readily at £19,670. The consequential loss policy paid £9,835. The split-up was of deep interest. David Harris's share was £1,000. Leopold drew £3,000, but slipped Riley back a tip of 850 one-pound notes. Riley was also openly rewarded with £300, recorded in the company's books as 'for his services'. The £4,000 which went to David and Leopold was shown in those books as 'expenses', which in reality was as near the truth as makes no matter. Satterthwaite, who never seemed to get a fair share of the loot, had only £200. This was passed as his fee for working out the claim due under the

consequential loss policy. That policy by its terms was to pay
a sum equal to half of any amount which should be paid on the
stock policy. Which means that Satterthwaite earned £200
for dividing £19,670 by two.

The insurers came off risk. For nearly three years Art
Publishers (Accrington) Ltd. could get no cover. Then on a
story from Riley that the 1929 fire had begun in the premises
of Kay (who he said 'had been paid to go') one of the leading
tariff offices was persuaded to take them back into the fold.
The grateful policy-holders were quick to profit by this good
fortune. Their turnover had dropped heavily. Some potent
stimulant was needed. What better than a fourth fire? It may
be thought, in view of their record, that they would be crazy
to take such a gamble. Must they not have realised that even
the most trustful of insurers would look askance at this un-
exampled series of catastrophes and probe a new claim un-
mercifully? Perhaps the gang expected that when the time
should come they would find themselves supported once more
by their trusted ally, Satterthwaite. Perhaps (and this is more
probable), like most criminals, their conceit blinded them to
the possibility of failure. In the event, on September 26th,
1932, the Art Publishers' basement stock-room at Blackfriars
Street, Salford, was ablaze from floor to ceiling.

*   *   *   *

Leopold lodged the claim at £28,000. He must have blenched
on learning that the insurers had put William Penney on to
check it. If genius means an infinite capacity for taking pains
Penney ranks as a genius among assessors. He fell upon that
claim like the Hand of Doom. His first words to Riley can
have done little to raise that scoundrel's spirits. 'Has anyone
got a grudge against you? *Because someone has set this place
alight!*' He dug into the claim day after day, night after night,
and tore it apart. There had been a lot of total destruction,
but, he was sure, nothing like so much as the claimants
pretended. Scouting around among the honest employees he

K

heard that one of them, a Mrs. Webb, had kept a stock-book of her own. This book was said to be missing. Under stern pressure from Penney, Riley not only 'found' it, but like an imbecile handed it over. He must have known that it would implicate him beyond all hope of escape. Here again is an example of what one may naturally expect from criminals—that is to say from abnormal folk—abnormal behaviour. The value of Mrs. Webb's record may be shown by a simple example. Certain cards, known as 'AA' cards, were admittedly burned to ashes. The claimant said there had been 615,000 of them. Mrs. Webb's book gave the true figure as 290,000. This one fraudulent item alone (and there were many others) inflated the claim by £3,500.

The claim was repudiated and died.

*   *   *   *

This completed the group of fifteen fires on which my prose-cution of the gang was to be based. To keep the story of each within the narrowest possible compass I have given no more than the barest relevant facts. Nor have I told of the many other fires which I reviewed only to satisfy myself, in the end, that they were mere 'factory waste'. They did not tie in with the operations of my particular quarry. This was a relief. The case was already too big. The last thing we wished to do was to make it bigger still. Our main problem would be to put it before the jury in a digestible form.

Where could we find short cuts to make this possible? Nothing more effectively simplifies a prosecutor's task than a plea of guilty. What were the chances of Leopold Harris being persuaded to throw in his hand? I had often thought he might do so if he could be tricked into talking freely about his frauds at some place where hidden and reliable witnesses could listen in. Could Capsoni lure him into an incriminating talk or any talk at all? There was bad blood between the two men. Capsoni had been putting pressure upon the gang. Law-suits which he had raised against Priest (ostensibly for dissolution of partnership) and against Jarvis (ostensibly for money due) were looked upon by Leopold and his co-adventurers as blackmail. During indirect and ill-tempered negotiations to buy him off dark hints were dropped that unless Cappa mended his ways he might be set upon and mutilated.

These threats came from a stupid creature, the very last person whom Leopold would have used as his agent in any capacity whatever. Few criminals are without good qualities. Among Capsoni's virtues was an invincible courage. The threats which were levelled at him he treated with contempt. So did I. But I asked him to pretend that he thought himself in physical danger, and to say that if he were attacked he would hit back and land the gang in gaol. Against this background I laid my trap.

Its nature will appear from the script which I issued to the *dramatis personae*. It ran as follows:

1. On Sunday, January 8th, 1933, R.C.W. (my partner Bobbie Whiting) *will call in a car driven by S.* (an obliging client) *at the surgery of Doctor B.* (who remains anonymous).

2. S. will proceed along Berkeley Street and enter Manchester Square arriving at precisely 6 p.m. (watches having been synchronised with railway time).

3. The doctor in his car will be a hundred yards in the rear and will stop to light a cigarette at the mouth of Lower Berkeley Street at a point where he will have the Wallace Collection in view.

4. Mr. and Mrs. X (the Capsonis) *will be strolling along the pavement in front of the Wallace Collection walking east—Mr. X. will be nearest the kerb. If it is wet he will wipe a streak of mud across his right shoe. If it is dry he will use dust.*

5. S., who will be driving an open Alvis car painted yellow with green wings, will, on seeing Mr. and Mrs. X., give three short blasts with his electric horn and will drive past Mr. and Mrs. X and make one circuit of the Square. He will reach Mr. and Mrs. X again when the latter are about the middle of the Wallace Collection building.

6. *The Alvis will drive within a foot of the kerb. Mr. X will step off with his right foot and fall back on to the pavement. The Alvis will swerve sharply to the offside and stop dead.*

7. *The doctor, who will by this time have lit his cigarette, will immediately drive on and pull up short of Mr. X. He will then get out of his car and examine Mr. X.*

8. *Mr. X will appear to be dazed and will complain that his right foot hurts him. The right foot will show marks of having come in contact with the car. R.C.W. will be within sight and will wait at an appointed rendezvous to be joined later by S.*

9. *The doctor will advise Mr. X to go to a hospital for examination, but this advice will be emphatically rejected and the doctor will then offer to drive Mr. and Mrs. X to their home in the vicinity. On discovering that Mr. X lives five floors up and that Mrs. X prefers her husband to go to a nursing home, the doctor will recommend the nursing home of . . . at . . .* (a little further anonymity). *Mrs. X will collect the necessary sleeping kit for her husband and the doctor will take her and her husband to the nursing home where the matron will receive them.*

N.B. Should it transpire that there is a policeman on duty in Manchester Square at six o'clock or that there are too many people for the comedy to be played in safety all the actors will disperse and the programme will be resumed at 7 p.m.

*   *   *   *

In consequence of what I have always thought an amazing coincidence the action was in fact delayed. Just as Capsoni was about to step into the road to be 'knocked down' some unknown nitwit innocently anticipated him and would have provided a genuine accident if S., the expert driver in charge of the car, had not made an emergency swerve and avoided him. The cast, all thoroughly scared, cleared off and resumed one hour afterwards to the tick. They put up a superb performance. Cappa surpassed himself. Indeed so convincing was he that Dr. B., already having qualms about his share in my

plot, feared that some miscalculation had turned a mock
collision into the real thing and landed him with a genuine
patient in urgent and serious need of attention. And the
nursing home matron herself rang me in a state of agitation
to ask, did I know my plans had gone wrong?; that Mr. X
was in a good deal of pain and had a leg bruise the size of a
cheese-plate! I wished I could take credit for that bruise. It
lent an authentic touch. But I had not arranged for any
bruising. It happened that by pure chance Capsoni had banged
his leg badly in stumbling out of a taxi-cab the day before.

*   *   *   *

A microphone ingeniously concealed at Capsoni's bedside
picked up everything he said, and carried it loud and clear to
my brace of witnesses in an upstairs room. They were R.C.W.
and an expert reporting stenographer posing as accountants
engaged on the nursing home's annual audit.

The trap was set. Could our prey be tempted to walk into
it?

*   *   *   *

'You and your threats!' said Mrs. Capsoni to the person who
had uttered them. 'Cappa stepped blindly in front of a sports
car and has only himself to blame for being bowled over. But
he swears there was a deliberate attempt to kill him and is
screaming revenge. Unless you can get Leopold to see him in
the nursing home and talk him out of this idiocy, Cappa will
go to the Yard with the full story of the fires. We shall then
all end in gaol which does not suit me in the least! Get busy!'
Confidential enquiries satisfied that very sceptical person that
Cappa had certainly been knocked down by a car. If confirmation was needed it could be found in the fact that the motorist
was to be summoned for driving with a licence one day out of
date! But neither that interfering person's unwanted advice to
Leopold that he should try to calm Cappa down, nor a direct

appeal which Mrs. Capsoni made to him in the same sense, had any effect.

Leopold Harris had the best possible reason for avoiding my trap. A traitor in my camp, none other than the Chief of the London Salvage Corps, Captain Brynmor Eric Miles, deep in my confidence, had warned him against it.

*   *   *   *

Security had been much in my mind ever since the investigations began. Many thousands of original and irreplaceable insurance documents came into my custody. Their loss would have maimed—might even have strangled—the intended prosecution. To lessen the risk of any such loss I took three photostat copies of every sheet which I judged to be of sufficient significance. Fate or malice could only have destroyed both the originals and their duplicates by striking simultaneously at four widely separated places (two of them fireproof and one a safe deposit).

None of the gang destined for the dock was of a type from whom there was the least reason to expect personal violence. Some of them would no doubt have welcomed my demise. All would have shuddered at the thought of doing anything to promote it. Solely to comfort my wife, who saw me in her mind's eye bludgeoned to death by an unknown hand in some dark entry, I habitually carried, very self-consciously, a small automatic pistol among the loose change in my trousers pocket.

Members of a criminal conspiracy find comfort in the belief, sometimes ill-founded, that no one of them can betray the rest without disclosing his own guilt and so losing his liberty. Among his former companions in crime it was no doubt thought most unlikely that Capsoni would risk gaol merely to vent his spite. But he was incalculable. They were uneasy about him. He realised, I think with amusement, that his Margaret Street flat was being watched and that when he left it he was being followed. The sleuths assigned to this task were normally engaged, he suggested, 'to take-a-da slips for da street book-a-makers'. They were earning a few extra shillings by miserably unsuccessful attempts to do that which calls for the highest degree of skill in a trained detective—shadowing a subject whose suspicions are already aroused.

Cappa loved dramatising himself. He was not above a bit of comedy. With his wife on one arm and a big basket on the other and a little dog scampering at heel he would set out on a stroll from shop to shop and so back home. The amateur sleuths trailing (conspicuously) along soon grew tired of these jaunts and were content to let Cappa go off unshepherded when his purpose was, as they judged, only to replenish the larder. All he had to do then, when called to confer with me or my colleagues at our secret rendezvous—a flat only three minutes away from his own—was to assume his cloak of invisibility—the shopping basket—and all was well.

That I myself should be shadowed seemed pointless. That a 'bloke' had been seen dogging my footsteps was brought to my knowledge (in the most shocking language) by one of my old favourites, a Cockney paper-seller whose pitch was just outside my main office door, at 21 Bucklersbury. I had regularly given him a weekly half-crown for luck. The fate to which he would have subjected any 'flipping creepers wot would tail a real gent' like me is unprintable. I displayed mild surprise at his news and asked him to do no more than watch what was happening and be ready to tell me about it if I should ask. Apparently the 'bloke' (there was only one) spent his time guarding the entrance to No. 21 and picking me up whenever he saw me go out. He was in fact guarding but one hole in an extensive warren. Few people knew (he clearly did not) of the private passage connecting our Bucklersbury premises with our 'overflow' offices in the adjoining Mansion House Chambers. By means of this I could emerge by any one of the several portals provided by that labyrinthine building and be lost in the crowds of Queen Victoria Street or Sise Lane without the lone agent having any reason to suppose that I had left my room. Ultimately a more experienced sleuth came upon the scene. He believed in the frontal attack. Marching boldly up to our telephonist-receptionist Tommy Thompson, he asked in a voice of authority: 'Has Mr. Capsoni called here recently?' 'I have not *seen* anyone of that name, sir,' was the polite reply. This was true enough. Tommy, a war victim (St. Dunstan's trained), was totally blind. The sleuth left with nothing to tell his principals beyond what they knew already.

Nineteen

THE FIRE CASE (FOUR)

I HAD long since determined that Mr. Roland Oliver, K.C.,[1] should be our leading counsel. Known to the profession as 'R.O.', he possessed all the qualities needed for the task: untiring industry, a powerful memory, an easy gift of almost conversational oratory and, in cross-examination, a level-voiced icy style which tore perjured testimony to tatters. At my first consultation with him I produced one of my most useful 'short cuts'. It was a large sheet of cartridge paper bordered by twenty-nine circles. Each circle represented a fire claim which I had investigated. They included the fifteen which I have described in the preceding chapters. In the middle of the sheet were other circles carrying such inscriptions as 'Harris Finance', 'Harris relative', and 'H. Gould & Co. Ltd.'. Lines were drawn from those inner circles to join those of the numbered fires which had respectively enjoyed the use of Harris money, Gould salvage or some other association with the Harris family. Similarly lines curved from fire to fire to indicate some other interrelationship, for example to trace where stock ('old soldiers') surviving their baptism of fire had passed along to be burned again.

This diagram demonstrated graphically and at a glance the general pattern of the conspiracy. Its criss-cross of gently curving lines suggested that it might have originated in the office of a railway engineer. For this reason it was known as 'Willesden Junction' and became the essential preface for anyone hearing the story for the first time. With the fifteen guilty

1. Later Mr. Justice Oliver (since deceased).

fires identified by name in the margin (no one was implicated in the crime regarding the other fourteen) this sheet served constantly as a most useful index for all of us who were concerned in steering the case through to its end.[1]

R.O.'s hobby was building models of historic sailing ships. He worked from drawings scaled down from the originals, many of which survive in naval archives. His years of close reliance upon such examples of the draughtsman's art may, I think, explain why informative documents of precision had a special appeal for him. Few preliminary consultations with leading counsel in cases of comparable magnitude can have ended with a happier and more concise opinion than that expressed by R.O. on this occasion. Giving 'Willesden Junction' an affectionate little pat, he said, 'My dear Crocker—you've got 'em!'

The Director of Public Prosecutions in England is only obliged to conduct the prosecution of capital crimes and a few others which affect government departments (e.g. the Mint in respect of counterfeiting). In practice, however, he concerns himself with any grave charge of importance to the public and is free to handle it in his own department if he so desires. His office is relatively small; he uses the police as his investigators. Our 'fire case' was clearly one which would claim not only his interest but, as we had always hoped, his support. The time came when we were almost ready to get our warrants. Then R.O. and I saw him and outlined our evidence.

The Director (the late Sir Edward Tindal Atkinson, K.C., K.C.B.) was most sympathetic and appreciative of what we had achieved without police help. On the one hand, he felt that in a matter of such gravity the prosecution must be under his aegis. On the other, he saw what inconvenience would arise if, contrary to the wishes of my insurance clients (who were quite ready to meet the costs involved), he should drop me and run the prosecution himself in accordance with his usual routine. With the approval of the then Attorney General

1. R.O.'s juniors in this case were the late Mr. Herbert D. Samuels, K.C. (afterwards Official Referee), and Mr. Lawrence J. Byrne (later Mr. Justice Byrne since deceased).

(the Rt. Hon. Sir Thomas Inskip, P.C., K.C., M.P.)[1] he escaped
from this dilemma most courageously by appointing me his
agent. I say 'courageously' because no London solicitor in
private practice has ever before been appointed to act for the
Crown in this way.

*   *   *   *

It was essential that, once the warrants had been issued, all
the arrests should be made simultaneously. Otherwise individual members left for the moment at liberty might destroy
incriminating evidence or decamp. How were we to avoid the
risk of reporters learning that an application for a sheaf of
warrants had been made to Mr. R. E. Dummett, the Bow
Street magistrate? The Director himself solved that problem
for us very simply. He asked Mr. Dummett to 'sit' during
lunchtime on February 1st, 1933, at the Treasurer's Office in
Gray's Inn. The Capsonis, Mathews and I appeared there and
deposed our respective statements in support of the charges
made. There was no publicity whatever.

Pocketing the warrants, I strolled with Sir Edward back to
his own quarters in Richmond Terrace off Whitehall. There I
was joined by Chief Inspector George Yandell[2] of the Criminal
Investigation Department, the officer who had been assigned
to me at my special request. He was the first police officer to
be let into our secret. I spent the next few hours going over
the tracks of 'Willesden Junction' with him and in detailing
the case on which, obviously, he and I and such subordinates
as he might choose to recruit from the C.I.D. would be working together for many months ahead. This Chief Inspector
('G.Y.' to everybody), like most top-ranking detectives, was
a countryman. He came from Somerset. I never heard him
mention such abstractions as 'loyalty' or 'duty'. But not for
all the gold in the Bank of England would he have betrayed
the minutest portion of the trust which went with his job. He

1. Afterwards Viscount Caldecote, Lord Chancellor, 1939–40.
2. Later Chief Superintendent.

won my heart from the start. At the end of our first inter-view—and despite what he may have thought of amateur 'coppers' in general (doubtless not much)—he said, 'You are the "O.C.", sir. I am the subaltern—what are your orders?'

The skill with which he effected the arrests of all the main members of the gang next day was masterly. He sent a fleet of Flying Squad cars, each under sealed orders, in charge of an officer concerned to collect only one of our victims with his papers and records. I had arranged for Neighbour, my own staff investigator, to watch the Finsbury Pavement premises of Harris & Co. where Leopold Harris, our first catch, was to have G.Y.'s personal attention. When I reached the spot my-self it was to receive a disquieting report. Leopold had been seen to leave his office building, but because of the thousands of pedestrians pouring into the City on their way to work at that early hour his return, if he had returned, had gone un-noticed. By a happy chance Harris & Co. (most of whose business was honest) were then presenting a fire-insurance claim on behalf of one of my clients, Mr. W. From a nearby box I called my own telephone operator, Tommy Thompson, and had him ring Leopold while keeping me in circuit so that I could listen in to the conversation. Thompson addressed Leopold: 'Mr. W. presents his compliments, sir, and wonders whether it would suit your convenience if he calls upon you in an hour's time, sir?' 'Certainly,' replied Leopold, 'I shall be in until one o'clock.' Three minutes later Leopold Harris was in custody.

I took up my observation post again a hundred yards or so from the Harris office and was talking with one of G.Y.'s assistants, Detective-Inspector Allan, when a strange thing happened. Neighbour hurried up to me and, pointing to a jolly little man who was strolling jauntily along, whispered, 'There's Priest!' Priest was thought to be in Stoke Newington, where Flying Squad men were waiting to pick him up. I passed the whisper on to Allan and said, 'Pinch him!' Allan hesitated for a moment. Then he beckoned to a slightly built young fellow whom I had not previously observed. He might well have passed for an undergraduate. This was Sergeant Arthur ('Gnat') Thorpe.[1] The three of us followed our unsuspecting quarry and he was arrested on the stairs of a building in Ropemaker Street. He took it bravely, even with a wan smile. Poor Priest! Fate had cast him for the role of clown. His was the clown's destiny to trip comically but rather pathetically over his own feet.

Nearly all those for whom we then held warrants were bagged in the first day's swoop. They were taken completely by surprise and had done nothing to destroy or conceal their books and records. We made a rich haul. One illuminating document told us that Leopold's intelligence system, the subject of so much guess-work in the past, was largely based on Christmas turkeys and cigars, rewards for firemen who took pleasure in phoning him the addresses of fires just signalled in their districts. Another gave the 'split-up' of the 'profit' (so labelled!) on the Marks Tobacco Shop swindle and carried down a balance for use in the next one.

No matter how gloomily Leopold may have received Miles's disclosures of Capsoni's activities he had not foreseen that gaol might be in the offing. One of the conspirators, learning what was afoot, fled overseas and was never heard of again. We were to have prisoners enough in the dock without him and did not mourn his escape. Simon Wolfe, through no deliberate evasion on his part, could not be found. Making no effort to conceal his identity, he had gone back to the only trade he really understood, fishmongering. Our Mr. Neighbour, on a hunch, traced him to Billingsgate Market and thence to his suburban lodgings. Next morning, when he left those lodgings to go to work, Simon, despite his fishy clothing and aura, was courteously invited to enter a well-appointed motor-car which awaited him. The C.I.D. detective in charge of that vehicle, after explaining why the car's destination on this occasion would not be Billingsgate but Bow Street, tactfully turned to a little small-talk. 'And how are you making

1. Later Superintendent Arthur Thorpe, Head of the Fraud Squad, New Scotland Yard (since deceased).

out with the fish?' he asked. 'Not so bad,' replied Simon, 'but *they won't burn!*'

Few could smile in the face of adversity as did Simon Wolfe and Harry Priest. Many a man with insurance frauds upon his conscience went in daily dread of apprehension. One such rogue with the added weight of years found life under this perpetual threat not worth living. He dived to death under a Tube train, first depositing his watch on the platform. David Harris and Loughborough Ball were not picked up with the first batch. They spent a day or two of tortured liberty before we had evidence enough to justify their arrests. They completed an impressive group of eighteen, namely Ball, Bergolz and wife, Bowman, Cope, Cross, Dywiene,[1] Gould, Leopold and David Harris, Herivel, Jarvis, Marks, Priest, Riley, Westwood and Simon and Ernest Wolfe.

Long before these gentry were in the bag the matter was putting a heavy load upon my firm. One of my then junior partners gave the whole of his time to it. Others lent assistance whenever the need arose. I, of course, was at it night and day. Counting all hands, partners, secretaries, senior clerks, photographers and investigators, we were giving the services of twenty-two individuals to this one case alone. I doubt whether we could have won it without the help of our photostat department. From its two machines had flowed, ever since my enquiries began, a steady stream of copies for my use, all of them, in the circumstances, top secret and many of them vital links in the chain of evidence.

Its indefatigable manager with two assistants all but worked the clock round for ten days when the papers taken from the prisoners' homes and offices by the police were passed to him for duplication. By the end of the case that department had produced and trimmed well over 200,000 prints, many of them against time and after office hours. In so doing it made a substantial but, I fear, unrecognised contribution towards our ultimate success.

*   *   *   *

1. A man released to give evidence for the prosecution.

The hearing of a felony charge in what is so often called the 'police court' is in substance a preliminary enquiry whereby the presiding magistrate may determine, after considering the evidence given for the prosecution and defence respectively, whether or not he is justified in sending the accused for trial before a judge and jury. The clerk of the court sitting below the Bench and facing the dock listens while the witnesses are being questioned and cross-examined. He writes down in long-hand the effect of their answers and so produces a coherent narrative. This is called a 'deposition' and if the witness, having read it, is satisfied that it faithfully records his testimony he signs it as correct.

Our application for warrants had disclosed enough about the case to let Mr. Dummett and his chief clerk (Mr. Lieck) foresee that the Bow Street hearing would be something in the nature of a magisterial marathon. Before it began I told Mr. Lieck that we should call over 150 witnesses (we called in fact 158) and that between them they would identify and put in over 500 documents ('exhibits'). They actually put in 563. He promised to bless any system of working which might properly be adopted to speed and smooth the trial. And he was better than his word.

It was clear that much time would be wasted unless the written records of one kind or another with which the herd of witnesses had to deal could be produced for them in court to identify without delay. These records, the preservation of which was a source of constant anxiety to me, were distributed among their appropriate files contained in the sixteen drawers of four fire-proof vertical filing cabinets. Please! (I asked) might these be brought into the court-room ready to my hand and remain there until the magisterial hearing should end (presumably with a committal to the Old Bailey)? When Mr. Dummett in turn was asked about this he thought it was a good idea. Since there was not a square yard of free space on the court-room floor where my cabinets could stand, he created a no-man's-land by roping off for my use about one-third of the dais which was his official Bench.

He went further. 'Exhibits', once they are put in evidence by either prosecution or defence, normally remain in the court's possession. They may be needed at any stage of the case for further reference, often for purposes of cross-examination. It would not be easy for the clerk of the court to run to earth the required paper in a collection of over 500 of them in all shapes and sizes. Mr. Dummett accepted a proposition that I might take over this duty. Each exhibit (so soon as it had been officially marked and numbered, i.e. had become 'evidence') regardless of its dimensions—anything from an adjuster's report to a visiting card—was to go into one of the stiff foolscap envelopes which we had prepared for this purpose. These were already printed with consecutive numbers and a form of words which, with a few strokes of the pen, could be adapted to give the provenance and sufficient identifying particulars of the contents. The envelopes were to be housed on edge in sturdy steel green-enamelled deed-boxes. How hateful these coffers became in the eyes of the prisoners!

The gang had gone to all sorts of shifts to hide the split-up of their spoils. We were able to bring these shifts out into the light of day with damning effect. But to give proof enough to satisfy the very strict rules of evidence which prevail in criminal cases we should have to put twenty-six bank officials into the witness-box. They would speak of transactions in sixty-nine accounts in thirty-four different banks. Their testimony would be sheer tedium. It would, for the most part, relate to isolated receipts and payments meaningless except to those in possession of the master plan. We told the magistrate that, with his approval, we would not try to explain, as we went along, the significance of what each witness was saying. Instead we proposed that once all the banking depositions had been completed, our accountant, Joseph Augustus Cook, would go into the witness-box to demonstrate with the help of printed 'J.A.C' schedules how those depositions, when pieced together, would trace from their sources the various sums of money with which the fires had been financed and would make plain the twisting paths by which the proceeds of those fraudulent fires had reached the pockets of the conspirators.

This technique was adopted without complaint—even from the defence. It was a wonderful time-saver, but, in a sense, was unfair to Cook himself. It was so easy. It gave no hint of the amount of skill and toil which the building of those schedules had entailed. One example may suffice. Bank of England notes have a short life-cycle. First they are issued to the head offices of the respective Joint Stock banks. These then distribute them among their branches to supply the needs of customers. Sooner or later, perhaps *via* a tradesman, the notes find their way back into some bank or other, thence to that bank's head office and thence again back to their starting point, the Bank of England. There they are punched with certain unmistakable signs of cancellation and are filed (in what is oddly named 'The Library') for any reference which may be called for in the future. With the single exception of the Post Office savings bank all banks receiving or issuing a note at the period with which I was concerned kept a record of its identifying code letters and consecutive number. On all of these 'dead' notes were found the small rubber-stamped mark of the branch bank in which it 'died'. Incidentally, on many of them one saw, endorsed by a shopkeeper, the lightly pencilled surname—or more often the abbreviated address (e.g. '7A Linden Av')—of a shopper who had used it to settle a household account. These markings were of great help to us in plotting the road by which such notes had travelled. It was well worth the trouble to look for them. No one could fairly say that J.A.C. did not 'look'. Before he was satisfied that the 'dead' notes in 'The Library' had told him their full story he had scrutinised over 22,000 of them and had occupied himself, two C.I.D. detectives and 'The Library' staff for the better part of three weeks. And this work represented only one small diversion in the labyrinth which had to be explored before the gang's finances could be reduced to a few pages of cold print in schedule form.

*   *   *   *

The Bow Street proceedings.began on February 3rd, 1933, and occupied the court for thirty days. All the prisoners pleaded 'Not guilty' and on June 1st (excepting only J. L. Dywiene, released to give evidence for the prosecution) were committed for trial at the Central Criminal Court, better known as 'the Old Bailey'.

The depositions ran to 150,000 words, the whole in the clear handwriting of the magistrate's assistant clerk, Mr. Hornby. I had them printed and bound with a cross-index by which under the name of the witness one could find the page and line at which he or she had testified and similarly (under the heading 'Subject') who had spoken about what and where. This particular venture cost a deal of money and I was accused of extravagance. Actually it proved to be one of the very best investments we could have made. In any type of case where many counsel are engaged in court at high fees to work the usual five-hour day the surest way to waste money is to waste time. And the cost is not to be counted solely in terms of pounds, shillings and pence. When a trial is held up while elusive passages are sought in lengthy documents impetus is lost—and the court's attention wanes. Those printed 'deps' were to save many hours and to help the prosecution drive smoothly on. By their use anything which had been given in evidence at Bow Street was found in a matter of seconds. They paid for themselves, over and over again. And, incidentally, they made appropriate mementos for the meritorious, such as Mr. Hornby.

*   *   *   *

It is said that a court has stood where the Old Bailey now stands ever since its site housed the *ballium* or guard room of the legionaries during the Roman occupation of Britain. The sole relic which they left there to remind us of them is, I believe, a leaden pipe still giving water in a remote corner deep beneath street level. But if the present building incorporates no other physical traces of the past it may proudly boast a rich heritage of ritual and tradition. The jurors scan with curiosity the dried herbs which they find strewn over their desks and across the court floor. They wonder why the be-wigged judge in his scarlet robes carries as part of his para-phernalia an old-fashioned bouquet in paper-lace. These, centuries ago, were devices to ward off 'gaol fever' (typhus) and to alleviate the stench which came from the filthy and diseased malefactors. It would be tantamount to sacrilege to suggest that such practices should be dropped as obsolete. Or that heavy blows on an oak door to herald the judge's entrance could be replaced by some less startling signal. Or that the usher (ignored by everyone except newcomers), with his cry of 'Oyez! Oyez! Oyez!', need no longer proclaim, in out-moded English, that business is about to begin.

This diehard love for the past held out small hope that those who ruled the Old Bailey would afford me anything like the facilities which I had enjoyed at Bow Street. I was to be agree-ably surprised. The Chief Officer of the Central Criminal Court —styled 'The Clerk'—the late Sir Wilfred Nops—grasped the nettle firmly. He set aside for me a spacious and well-furnished apartment where I could lodge our battery of filing cabinets, with a small staff to look after them. He followed Mr. Dummett in allowing me to have control of the exhibits. He certainly blenched a little when I asked him to let me install a specially designed telephone for use in court at the solicitors' table. It would be in the shadow of, but invisible from, the Bench. It would be noiseless. Incoming calls would light up a tiny red glow-lamp. Outgoing calls, made in a soft whisper, would be so amplified as to travel, loud and clear, as far as John o' Groats. Without such an aid, I pointed out, a constant stream of runners would pour in and out of the court-room, fetching papers for us, collecting and passing messages for the timely arrival of witnesses and for a multitude of other pur-poses as need might arise. With it I should be able to cut such traffic to a minimum, produce order in place of chaos and speed the trial to everyone's advantage. The learned clerk kept a grim silence. Was he mentally selecting suitable words with which to damn my insolence? Or had he concluded, albeit reluctantly, that even Old Bailey traditions must bow to the march of time? I breathed more easily when he said, 'I will speak to the judge.' And the judge said, 'Let the phone be put in. But if it creates the slightest nuisance it will be removed instantly.' I had won! The Post Office engineers, deeply interested in their novel job, built and fitted a superb instrument It did all I had guaranteed and more.[1]

I became Sir Wilfred's debtor in one other important respect. He gave me a fine room in which (thanks to a friend of mine, a famous *maître d'hôtel*) I could offer on the spot, to the many senior insurance executives who would be attending the hearing, a light meal as good as my guests could have found had the usual hour's luncheon break given them time enough to go to the Ritz for it!

---

1. It is still there.

Twenty

THE FIRE CASE (FIVE)

BOW STREET had been akin to a dress rehearsal testing the quality of our production. It had revealed no weaknesses. Of defence, so far as we could see, there was none. Two of the accused resigned themselves to that view. When the Old Bailey trial opened on July 4th, 1933, Gould pleaded guilty in respect of conspiracy to fire Continental Showrooms, Franco-Italian, Barbican and Mantgown. Bergolz accepted sole responsibility for the Poland Street fire. They both went down to the cells to await sentence. We moved for a verdict of 'not guilty' in respect of Mrs. Bergolz. To our great content she left the court a free woman. The rest, all fourteen of them, seemed resolved to soldier on, doubtless in the forlorn hope that rescue might be found for them in the forensic skill of their advocates, of whom there were, at the start, twenty-one.[1]

1. These included the late Sir George Jones, K.C., M.P., and Mr. F. Ashe-Lincoln (now Q.C.) for Leopold Harris, the late Sir Henry Curtis-Bennett, K.C., and Mr. R. F. Levy (later Q.C. and Chairman Monopolies Commission since deceased) for Louis Jarvis. Mr. Norman Birkett, K.C., who became the Rt. Hon. Baron Birkett of Ulverstone, P.C. (since deceased), Mr. G. D. ('Khaki') Roberts (later Q.C. since deceased) and Mr. Richard L. Jackson (afterwards knighted and Assistant Commissioner of Metropolitan Police) for A. J. Loughborough Ball, Mr. T. Christmas Humphreys (now Q.C., a Commissioner of the Central Criminal Court, etc.) for H. C. Priest and J. R. Cross. The late Mr. Fearnley Whittingstall (afterwards Q.C.) for V. E. Cope, Mr. Eric Sachs (now a Lord Justice of Appeal) for W. E. Westwood, Harry Gould's senior Counsel was Mr. Walter Monckton, K.C. (the late Rt. Hon. the Viscount Monckton of Brenchley). Mr. Henry Elam (now Deputy Chairman London Sessions) for Ernest and Simon Wolfe was his junior.

Two things were obvious: that the trial would last at least a month and that until it ended I could expect very little sleep. To ease my load, and so that I might always be on hand to deal with the unheralded snags which always bedevil lengthy litigation, my wife and I left our home in Kent and moved to the May Fair Hotel. The court would rise at 4.30 p.m. This gave me an hour or so in the City to deal with my share of the paper-work. Then in our hotel suite over a cool drink the problems of the moment would be discussed with whoever might be caught up in them, men from Lloyd's, from the insurance companies, from adjusters' firms and from the C.I.D. We rarely sat down to our evening meal before ten o'clock. And then, more often than not, it was to continue a conference with guests at the supper table. Never in my life have I gone nearer to 'filling the unforgiving minute'. But we felt no fatigue; the heat of the chase lifted us above it.

The importance of the machine-like system by which we kept the wheels of this gargantuan prosecution turning smoothly, and remorselessly, could not be over-emphasised. Thanks to the Bow Street run we knew at the Old Bailey approximately when each witness would be needed, and how much court time each would occupy. We had them lined up ready to give their testimony at a moment's notice. Exhibits with which they would deal were on hand for instant production. This was all arranged with the greatest ease over the whispering phone. For the judge, for the jury, for our counsel and for ourselves we had large scrap albums in which photostats of the exhibits were stuck after the originals had been put in evidence. There were fifty of these volumes. Sometimes when the day's intake of exhibits had been heavy it was an all-night job for my staff to do the photography and mounting, to bring the albums up-to-date for use on the morrow. But it was labour well spent. Without these photostats always before them I doubt whether the jury could have followed the case as they did, through all its twists and turns. Although I was never free from the dread that we might run into a jam of some sort, none developed. The prisoners, already shaken by the collapse of Gould and Bergolz, grew more and more gloomy as the case for the Crown flowed on.

Roland Oliver spent the whole of July 3rd in opening fire by fire. His style was quiet, almost casual. But the story as he unfolded it had the quality of a real-life thriller. The jury were enthralled. Nor did they seek to hide a smile now and then. The evidence of our No. 1 and No. 2 witnesses, Cornock and Matthews, who spoke of Harry Priest's clownish attempt to recruit them into 'The Prince's' gang, was touched with farce. They were followed by our star turn, Capsoni, who was to lift the case into the realm of pure theatre. He inevitably started under a dark cloud. We were obliged to offer him as a self-confessed criminal whose word should only be accepted where it was backed by substantial corroboration. I had given him beforehand the most solemn warning that only by answering with absolute truth every question which might be put to him, could he hope to capture the jury and neutralise the stinging cross-examination which he would have to face. He swore to obey me in this to the very letter.

That he did so is beyond all doubt. He was a handsome rascal. His manner in the box was just right, neither smug nor cocky. His Italian accent was attractive. I was delighted to see the initial hostility of the jury gradually soften into sympathy. Did I deceive myself in thinking that even the learned judge was losing some of his accustomed frigidity? Cappa's confession was true on the face of it. There was ample corroboration. He took with dignity a savage but ineffective mauling at the hands of Norman Birkett. When it was suggested that one of the prisoners at a certain stage had threatened to thrash him, Cappa threw back his head and laughed. And the jury, comparing his athletic physique with those of the sedentary bunch in the dock, laughed with him. The jury were obviously on his side and in consequence Mrs. Capsoni had an unexpectedly easy ride. Her fault, an amiable one, was that she had put love for her man before her duty as a citizen. Juries do not find it difficult to forgive such lapses.

*   *   *   *

We had an exceptionally intelligent jury. For them it was all new. For me it was a twice-told tale and, at times, a little boring. My job was a mechanical one. It was to sit in court and see that our cogs were all in mesh, and to wait for something to go wrong. But with our own ample staff, plus Scotland Yard and the whispering telephone, we were never caught out. The nearest we came to this was one day when the judge suddenly expressed a wish to recall Henry Butcher, a witness who had given evidence earlier in the day and been excused further attendance. I phoned Butcher's office. He had gone home to Bognor. I phoned his Bognor house and spoke to his very bright cook. Mr. Butcher was sea-bathing. I asked her how he reached the fast trains from Lewes (thirty miles off). She said he always hired a car for that purpose. Both cook and garage were co-operative. Cook trotted to the beach. Butcher was summoned from the water, allowed to dry and dress, put in the waiting car (with a sandwich lunch by courtesy of the garage), whisked to Lewes, picked up at Victoria by a police car, driven at top speed with siren screaming past traffic lights and handed over to us pale and shaken just in time, ten minutes before the judge was to rise for the day.

Our case against Loughborough Ball was in the main that he had passed, as honest, claims which he must have known were false. The inference was that he had been bribed. Gould, in a helpful mood after his plea of guilty, went into the witness-box and gave evidence for the prosecution. Among other things, he swore that shortly after the Franco-Italian fire he had sent to Ball's country home by registered and insured post 400 £1 notes in a glove-box. Gould's manager, Arthur Turvey, swore to having addressed the parcel and posted it. Norman Birkett put it bluntly to both in cross-examination that they were perjurers and that the story of a sending at any time by registered mail was wicked fiction. Never for one moment had his upright and honourable client suspected that he was dealing with rogues, or that the claims they presented were fraudulent.

Among our C.I.D. team was Detective-Sergeant Hatherill.[1] Very tall, very quiet, soft-spoken and contemplative, he had two outstanding characteristics for which all the truly great detectives of my acquaintance have been notable. Firstly he did not look in the least like a policeman and secondly he would never drop an investigation until he had methodically and patiently followed every possible line of enquiry, whether promising or not, to the point of complete exhaustion.

Turvey under cross-examination admitted that the firm A. T. Lewis & Co trading from his address was a dummy and had never functioned. But he denied all knowledge of the fact that its bill-heads were used to bolster false fire claims. Hatherill paid him a routine visit to see the A. T. Lewis records. Having done this he asked Turvey whereabouts in the office of H. Gould & Co. Ltd. registered package receipts were kept. The reply was: 'Nowhere! I just stuffed 'em in my pocket along with the other odds and ends that pile up in our job.'—'And when your pocket got too full—what then?'—'Oh! I would tip the lot into a drawer in my bedroom.'—'Let's have a look at the drawer,' said Hatherill.—'What's the good? It's only a heap of rubbish!' 'No matter,' replied Hatherill. 'Rubbish interests me—let's go!' And so the drawer's contents —the accumulation of years—were turned out on to the bed and systematically examined scrap by scrap. Nobody was more surprised than the slightly derisive Turvey when Hatherill at last found the registered-package receipt which quite clearly had covered the £400 glove-box addressed to Loughborough Ball in June 1930. One could not have a better illustration of a good detective 'cleaning up'. The receipt was the last nail in Ball's coffin.

*   *   *   *

On the tenth day of the trial Leopold Harris and Louis Jarvis bowed to the inescapable. They confessed their share in the arson conspiracy. Jarvis pleaded guilty specifically to

1. Commander George Hatherill, c.b.e., Chief of Staff, C.I.D., New Scotland Yard (retired).

the Fabrique de Soieries swindle. Leopold pleaded guilty to
that and nine others.[1] They went down to the cells to be sentenced in due course. Ernest Wolfe unexpectedly insisted on
admitting his fraud in the Glen business but denied complicity
in raising the fire there. And so he was one of the dozen still
left in the dock to fight a losing battle.

What happened after the surrender of Leopold and Jarvis?
In a blurred jumble of memories I recall first an oppressive
summer heat and the cooling system of Court 1, trying with
small success to moderate it. Then I see a rather dreary pro-
cession of witnesses—206 of them. Many of ours, giving only
formal proof of indisputable matters, suffered no cross-
examination, and therefore emitted no forensic sparks to
lighten the general monotony. But monotony vanished once
the dramatic Norman Birkett was on his feet. I shall never
forget either his golden voice or the gallant battle he waged in
the forlorn hope of saving Ball from gaol. Nor am I ever likely
to forget our constant fear that a member of the jury or even
the judge himself might go sick—or die—and so scuttle the
trial and force us to start afresh. But we worried unnecessarily.
Everyone stood the strain without turning a hair. And at long
last, on August 19th, 1933, the trial was over. Leopold Harris
was sent to prison for 14 years, Gould to 6, David Harris to 5,
Marks to 3½, Jarvis to 3, Ball (found guilty only on the Franco-
Italian charges), Riley and Priest to 3 years each. Cope went
down for 21 months, Bowman, Herivel and Simon Wolfe tied
with 18 months apiece. Ernest Wolfe had 15 months, Bergolz 12
and Cross 9. Westwood, who was thought to be not too strong
in the head, was given a sympathetic sentence of 4 months only.

*   *   *   *

This was then the longest Old Bailey trial in history. If
anyone wishes to know how many days it consumed—the
answer is thirty-three.

1. The 'Not guilty' pleas by Jarvis were in respect of Margaret Street
and Franco-Italian and by Leopold Harris in respect of Margaret Street,
Bergolz, Art Publishers (1929 fire) and Mantgown

Twenty-One

THE FIRE CASE (SIX)

THE Fire Case was rich fare for a news-starved Press in the 'silly' season of 1933. Some journalists dubbed me 'The Sherlock Holmes of the Insurance World'. To others I was 'The Gang Buster'. They all fostered the idea that being a solicitor was purely incidental to my full-time work as a sleuth. But our clients knew better and the practice did not suffer from this flood of potentially harmful publicity. Although the case lives on with the persistence of folklore, detail is forgotten. And in the vague surviving recollection of it I am pegged I hope firmly as a solicitor who somehow or other helped to bring an arson gang to justice. I say this in spite of the *sotto voce* comment overheard by one of my daughters in the Savoy lounge. It was made by a stranger pointing me out to another: *'That's Crocker the Fire-Raiser.'*

* * * *

When the trial ended there were presentations. Mr. Justice Humphreys gave my late wife his ceremonial nosegay. He accepted, under protest, from the barristers engaged in the case an inscribed inkstand. Lloyd's gave me a silver model of a 'Merryweather' fire engine on an onyx plinth. I gave George Yandell a gold watch and made his only son a solicitor. Inscribed cigarette cases went to G.Y.'s C.I.D. team. 'Beck' merited something special. She had slaved with me on this enterprise all the way from start to finish. With her background knowledge of fraudulent claims, her card-index memory and her easy control of our operational procedure in court her services, rendered without fuss and without pause (she was never so much as half a day off duty), were seen by all of us as beyond praise. Dr. Harold Dearden, author of *The Story of Leopold Harris and his Gang*,[1] was particularly struck by her role in this drama and above all by her ability to keep a secret. He wrote: '. . . in the matter of discretion it may be said with safety that, compared to her, the Sphinx is a garrulous and confiding old lady'. I thought something stressing this quality would make her a suitable memento. A sphinx might have done, but the oyster, with its unchallenged reputation for taciturnity and none for ambiguous prophecy, was easier. My friendly (Old Bailey) *maître d'hôtel* found one for me, fat and flawless. My jeweller made casts from the two half-shells in silver, dipped them in gold and hinged them together. From mother-o'-pearl plates he fashioned a shallow dais—not much larger than a playing-card—to which this golden bivalve could attach itself as though in its natal bed at Colchester. When the shell was opened a tiny matching clock sat up. If she looked upon the few words of recognition and esteem engraved in the lower shell as ridiculous exaggeration —and she probably did—this was just one more secret to be tucked away and forgotten.

Leopold Harris was a sick man. He had pernicious anaemia. Science, in 1933, could prescribe only one treatment for that disease—the eating of raw liver to the exclusion of all other food. A patient at liberty might well have thought good food and death a pleasing alternative to such a revolting diet. For Leopold there was no alternative. In gaol he ate raw liver or starved. Under the care of an able prison doctor he regained his health. He was philosopher enough, in weighing his crushing sentence, to value this reprieve as 'some soul of goodness in things evil'. Moreover his philosophy extended to giving me credit for having conducted the prosecution with scrupulous fairness. So far as I could see he bore me no grudge. On

1. *The Fire Raisers* by the late Dr. Harold Dearden, London, William Heinemann Ltd.

the contrary, when his world crashed about him and he sought desperately for the emotional relief afforded by confession, it was to me that he opened his heart.

*   *   *   *

George Yandell and I then made scores of visits to Maidstone Gaol. Leopold's information was extensive and precise. Our first concern was to hear from him the story of his guilty relationship with Captain Miles, the London Salvage Corps Chief. Next Leopold helped me to strengthen charges which I was about to launch against a brace of fire claimants and against three provincial adjusters. To Miles' fate I shall turn presently. To the fire claimants I return thanks for a happy recollection. It was my hope that the mistress of one of them, who held vital information, might be persuaded to talk. It was my luck to see the lady while she was still bruised, shaken and furious just after her master had given her a beating. She was communicative. This particular jigsaw was thereby completed and two more rascals went to gaol. The case which we made against two of the assessors was so overwhelming that they pleaded guilty. As they left the dock to begin their prison terms I passed a note to prosecuting counsel, who was, of course, R.O.: 'The bag to date is eleven brace.' He returned it with the added words: 'All cocks.' As for the third adjuster, the late Marcus Fleeson, he had been bribed to pass an impudently fraudulent claim arising from a 1929 fire at a provincial store. Leopold, giving me chapter and verse for it, ran his eye over one of my 'J.A.C.' schedules and pointed to a £300 entry. 'This,' he said, 'was the cheque with which I got the notes to give Marcus.' 'That,' I replied, 'cannot be so. The bank certified that it was not cashed over the counter. It passed through the Bankers' Clearing House.' 'The bank is mistaken,' said Leopold, 'check on it—you will find I am right.' *He was.* This I mention as illustrating the fantastic power of his memory. Unfortunately I had no means of tracing the money into Fleeson's hands. But Leopold, with a smile, put me on the track of other irrefutable if unusual evidence of the swindle. Two expensive electric trains had been ordered from Messrs. Hornby, the model builders, *after the fire*, through the store's toy department. These figured in the claim as having been totally destroyed *in the fire* and were paid for under the insurance policy.

Leopold recalled that the trains reached the Harris and Fleeson homes by railway van. A helpful railway official after a lengthy search was able to provide me with the consignees' receipts. For technical reasons we decided rather sadly not to prosecute but to sue the store for damages. Rather than face trial in open court the defendants met our demands in full. No one could fairly say in this connection that I erred on the side of mercy. It is true that Fleeson kept his liberty. But if after the settlement of this action one met him at all in business it was not as an adjuster for his former clients, the insurance companies. He would be found acting for the claimants. His flourishing practice had withered away. To that extent at least one could feel that condign punishment had been inflicted.

*   *   *   *

Shortly after the gang's arrest Captain Brynmor Eric Miles made one of his, by then, rare visits to my office. 'Most of us have a skeleton in our cupboard,' he said, 'mine is that my bank overdraft is guaranteed by Leopold Harris.' I was stunned. 'Have you ever had any other financial dealings with him?' I asked. 'Never!' he replied with immense emphasis. This was a lie.

Miles as Chief of the London Salvage Corps enjoyed the full trust of his employers, the insurance community. He was on terms of close friendship with some of the general managers. He went to shoots at their country homes and for social week-ends. His job was ideal for a young retired army officer. It carried a good salary, a free and spacious flat over the Corp's H.Q. in Watling Street, a personal manservant and the use of a chauffeured car. I do not know to this day what crisis or stupidity induced him to accept money from—and so put himself at the mercy of—the man whom his employers regarded as their arch enemy—Leopold Harris. But he did.

I learned the whole sordid story from Harris in Maidstone Gaol and had the wretched task of finding evidence to corroborate it. Unless corroborated, as I have already said, the evidence of a convict is of no value. I was satisfied that Harris, while a prisoner, was most careful to tell me nothing but the strict truth. He knew so much in general about the range and nature of my researches into his past, and in particular about the 'motor accident' trap, that it was clear he had been warned by a friend and that the friend must have been Miles.

Bank records, as before, were to provide the corroboration I sought. For example, Harris said he had drawn from one of his own accounts £500 in £1 notes and given them to Simon Wolfe to pay into Miles's bank in Chancery Lane. Harris, who did not miss many tricks, had kept the paying-in slip which was in Wolfe's handwriting. Harris said that for a price Miles, at a secret rendezvous in Hyde Park, had warned him of my contact with the Capsonis and had advised him to destroy all his papers and fly the country. The price £150 was paid in £5 notes. Twenty-seven of those notes were traced by their serial numbers as having been paid into one or other of Miles's banking accounts. At the time of Harris's arrest the bank overdraft which he was guaranteeing for Miles stood at roughly £800. In other words Miles owed Harris that sum.

The facts were reported to the Director of Public Prosecutions. He gave me instructions to charge Miles with bribery and corruption. Harris spoke once again at the Old Bailey, this time from the box as a witness for the Crown. His former place in the dock of No. 1 Court was taken by Miles. The verdict on the major counts was never in doubt. The judge in sending the prisoner to penal servitude for four years said the case was one of the worst of its kind he had ever heard.

This was the sort of case which leaves one sick at heart. I loathed every moment of it.

* * * *

On his release from prison Loughborough Ball published a book, *Trial and Error*,[1] to 'prove' that he had been the victim of a tragic miscarriage of justice. For sheer cool cheek it would be hard to beat. But casual readers, lacking detailed knowledge of the case, would not realise that in 'proving' his innocence Ball was merely reiterating the arguments which had been advanced in his favour, and was conveniently omitting any reference to the evidence which had damned him. For example, the episode of the glove-box containing £400 which Gould sent to him by registered mail was not mentioned at all. Nor did he quote the remarks addressed to him by Mr. Justice Humphreys in passing sentence. '. . . it is impossible for anyone to believe that this [Franco-Italian] is the only case in which you received bribes because there have been traced to you sums which you yourself, clever man as you are, educated man as you are, could not deal with when you went into the witness-box; you had no answer. . . . I say to you that the view which I take is that a man who has had the advantages of an excellent education and who is in the enjoyment of a substantial income is worse when he descends to fraud than the man who has not those advantages and may have the temptation of poverty. . . .'

* * * *

Loughborough Ball always protested that his arrest, utterly unexpected, fell on him like a thunderbolt and that never for a moment had he doubted Gould's complete honesty. As against those protestations there is the fact that Guy Durnford, Ball's legal adviser *before Ball's arrest*, called first upon

1. *Trial and Error—The Fire Conspiracy and After*, by A. J. Loughborough Ball, Faber & Faber (1936).

me to know whether I was after his man and then upon an intermediary to say that, from what Ball himself knew, Gould must be convicted and that if Gould, after Ball's arrest, would testify to that gentleman's innocence suitable financial provision would be made for Mrs. Gould during her temporary widowhood.

*   *   *   *

There may be such things as 'The Perfect Crime' and the faultless criminal. I have never happened to run across either. In the Fire Case, blunders, big and little, in one way or another, gave us our trump cards. I have already touched upon some of them in the course of my narrative. One of more importance to me than all the rest put together sprang from the Fabrique de Soieries adventure. Capsoni, with his £1,000 fire-lighting fee in his pocket, slipped off to Paris by himself 'to have a good time'. But he found without his wife the world was empty. He came back miserably repentant and implored forgiveness. His desertion, he said, had been inspired by Jarvis to whom the lady, with her preference for an honest way of life, promised to be a clog on Cappa's future usefulness as an arsonist. From that moment her determination was that sooner or later she would have the head of Jarvis, her husband's evil genius, delivered to her on a charger. All things considered I thought this not an unreasonable ambition and was willing enough to provide the platter. When Louis Jarvis was led from the court to begin his term of imprisonment Mrs. Capsoni whispered to me demurely, 'Thank you very much.' The greatest mistake one can make in affairs of this world is to under-estimate the power of a woman.

M

Twenty-Two

CLARKSON'S WILL

FOR half a century before Willy Clarkson's death in 1934 most theatre programmes in the British Isles bore the legend 'Wigs by Clarkson'. He supplied from stock at a few hours' notice the scenery, 'props' and dresses for any show capable of stage presentation. To him *Cinderella, Charley's Aunt,* or Ibsen's *Ghosts* came alike. No first night was complete without him. And it was impossible to mistake him for anyone else. He produced himself theatrically, one might have thought from stock, with attire and hair-do exclusive to the role. An extra-long frock-coat gave height and even distinction to his stocky figure. His hair, dyed a near-chestnut, was curled poetically. The heavy moustache, like the horns of a cow, turned up a little at either end. The beard, modelled on those of the Sikhs, was parted in the middle and brushed wide open. His chubby cheeks were lightly touched with rouge. His low stand-up collar, of a design peculiar to Willy, gaped to display his neck and was swathed in a prodigious foulard cravat. From his shiny buttoned boots to his ladylike coiffure he was artificiality personified. He cast himself for the part of the artistic simpleton, a business man *malgre lui* of whose coy, languishing innocence everybody, *just everybody*, took advantage. The amateur dramatic performances which were the *dernier cri* in Victoria's closing years and during the succeeding decades gave Willy the entrée to the London and country mansions of the great and even to the royal palaces themselves. With this

advantage and by cultivating every other worthwhile contact
he reached the zenith of his ambition, which was to be known
by sight to everybody and to be on speaking terms with most
of those to whom the social columns referred as 'celebrated'.

One could dine out on the latest Willy Clarkson story. Sir
George Alexander told of a supper given on the St. James's
stage after a first night when he asked Willy what he had
thought of the show. 'My dear!' gushed Willy—who had made
Alexander's wig—'it was just *too* marvellous, even from my
stall in the third row I positively couldn't see your join at all!'
Clarkson's own accounts of his adventures were always in
character. It was with giggles of happy pride that he related
his encounter with King Edward VII in the Royal Enclosure
at Ascot: 'Teddy slapped me on the back and said, "Well,
Willy, you old b——, how are you?" Wasn't it *sweet* of
him?'

I first met this amiable eccentric during World War I, when
I was a second lieutenant in the Dorset Regiment. The special
duty to which I was assigned required that I should be prepared to doff my khaki, disappear from circulation for a while
and go to work as a docker. A trustworthy Custom's officer
whom I knew bought for me the working clothes of a real and
incurious docker who was built to my size. But my features
raised difficulties. In the first place they were already fairly
well known in the district where I was to labour. In the
second place my rather ruddy complexion would have attuned
ill with the sallow faces of the local comrades. I accordingly
travelled to London, gave Clarkson a suitable if not wholly
veracious explanation of my needs and witnessed a wonderful
demonstration in the art of disguise. It was so masterly that
I found it almost possible to ignore his mincing gait, the
fluttering eyelashes, the ladylike giggles, and the affected
French phrases with which he punctuated his performance.

In my ignorance I had assumed that my face alone needed
attention. 'My dear!' he said, 'the face is the very *last* thing to
worry about. We can fix that in a jiffy, cut down the eyebrows
to a ribbon, shave off a *centimetre* at the inner ends to widen

the gap above the nose, lengthen the eye with a spot of fast colour, bring your hair down in a 'bang' over your forehead so, and stain your teeth *almost* brown. I'll give you a sallow wash for the cheeks which will *only* come off with Willy's *own* remover [giggle] and I'll defy *anyone* to see the make-up, no matter how close they are. But, my dear, everyone, *je t'assure*, *everyone* would know you from behind. So what do we do, *hein*? We cut down your heels and we pad out your shoulders and give you width and we round your back *un tout petit peu* and we alter your silhouette and we make you look positively *short*. And you will learn to alter your stride? A slight nautical roll is easy. Practise a bit, *n'est ce pas*?'

When I reached home I made myself up for a rehearsal. Creeping away quietly I slouched back to my front door and rang the bell. My wife appeared and looked in some alarm at the big tough who stood in the porch touching his cap to her. When I spoke she knew my voice and realised too late the sort of man she had married. She burst into tears—Willy Clarkson never earned a greater compliment.

In 1932 I consulted him again when I wished to pass as a Carter Paterson van-driver for the purposes of a delicate matter upon which I was then working. I found him greatly aged, seedy and nervous. Stageland, in spite of his manifest homosexuality, still found excuses for him. No one took him seriously. But in 1933 it fell to me to take him very seriously indeed. On September 15th of that year his stores in Ramillies Place, Oxford Street, went on fire and he sought to recover from his insurers £36,748.

On behalf of those insurers I made investigations which ranged wide and deep. They led me to conclude that the simplicity and guileless innocence which Clarkson showed to the world was a false façade. Behind it there operated the real Clarkson; a man of filthy secret life, associating with gaol-birds, a miserly rapacious criminal ripe for retribution. I found that the fire, the subject of my immediate enquiry, was his eleventh. On the tenth, which had occurred only two years before, his fire policies had paid him £26,174.

There is in the United Kingdom no central insurance bureau where tally is kept on all claims paid to any one person or concern. It is only when a particular loss happens to throw doubt upon the claimant's honesty that sometimes (by no means always) his hidden history of earlier losses emerges as the result of enquiries directed to the fire or accident offices, to the leading loss adjusters and to similar likely sources of information. It was with something of a shock, therefore, that the insurance community learned how very combustible Clarkson's enterprises had proved in the past.

The assessors appointed by Lloyd's and the insurance companies to examine his two most recent fires had found it impossible to check with accuracy Clarkson's estimates of his losses. To pin him down to detail was, in H.G. Wells's simile, like trying to introduce a jelly-fish into a ginger-beer bottle. 'I am,' said he, *'tout simplement* an artist—business as such is repugnant to me. I know my system is *vraiment* a system *pour rire*. You ask me for lists of this, lists of that—I reply I have none. Where did I buy this, what did I pay for that? I do not know! It must seem awful, *incroyable*, to a trained *homme d'affaires* like you and you will be cross with me. But *malgre tout* my establishment is of international fame and it works the way I like it to work. I muddle along successfully and happily and now for that you will punish me by paying much less than my beautiful wigs and dresses and things were worth! *Alors! tant pis.'*

What were the assessors to do? There was no reason to suspect that this world-famous figure was a scoundrel. If assessors when faced with an apparently honest but muddled claim were to call in accountants and other experts to check it the expense entailed would rarely justify itself. On the contrary, the loss to the insurance company would in all likelihood be increased to the extent of the experts' fees while the assessors would be cursed both by the claimant and by their own principals for wasting time and money. And so the insurers had been persuaded to waive the strict proof which their assessors would have liked to see and Willy had been able to collect on his tenth fire a very profitable £26,174 'by way of compromise'.

When I came upon the scene to delve into the eleventh fire, the £36,748 one, I did not need to ask myself whether or not the claim was honest. From information which came to me after the Fire-Raising Trial, I already knew that I was dealing with an impudent swindle. By disentangling the deliberate chaos of Willy's records, and by recourse to the usual methods of detection, I felt sure we could, although at heavy cost, obtain enough evidence to prove Clarkson's guilt.

Once, when travelling in the Blue Train to the Riviera, I had chanced to share a carriage with Clarkson. He was playing cards with a young man and wanted a pencil to keep the score. He produced a battered old biscuit tin which held what looked like a lifetime's accumulation of pins, buttons, studs, twists of thread, pieces of string, bits of chalk, grease-paint and odds and ends in bewildering confusion. Rummaging about in this hoard he finally found a scrap of lead pencil perhaps an inch long, and giggled a triumphant, '*Voilà!* I *knew* I had one somewhere!' He had a niggardly hatred of discarding anything. This characteristic was to contribute to his undoing, for buried away in the disorder of papers and rough records with which his shop was littered there existed a mass of raw material. From this my patient accountant-detective, with his staff, given time, knew it would be possible to reconstruct balance sheets showing nearly enough what Clarkson's true stock position had been before and after the fires of 1931 and 1933.

That task of reconstruction, which occupied over two years, represented a substantial investment in accountancy fees alone. It was, however, a good investment and produced (on some 80,000 cards) sufficient evidence (without the trimmings obtained from other sources) to prove to demonstration that both claims were fraudulent. 'The wicked flee when no man pursueth.' Long before suspicion fell upon him Clarkson was haunted by fears of being found out. He was one of the many scamps who imagined that my success in the Fire-Raising

Trial was due to a form of white magic, in the face of which bogus claimants might just as well give up hope and plead guilty. This reputation, ridiculous though it was (my *ju-ju* being nothing more magical than dogged hard work), occasionally stood me in good stead. Clarkson, for example, might have made things difficult for me in many ways. He could have thrown me off balance, might even have beaten me, by forcing his claim to arbitration before I was fully prepared. But his courage, never high enough for the frauds on which he ventured, seemed to ooze out of his boots when I came up against him. The mild squeals of protest which he let out when I refused to talk compromise before his claim had been 'examined' were the squeals of the rabbit who in imagination already feels the ferret's teeth. In his extremity he turned for help to William Cooper Hobbs.

*　　*　　*　　*

William Cooper Hobbs was born in 1864. After board-school education he became office boy to a solicitor in a small way of business. He did not stay long in that post, but it gave him a taste for the law. After a short spell as a bookmaker he drifted back into the legal profession, this time as clerk to a barrister with a practice among criminals. While in that comparatively respectable situation he acquired, by means unknown, an interest in Cahill & Co., a money-lending firm. That interest even more mysteriously soon developed into virtual ownership. The nominal owner then died, and Hobbs, in order to enjoy the support of the law against unscrupulous borrowers who failed to repay his loans, was obliged to become a registered money-lender himself. This was annoying; money-lenders are not held in high social esteem and the register in which such gentry have to enroll themselves is most inconsiderately open to public inspection.

Another source of annoyance to Hobbs was that in relation to Cahill & Co. and to some other profitable pursuits in which he dabbled from time to time he found it necessary to employ solicitors and to pay their fees. He put a stop to this waste by teaming up with one C. F. Appleton, a charming but young and weak solicitor, then practising alone. To the world at large Hobbs became Appleton's managing clerk. In fact he ruled the roost with absolute authority.

This arrangement lasted for twenty-two years. Appleton received from it nothing like his fair share of the swag, but he picked up more spending money than he could have hoped to earn otherwise and was content.

I first met Hobbs in 1908 and continued to meet him periodically during the next twenty years. He habitually acted for claimants who had been injured (or were said to have been injured) in street accidents. It often happened that I represented the insurers of the offending vehicles. His claims, most grossly exaggerated, were frequently supported by perjured evidence. One had only to be opposed to him in a few of these cases to learn the depth of his cunning and rascality.

Luck, to which I owe so much, came to my aid in the very early days of my acquaintance with Hobbs. Details of his past and current activities were given to me by an aged clerk who had worked with and hated him. Some of those details were capable of proof. Some I accepted with a slight reserve, although later I came to regard them as understatements. Hobbs, as a sideline, battened on feckless young fools with expectations, ready to sign anything in exchange for some spot cash to invest in a slow horse or a fast woman. Teddy Robinson, the spendthrift son of Peter Robinson, the millionaire store proprietor, was plucked in this way by Hobbs. The scene of the plucking was the flat over Willy Clarkson's shop in Wardour Street. I was told also that Hobbs cultivated the society of male perverts solely because he found among them rich opportunities for blackmail. Once when I called on him at his office I found him full of a defence which he was then conducting upon behalf of a gentleman charged with keeping a male brothel. I asked whether there was any money to be made in that rather special line of legal endeavour. Hobbs replied: '*Money?* There's money to burn—money to burn!'

Unlocking a drawer in his desk he took out a thick packet of letters. Slapping them, he said: 'All from men of good standing, and *rich* clients of the prisoner *begging* to be allowed to help him!' How much, I wonder, did Hobbs 'allow' those unfortunates to contribute towards his personal fortune? Rarely can a blackmailer have possessed more superb material than was comprised in that bundle of correspondence. And as a blackmailer Hobbs was supreme: he had no more compunction than a rattlesnake and was insatiable.

It was not until 1919, when increasing years had blunted the keen edge of his powers, that he over-reached himself in a blackmailing venture which the Press called 'The Mr. A. Case'. The victim, Sir Hari Singh, to be known to the public only as Mr. A., was heir to the immensely wealthy Maharajah of Kashmir. His British equerry, Captain Arthur, was a scoundrel. For his intended purposes Hobbs had to find a warm-hearted lady with a hint of blue blood, and possessing that rarest of all gifts, the ability to enslave any man of her choice on sight. This role was sustained with resounding success by a Mrs. Robinson, who in the sense that she had no knowledge of the plot was an innocent tool. A cleverly engineered but seemingly chance encounter of that lady and 'Mr. A.' ripened so rapidly that soon they were secretly sharing a guilty bed in Paris. A rather amusing rascal—Montague Noël Newton—playing the part of the outraged 'husband', burst into their room in the small hours of the morning crying, 'Now I've got the evidence I want!' The real husband, when told of the liaison (but not of the plot), authorised his informant, Hobbs, to file a petition for divorce citing 'Mr. A.' as co-respondent and claiming damages. On the advice of the traitorous equerry, 'Mr. A.', rather than risk publicity and perhaps jeopardise his succession to the Raj, agreed to pay £300,000 for a quick and quiet settlement. He drew two cheques for £150,000 each, one to be met at once and the other when funds should permit. Having opened an account for himself in the name of 'C. Robinson', Hobbs endorsed the first cheque paid it in to that account and in due course had the whole of the £150,000 to his credit. He told the Robinsons that he had settled for £25,000 and handed over that sum less £4,000 'for costs'. Mrs. Robinson subsequently swore that Newton took £10,000 of this from her by force, but the balance, £11,000, was left in her hands. The wronged spouse, who was not a party to the scheme, refused to take a penny of it.

The equerry's share of the plunder was £40,000. One might reasonably assume that everyone who had been engaged upon the receiving side of this project was satisfied with the outcome. Mr. Hobbs, however, as I have said, was insatiable. After a while he sought to cash the second £150,000 cheque, but 'Mr. A.'s' solicitor intervened and payment of it was stopped. Contemporaneously Hobbs's conversion of the first £150,000 to his own use came to the knowledge of Mr. Robinson, who sued the bank for facilitating that conversion. He lost the action. But it had aroused the interest of the Director of Public Prosecutions. Hobbs was put on trial for conspiracy.

The solicitor acting for Hobbs in this disastrous matter was Edmond O'Connor. I had known him, as everyone else did, as 'Ned' ever since the days when he and I were articled clerks. He was a reckless gambler and was cursed by alcohol in one of its worst forms, where long periods of total abstinence are followed by complete surrender to bouts of uninterrupted intoxication. When in the throes of these he would hide himself away in a low dockside pub and drink himself to the verge of insanity.

The craving for the time burned out, O'Connor would return like a spectre to resume his practice which, as the years rolled on, grew ever more shady.

In spite of the best efforts of Ned O'Connor and of that able advocate, Sir Henry Curtis-Bennett, the blackmailing of 'Mr. A.' earned Hobbs two years' hard labour. Still full of fight, Hobbs appealed. Pending the hearing of that appeal he was let out on bail. It was widely believed, not least by the police, that he had a lot of money salted away abroad and might try to flee the country. He was therefore kept under continuous observation. The shadowing was unexciting: the quarry carried on a normal life, went quietly about his affairs and, if he was conscious of being followed, he did not allow it to disturb him in the least. One morning, however, while Hobbs was pottering about London in this way, under the eyes of his inconspicuous guardians, the Dover Harbour police telephoned through that the said Hobbs had just been prevented from boarding the Calais boat and was being held pending instructions. The London 'Hobbs' (I never heard his real name) had been made up to look so like the real Hobbs that I am assured the two could have passed as identical twins. The artist responsible for this *chef d'œuvre* was, of course, William Berry Clarkson. Scotland Yard, having had their leg pulled in this manner, but having had the last laugh, took the trick in good part. They sportingly forgot about it. Nevertheless, the real Hobbs received a hint that he had better remain in England until his appeal had been heard. To help him take that hint seriously he was told that his name figured on the 'stop' list at all the ports of exit anyway.

*   *   *   *

The first approach which Hobbs made to me on the Clarkson fire claim was staged with his usual craftiness. He had been out of prison for seven years, but he knew that he was still regarded with the special detestation which attaches to blackmailers. He must have known I would not let him into my office; so he lay in wait for me outside the Law Society and accosted me as I left. He looked aged and ailing; his former domineering style had given place to one of servility. Raising his hat, he asked whether he could be of use in negotiating a compromise between the insurers and his old friend Willy. My answer was: 'You have been in trouble enough already, are you looking for more?' This interview lasted less than a minute. I guessed (wrongly) that Hobbs—who thanked me for my friendly advice—would leave the Clarkson matter severely alone and perhaps content himself with a few quiet deals in his old standby, the 'fencing' of stolen property.

Our examination of Clarkson's affairs was going along with painful if excusable slowness, but we were getting some impressive results. In my optimism I could see the day not so very far ahead when Willy might share the fate of the other and better fire-raisers who had preceded him. I was, however, frustrated. On October 12th, 1934, before I was ready to strike, he had a seizure and within a few hours was dead. Sir Bernard Spilsbury certified that death was due to natural causes. Unofficially he agreed with me that fright may have been a contributing factor.

Clarkson's death at once brought Hobbs back upon the scene. He was, surprisingly enough, one of the two executors named in a will of 1927 which Clarkson, with typical stinginess, had made on a sixpenny will form bought from a stationer's shop.

Now the layman who, without legal training, embarks upon the making of his own will may be likened to one who never having trained as a jockey tries to ride the Grand National course at Aintree. The chances are that he comes a cropper. Willy was no exception. He followed 'the clear directions on the packet' to the extent that he employed, most unusually for him, his full name, 'William Berry Clarkson', and he set out similarly the names of several legatees with the sums they were to receive. He even successfully jumped the fence at which so many testators fall, i.e. the signing and witnessing of the document in the strict manner provided by the Wills Act. The sixpenny form is accompanied by a picture of a testator and the witnesses grouped ready to carry out those very necessary formalities. All Willy had to do was to 'produce' that scene in accordance with the script. However, he made one serious blunder: having dealt with the legacies he forgot to say what was to happen to the balance of his fortune, worth, it was thought, something like £60,000. He had saved the few guineas a lawyer would have charged to prepare an adequate will and in attempting that economy had, for all practical purposes, died intestate.

The situation thereby created was one which, as I realised

with grim enjoyment at the time, Hobbs would find intolerable, and for this reason: Clarkson was a bastard. The estates of bastards who do not dispose of their property effectively by will pass to the Crown. It was obvious, therefore, that almost everything of which Clarkson died possessed would evaporate in that way unless Hobbs, the tactician, could devise some suitable corrective action.

Had he been the sole executor, free to exercise his habitual dishonesty upon Clarkson's fortune, the Crown's share would have been a small one. But he was not sole executor. The problem which faced him could not be solved by simple theft.

If you are making a fortune as a swindler it may be a good idea to have a fully qualified swindler as your executor, to complete any of your frauds which may be in train at your death. But since implicit trust cannot be placed in a crook executor it is advisable to have a second executor, an honest one, to watch him. This may be how Clarkson's mind moved when he appointed an old and thoroughly reputable friend, Mr. Walter Hyman, to serve as joint executor with Hobbs (just out of gaol). On the envelope containing the sixpenny will those two names were endorsed. That Clarkson, at some later and unknown date, repented his choice was shown by the fact that he had re-endorsed the envelope, substituting his solicitor's name, Mr. H. Clark, for that of Hobbs. This re-endorsement had no more effect on the will than the alteration of the label would exert upon the contents of a bottle. Hobbs and Hyman remained the executors and Mr. Clark, on their instructions, applied for probate. This, so far as Hobbs was concerned, was the merest gesture. He had thought up an alternative and a more profitable plan for handling the situation.

I first realised the nature of that plan on January 24th, 1935, when Hobbs, accompanied by Mr. Clark, honoured me with a visit. They then told me that the testator had revoked the 1927 will by one made in 1929 and recently discovered in the offices of Messrs. Edmond O'Connor & Co.

Edmond O'Connor, to whom I have already referred, was the 'Ned' who had acted for Hobbs on scores of occasions. Hobbs had the run of his office. That the old and trusted convive Ned should now be referred to with such stiff formality was ludicrous. When it was revealed to me that the sole surviving executor and happy residuary legatee under this new will was none other than William Cooper Hobbs I laughed aloud. I was not asked to explain why. My callers saw no cause for mirth.

It transpired that Hobbs was not alone in regarding this new development as unfunny. One Fred Brezinski (alias Brezin), a comedy juggler, had expected that he and his daughter Simone, as Willy's oldest and dearest friends, would inherit the bulk of the Clarkson fortune. Mr. Brezinski contended that a third will, even later than the 1929 one, had been made to that effect and had vanished. He challenged Mr. Hobbs to fight it out in the Probate Court. The learned judge of that court, in circumstances over which I will draw a tactful veil, gave his blessing to a compromise. The respective solicitors for Hobbs and Brezinski were appointed to administer the estate until the nuisance I was creating over Willy's fire claims could be abated. The assets thereafter available would be distributed in accordance with what the Probate Court had decided must have been the true intention of the deceased. In other words, the legatees mentioned in the 1929 will were to be paid and the residue was to be shared between Hobbs and Brezinski!

By the early months of 1935 our rebuilding of Clarkson's business records from scratch had gone far enough to justify the issue of proceedings. In those proceedings (they took two years to reach trial) we asked that Clarkson's estate should be made to disgorge the money of which the deceased had defrauded his insurers in respect of the 1931 fire. The executors repudiated that claim and asked for payment of the £36,748 which they said was owing in respect of the 1933 fire.

Where a law-suit embraces issues of fraud to be resolved largely by the examination of masses of figures and business documents, the litigant who has the better case may be congratulated if he can avail himself of the finest of all tribunals, a judge sitting with a City of London Special Jury. Subject always to the luck of the draw (for the names are drawn by ballot) one may expect to find on such a jury accountants, bankers, brokers, shippers and merchants; that is to say, a good cross-section of City principals. We had a City of London Special Jury for the Clarkson fire case and felt safe. They listened with the utmost patience throughout the seven days' hearing and, in spite of the brilliant performance put over by Sir Patrick Hastings on behalf of the defendants, both 1931 and 1933 claims were declared fraudulent. The jury were unable to agree whether or not Clarkson had, as we alleged, employed two men (whom we named) to light the 1931 fire. The fact that this issue was left undecided was of no consequence. We obtained the judgment we had sought and Clarkson's administrators faced a gloomy prospect: an asset of £36,748, which they had hoped to collect, had vanished and a liability of £26,174, which they had hoped to escape, was now judicially established.

*   *   *   *

There is no line of investigation more fascinating than that relating to 'questioned documents'. It is a favourite theory of mine that a crook who relies upon a bogus document is given away once that document comes under suspicion and is studied with sufficient care. I have yet to meet a case which shakes that theory or a professional detective who rejects it. No matter how adept the forger may be, he blunders, just as the merest tyro does. Hobbs, it is thought, used forgery as an aid to business all his adult life. With that experience he must have deemed it child's play to forge a will such as Clarkson might actually have made on the date chosen for it, i.e. June 24th, 1929, at the place chosen, i.e. O'Connor's office, and in the presence of the chosen 'witnesses', i.e. O'Connor and O'Connor's clerk Mitchell.

But Hobbs, for all his cleverness, ran into two manifest errors. On the date of the forged will Clarkson was in Le Touquet and Mitchell had not yet entered O'Connor's service. Moreover, legatees who had been in Clarkson's employ upwards of thirty years were misdescribed in a manner which Clarkson would never have passed; for example, a Mr. Rogers was called 'Mrs. Rogers', Arthur Stevens was called 'Charles Stevens', Herbert Blomfield was called 'Mr. Herbert' and Mrs. Dorothy Bowsden was called 'Miss Dolly'. Dennis William Hawker Helyar, Clarkson's own godson, was called in the forged will 'Hawker Helyar', while the name of Clarkson's oldest friend, Brezin, was misspelled 'Breizin'.

Again one was expected to believe that the 'witness', J. Mitchell, an experienced law clerk (comfortably dead long before Clarkson), had been content merely to sign his name and to give neither his address nor description, and that the highly experienced O'Connor, witnessing the will jointly with Mitchell, had countenanced this unheard-of laxity.

Still blundering, Hobbs arranged for the will to be 'found' in circumstances which were incredible. He knew, so his story ran, that there was a 1929 will because the testator had written him that Mitchell of O'Connor's had made it for him. In the light of that knowledge (but forgetting he had not introduced his friend Mitchell to O'Connor until 1933!) he had caused Mr. Henry Clark, the solicitor, to write Messrs. Edmond O'Connor & Co. to search for the will which was 'most probably' in their office. O'Connor's reply was that he had made no such will and knew nothing about it. Upon further enquiry O'Connor repeated that he could find no trace of it. Ten days later, in spite of the earlier searches having proved fruitless, Messrs. Edmond O'Connor & Co. 'found' the will after all and sent it to Mr. Clark.

To any one who knew (as so many of us did) that Hobbs and O'Connor were bosom pals, literally as thick as thieves, the idea that Hobbs, honestly believing that Ned had a missing will, would send him formal letters about it through another lawyer fell into the sphere of fantasy.

To Brezin, familiar with Clarkson's business affairs and knowing all the staff well, the falsity of the 1929 will screamed aloud. He was, however, disappointed in his hopes that the screams would arouse the Treasury. He reported the fore-going facts to them, thinking they would move against Hobbs to recover for the Crown the unwilled residue of Clarkson's estate. Neither the Treasury nor any other government department showed the least interest in the circumstance that a notorious ex-convict was well on the way to enrich himself by one of the gravest crimes in the calendar, the forging and uttering of a last will and testament. In short, authority was content to treat Hobbs on this occasion as an honest man. Mr. Brezin, as I have already indicated, was left to fight it out with him in the Probate Court on that basis.

*   *   *   *

When after ten months' sick leave I returned to the City at the latter end of 1935, I found that Hobbs was clearly regard-ing himself as no longer in any danger. I set to work and picked up the main threads of the story. Bit by bit I gleaned enough to leave no doubt in my mind that if a good man from Scotland Yard were put on the trail Hobbs and O'Connor would inevitably land in gaol. After my work for him in the 1933 Fire Case Sir Edward Tindal Atkinson, the Director of Public Prosecutions, treated me as a friend. When I took advantage of that pleasant relationship to give him un-officially an outline of the Clarkson will conspiracy, he was good enough to agree with me (still unofficially) that if the matter should reach him 'through the usual channels' he would certainly direct a thorough enquiry. It did so reach him. The Treasury solicitor who had declined to intervene changed his mind. He sent a memorandum to Sir Edward, who in turn instructed the Yard. The investigation was assigned to 'Len' Burt, then Chief Inspector, but destined to become Commander Leonard Burt, M.V.O., C.B.E., Chief of the

N

Scotland Yard Special Branch, and justly recognised as one
of the world's greatest detectives. Within a couple of months
he had put in his report and had recommended criminal proceedings. And nothing happened. Week after week went by
with no decision. One might have been excused for thinking
that Hobbs enjoyed the protection of some Satanic power.
Again I erupted, blasting and cursing even within the walls
of the Temple itself. Finally a learned barrister for whom I
entertained the highest regard, slow in making up his mind,
cursed back at me, but finally advised the Director that there
should be a prosecution.

Half a year passed before the Bow Street magistrate was
asked to grant warrants for the arrest of Hobbs and
O'Connor. This application was refused, presumably because
the magistrate, Mr. Fry, did not grasp the strength of the
case. Satan was not yet beaten. Happily Sir Norman Kendall,
then Assistant Commissioner of Police in charge of C.I.D.,
was very much on the side of the angels and I guess that
under his influence Mr. Fry had second thoughts. The
warrants were issued.

*   *   *   *

What a chapter Edgar Wallace could have written around
the arrests! There would have been no need for him to introduce a single note of fiction.

Hobbs, with a silvery beard hiding his cruel mouth, had a
look of Old Testament respectability about him. On the
evening of January 13th, 1938, he sat by the fireside in his
New Malden home quietly reading. Chief Inspector Burt and
his henchman Sergeant Tapsell, having peeped through the
blinds to make sure of their quarry (risking attack from the
savage Alsatian dog which was on guard), rang and were
admitted.

Leonard Burt does not look anything like the detectives of
stage and screen. Of medium size, gentle, sympathetic, good-
humoured, absurdly modest, no theatrical producer would

dream of casting him for a hawk-eyed, stern, dynamic arm of the law. On the other hand, no producer in search of comedy relief could have bettered Sergeant Tapsell. That excellent officer, whose brain worked like lightning and whose memory stored with effortless ease every detail of the cases on which he worked, loved to play the simpleton. In crime detection it is sometimes worth while to 'cover discretion 'neath a coat of folly'.

Hobbs, when the warrant was read to him, had a heart attack and looked near dying. The Chief Inspector, not wishing to have a corpse on his hands, ran to fetch medical aid. While he was gone Hobbs pulled himself together and anxious to know the strength of the case against him tried to pump the Sergeant. Tapsell went into his routine performance. Shyly fiddling with his fingers and looking abashed, he said, 'It's Mr. Burt's case, sir—I don't know the *details* myself, sir,' and fell dumb. This gross understatement tickled the Sergeant's sense of humour and reduced Hobbs to despairing silence until Burt's return with the doctor.

Hobbs was too ill to be moved and remained at his home under police guard for a week. This delay gave us a chance to look for Edmond O'Connor, who, having stolen large sums from his clients, had vanished in June 1936. A warrant was out for his arrest. His friends were many and, apart from himself, he had no enemies. None who knew of his hide-out— they must have been few—were likely to betray him. Hopes of finding him seemed dim. But I learned, by chance, that after his flight from London he had been treated in an Irish hospital for serious injuries received in a motor accident. And I also knew an ex-I.R.A. officer who had sought my advice about establishing an enquiry agency in Eire. His experience and access to the former I.R.A. grapevine seemed to equip him most admirably for my purpose. He was grateful for my help in the past and I thought in return he might help me to find O'Connor. Armed with the hospital clue this young man traced Ned, who was using the name 'Moran', and expressed relief when the Irish C.I.D. tapped him on the shoulder.

Chief Inspector Burt went to Dublin at once to collect a very pathetic O'Connor reduced to penury: his worldly possessions were the shabby suit he stood up in, an inch of shaving stick, a safety razor and a florin. It is distressing to see an old colleague in the dock and all the more so if one has helped to put him there. For the ten years before his downfall Ned had been one of London's best-known police-court advocates. Burt could not bear the thought of such a man coming before the magistrate looking like a tramp. So he made him a present of a shirt and collar and tie and sent me down to see him in the awesome underground cells at Bow Street, where an inch of sawdust lay on the floor to soak up the condensed moisture which ran down the tiled walls. It was a harrowing interview. I made it plain to O'Connor that although I had no official standing I was closely identified with the prosecution. He saw that I was sincerely sorry for this; with all the goodwill in the world he shook me warmly by the hand and almost gaily told me not to give it another thought.

I begged him to tell the truth, which was that he had been led into the conspiracy when he was distraught through his desperate financial position and consequent illness, and that, as we all recognised, his tempter had been the arch-villain Hobbs. None knew better than O'Connor that to adopt my proposal could do him no harm and might shorten the sentence he must otherwise expect. But the idea of betraying even a rat like Hobbs was repugnant to him; he decided to fight it out to the bitter and inevitable end. There was more good than bad in poor Ned O'Connor's make up.

*   *   *   *

The forged will, in respect of which Hobbs had sought probate, was in the custody of Somerset House. It was not open to examination by anyone except with Hobbs's authority. Once the prosecution of Hobbs and O'Connor had been launched, the will, of course, became the centrepiece in the case for the Crown and was put at the disposal of the police. As a matter of routine they photographed it under the ultra-violet ray. It is now fairly widely known that ink writing, although bleached out by chemical means so as to be no longer apparent to the naked eye, is recaptured and clearly seen in the form of fluorescence when submitted to the 'dark light' or band of invisible rays, which is found beyond the violet end of the solar spectrum. The evidence which this process brought us was of a dramatic character. In the forged will of June 24th, 1929, Clarkson was leaving legacies of £100 to certain persons '*if still in my employ at the date of my death*'. Through a space which had been left among the names of these legatees two horizontal lines had been drawn. The assumption was that the forger, intending to fill in the blank with the name of yet another legatee, had, for some unknown reason, changed his mind. The precautionary use of the cancelling lines would be in accordance with common usage in law engrossing. The ultra-violet rays showed, however, that before those lines were drawn the space had been occupied by the name 'Ivan Godwin'. Now Clarkson at the date of the forged will had been wholly unaware of the existence of Ivan Godwin, who first joined him many months later in answer to an advertisement.

This fact came to the knowledge of the forgers, it is believed, shortly before the will was uttered. The wisdom of keeping all members of Clarkson's staff happy with legacies was apparent; only those left out would be likely to question the will's authenticity. It was equally apparent that the testator, in a genuine will, could not without the gift of prophecy leave money to a man of whom he had never heard '*if still in my employ*'. And so the 'Ivan Godwin' blunder had, somehow, to be corrected. With a chemical bleacher the forgers took out the name and thought in doing so they had reached safety again.

* * * *

The prisoners were committed for trial at the Old Bailey. The result was never in doubt. The attack had all the luck and the defence continued to blunder. If Clarkson's former secretary, Mrs. Eakins, had been disposed to 'give certain evidence' it might have helped Hobbs considerably. Her husband said he was approached by Clarkson's ex-manager, George Milne, and told that such evidence would have an attractive cash value. Mr. Eakins was a retail chemist and, faced with this proposal, turned for advice to the police officer who in former years had called upon him from time to time to make routine inspections of the shop's poison register. The name of the officer was Leonard Burt! Mrs. Eakins, 'acting under police directions', accepted a handful of notes —£25 worth—and forthwith turned them over to Burt, who was concealed nearby. When this episode and the bundle of notes were put to Milne at the Old Bailey he denied all knowledge of either. But the jury seemed more amused than defending counsel.

*   *   *   *

The testimony of Mr. G. F. Gurrin, the famous handwriting expert, and of the late Colonel W. W. Mansfield, another expert in that field, damned the will as a forgery. After a six days' trial Hobbs was sentenced to five years' penal servitude and O'Connor to seven. Hobbs, a rich man, had left his victim, O'Connor, to get on as best he might and had refused to put up so much as a penny for his defence. It was typical of the two men that O'Connor, utterly ruined, took his punishment chin up and without any sign of self-pity. Hobbs whined for mercy and ended his plea to the judge with the miserly words: 'Punish me if you like but don't take —*my money*!'

After serving his sentence he lingered on wretchedly until he was eighty. What was left of the Clarkson assets ultimately passed into my hands. The salvage recovery of £27,323 net was divided among the insurers on whose behalf this long battle had been waged.

Twenty-Three

THE MOST HAUNTED HOUSE
IN BRITAIN

M Y WORK in fire claims brought me another and some-
what outlandish case. The background to it was this:
The late Harry Price had a strange hobby. He spent most of
his life and much of his money in search of ghosts. Ghost
stories came to him by the score. It was his joy to dig into
them and root out the truth. This after years of such work he
did not find hard to do. But among those who thought they
had seen a 'Thing' from the Beyond were many who wished
to stay with that belief. It irked them to know that what
they had seen was no spectre but an everyday thing—even
a silly thing such as laundry on a clothes line given spectral
form by some quirk of light and shade. To these folk Price
was a cynic, a cross to be borne. To fraudulent mediums he
was a knife through the heart. To the world at large he was
Honorary Secretary of the University of London Council for
Psychical Investigation, and to use his own words 'utterly
sceptical as regards spirits'. In his oddly chosen branch of
science he had no serious rivals. What a triumph, then, it was
for dedicated spiritualists when this tough adversary was at
last converted and explained why in his book, *The Most
Haunted House in England. Ten years investigation of Borley
Rectory*.[1]

*　　*　　*　　*

Haunted houses sell cheap. One would have thought
Borley Rectory dear even as a gift. Ghosts apart, it had no

1. Published by Longmans, Green & Co. (1940).

piped water, no central heating, no gas or electricity or neighbours. It was as ugly as the bad taste of 1863 could make it. Despite all these natural and supernatural disadvantages, the late Captain William Hart Gregson, R.E. (retired), bought it on December 16th, 1938, with its three and three-quarter acres, its twenty-three rooms, its cottage and its farm buildings. He paid £500 for it. He took ghosts with a grain of salt. Even when, some ten weeks after moving in, the place was burned to the ground he did not put the blame on poltergeists.

Answering an enquiry from Price, he conceded that during his short tenancy a few 'unaccountable' incidents had occurred: frightened dogs had run away for good, articles had been shifted or broken and so on. But he had no belief in ghostly responsibility for these happenings. As for the fire itself—which he explained arose through a pile of books falling on to a lamp and upsetting it—he said: 'The only suggestion of any mysterious influence lies in the fact that I had stacked the books quite carefully, and that in ordinary common sense they should have remained in their stack without falling over at all.' If Gregson still had his doubts, Price had none. He described the fire as 'an event that . . . dramatically brought down the curtain on the most extraordinary and best-documented case of haunting in the annals of psychical research'.

*   *   *   *

Legend said that the rectory stood on the site of a thirteenth-century monastery, one of whose monks had fled in a pair-horse coach with a nun from a nearby convent. The guilty couple overtaken had been put to death; the nun by being bricked up alive in the convent wall. That their restless apparitions—and that of the coach—passed silently through Borley from time to time thereafter was a sequel to be expected from such a tragedy. Price, in his down-to-earth manner, exploded this tradition for two reasons: firstly because no such type of coach appeared in England until 1555 and secondly because the immuring of nuns is a myth wholly lacking historical proof. But Borley's story went far beyond the legendary and Price made plans to get at the truth of it. Renting the rectory for twelve months from May 19th, 1937, he kept continual watch on it, helped by a team of honourable (and honorary) volunteers recruited through a *Times* advertisement. They numbered about forty, all cultured, well trained and judicious, with a sincere interest in the project. Price in *The Most Haunted House in England* says he did little more than edit the 'oral and written testimony' of which in the main that teamwork was the source. The book had so great a success that in 1946 the author published a second, *The End of Borley Rectory*. And at the time of his death in 1948 he was contemplating a third.

*   *   *   *

But this famous psychic investigator and his Borley investigations became the subject of an investigation in their turn. It was conducted by Dr. Eric J. Dingwall, Mrs. Kathleen M. Goldney and Mr. Trevor H. Hall. The report of this skilled trio, *The Haunting of Borley Rectory*,[1] is a classic of detection and could well have been called *The End of Borley Rectory* had Price not already appropriated that title. With access to his papers they were able to reveal how he had 'edited' some of the 'testimony'. He said, for example, that the most convincing evidence for paranormal happenings at the rectory came from the Rev. I. A. Foyster, the parson who lived there with his wife from 1930 to 1935. He listed Mrs. Foyster as having seen a 'phantom' of a former Borley rector, heard various ghostly noises, smelled inexplicable odours, witnessed the shifting and aerial flight of objects and been the subject of poltergeist assault. He was at table with her when 'her

1. Published by Gerald Duckworth & Co. Ltd. (under the auspices of The Society for Psychical Research), 1956 (16s.).

wine turned to ink'. In his editorial discretion he disclosed
nothing of what he wrote to a friend about this lady: '. . . we
were convinced that [she] . . . was just fooling us, for some
reason best known to herself. . . . Of course we told Foyster
we thought that his wife was cheating, and that made him
very cross. . . .' Nor did Price let his readers know that the
Borley 'manifestations' were easily explained. Trailing
branches scraped and tapped with eerie fingers on walls and
shutters, 'horrible sounds' from a locked room were made by
the flapping of a frightened bird which had tumbled down the
chimney; others, whispers, footsteps and such, which seemed
to come from inside the house came in fact from outside and
were disguised by the peculiar acoustic properties of the
courtyard around which the rectory was built; the lights seen
from the garden in the windows of empty and unlit rooms
were reflections from the lights of passing trains; the ghostli-
est of all the spectres, 'a decapitated man', was the maid-
servant's boy friend who liked to wear his jacket country
fashion over his head; a white-clad figure—assuredly the
'monk'—gliding through the twilight—was the smoke of a
dying bonfire.

*   *   *   *

What makes a gamekeeper turn poacher? Is it always
greed alone? What made Price turn cheat to peddle just
such 'paranormal' trash as he had spent his life in scupper-
ing? Maybe cash was not the only bait. Perhaps scorn had
something to do with it. Of those ghost-seers to whom he tried
in vain to show the truth he is alleged to have said: 'They
don't want *debunk*, they prefer *the bunk*, and that is what I'll
give 'em!' And he set about so doing with a shameless skill
which few but he would have dared to exercise.

Mr. Charles Sutton, visiting Borley with Price in 1929—
'after much noisy phenomena'—was struck on the head by a
'poltergeist' pebble. Sutton—then a *Daily Mail* reporter (not
easy types to bamboozle)—seized Price and found his pockets

full of pebbly ammunition. Another seeker after truth, suspicious of certain 'paranormal rustlings', managed to peep into Price's suitcase and saw a long roll of cellophane with a jagged edge which could—and no doubt did—produce them.

The Dingwall Goldney Hall Report which makes much more fascinating reading than any fictitious 'Who Dunnit?', lets Price out with no hard words. Its authors are content to say: 'The question as to whether Price presented a deliberately distorted account of the Borley affair in his books is not, we think, now in doubt. . . .'

*   *   *   *

My part in that affair was to act for Gregson's insurers and look into his fire claims. In that amusing task I worked with Colonel Cuthbert Buckle, an adjuster with some 20,000 such claims already to his credit.

The first 'paranormality' to strike us was that the £500 Gregson paid for the rectory came out of a mortgage he raised on it for £600. And the second 'paranormality' was the fire itself. What caused it? I have already quoted the explanation which Gregson gave Price (the upsetting of a lamp by the collapse of a stack of books 'which in ordinary common sense should not have fallen over'). He improved on this when he broadcast from the B.B.C. in June 1947. With no mention of the book-stack he said: 'An oil lamp, which in the ordinary way I should have considered perfectly safe, suddenly fell over automatically it seemed and in a matter of seconds the whole library was ablaze. . . . I really was a little startled when someone who had known nothing about the supposed hauntings came to ask me who were the cloaked lady and gentleman who had come out of the rectory and joined me on the lawn when the fire was at its height. *You see I had been quite alone at the time.*'

A third version, the first in point of time—perhaps before he had gauged the depths of human credulity—was that which Gregson gave to Colonel Buckle while the Borley ruins were still smoking. In this the books, 'affected by damp', were spread out to air in the hall. On a large drawing-board, resting on a small chest of drawers and a two-tier medicine cupboard, was a lighted paraffin lamp and also a pile of some hundred books. Gregson suddenly noticed among them an odd volume of *Chambers' Encyclopaedia.* 'In extracting this to put it with its fellows the pile of books collapsed and knocked over the lamp. Immediately there was a blaze.'

We liked this version better than the other two. But all three were weak in one respect: they were false. So was the claim. Gregson's underwear provided one illustration of this. Richly described and highly priced, the chest of drawers was full of it. The chest, although carbonised by the flames, had not fallen apart. For lack of air among the tightly packed garments these had been no more than singed. They were of the poorest quality, darned, worn-out and fit only for the rag-bag. Better still, Gregson said he lost in the fire a collection of ancient coins insured for £50. Looking more for indisputable proof of fraud than for the coins themselves, we had our salvage team pass all the relevant debris through quarter-inch-mesh sieves. The heavy cost of this search was justified by the total harvest: one Victorian farthing.

*   *   *   *

On his Borley property—bought for £500—and on his personal belongings—worth at the most £100—Gregson managed to effect insurances for over £10,000.

We repudiated his impudent claim for 'accidental loss by fire'—£7,356, pleading bluntly that he had fired the place himself. It was never our wish that the guiltless mortgagee should lose his £600 and when—at the eleventh hour—we were told the matter could be settled on a nuisance basis for £750 and costs, in all less than our own costs would be to beat Gregson—and get an empty judgment against that man of straw—we hid our chagrin and paid.

From Colonel Buckle, who played the chief part in this rural comedy, I received a pleasant memento. It was Price's *Most Haunted House in England*, generously inscribed: 'To William Charles Crocker—Layer of Ghosts—C.B.'

Twenty-Four

BUDGET LEAKAGE

HAVING once appointed adjusters or lawyers to deal with a claim few underwriters either hear, or wish to hear, anything more about it until it is either ripe for settlement or calls for some important decision. I always assumed that if an underwriter wished to talk with me at home it would be about something other than his underwriting. And so, when my friend the late A. H. Dancey rang my house one April evening in 1936, I guessed he would speak about his will (he had already offered to mark my draft of it 'held covered'). To my surprise he had a very different story to tell, and a Lloyd's story at that. Year by year, when Budget Day drew near, merchants and others whose pockets would be hit by changes in taxation were in the habit of insuring against the risk of such changes being introduced. The F.R.B. syndicate, for which A. H. Dancey underwrote, 'made a market' in these risks, subscribing the policies on P.P.I. terms (which is to say that the proposer was not obliged to disclose any insurable interest, the policy itself being accepted as proof of such interest). Thus John Citizen, with a hunch that any specific tax would go up—or would go down—could back his fancy at odds set by the law of supply and demand. But Dancey was not a gambler. He merely 'sold' at high rates slices of a large Lloyd's cover which he had negotiated months earlier in favour of his syndicate at much lower rates. The demand for insurance in respect of the 1936 Budget, Dancey said, had not been abnormal. His own cover was far from exhausted. His 'take' under that cover would much exceed the losses he had to meet. But there had been a remarkable last-minute placing of insurances against an income-tax increase. 'Supply' had shrunk and rates had risen sharply. In fact, it happened that the Budget raised income tax by threepence. Was there any truth in the rumour that the forthcoming Budget had 'leaked', presumably through someone close enough to the Chancellor of the Exchequer to know what taxation changes would be put before Parliament? And had some persons improperly in possession of that knowledge sought to cash in on it at the expense of the underwriters? My instructions were to sort this out.

Preliminary enquiries satisfied me that certain of the insurances against an income-tax rise effected in the names of different individuals might really represent insurances effected not for the benefit of those individuals but for the benefit of two small groups of operators. As soon as they heard of my enquiries the committee of Lloyd's called me into consultation so that the information I was collecting might be collated with theirs. The story which emerged began to look significant. The 1936 Budget Day was April 21st. One Alfred Bates had obtained policies for £3,000 and £2,000 respectively on April 15th. Using his fuller name of A. C. Kosher-Bates he placed a third for £3,000 on April 20th. Edward Bates, his co-director in the family business, obtained a £1,000 policy on April 16th. The Bates company's solicitor, on April 20th, using two separate brokers, obtained policies for £1,000 and £2,100, one in his usual name of 'Harold Eves' and the other in that of 'Major H. Eves' ('and/or as agent'). Having sent his personal cheque for the premium on the former, he hastily withdrew it and substituted a banker's draft. Mrs. W. E. Stubbs had a policy for £1,500. Miss W. E. Scott had one for £1,000. Mrs. Stubbs *née* Scott was A. C. Kosher-Bates' secretary. So much for the Bates' group.

*　　　*　　　*　　　*

I analysed six policies, two covering a total of £1,200
against an increase in the tea tax, the rest covering a total of
£6,750 against an increase of income tax. They were all
placed on Budget Day itself. In five instances the policy-
holders proved to be partners in a stockbroking firm. They
admitted being nominees for their client, Sir Alfred Butt.
This gentleman was both a Member of Parliament and an
underwriting member of Lloyd's through the agency of
Messrs. Gardner, Mountain, and D'Ambrumenil. Sir Alfred's
son, Kenneth, worked in a clerical capacity for that concern,
and, like his father, was a name in their syndicate. It seemed
odd that in placing four of these six policies (and a small one,
£100 for himself) Kenneth had used not his own employers
but five other brokerage firms, and this without his employers' knowledge. Why all this secrecy if Sir Alfred Butt, M.P.,
had nothing to hide?

*   *   *   *

A statement which I took from my friend the late Jimmie
Matheson of Lloyd's threw some light upon that question.
He specialised in placing contingency risks for fellow brokers
less familiar with the contingency market. During the afternoon of April 20th he telephoned Sir Alfred Butt (for whom
he had done insurance business in the past) and asked what
he thought about the risk of income tax going up. Sir Alfred
thought there was none and offered, as an underwriter, to
accept such risks up to £5,000 at a rate of fifteen guineas
per cent. Matheson doubted whether he could command so
high a rate and was given an order to deal at ten guineas per
cent. This he did to the tune of £3,000, telephoned reporting
and that evening wrote confirming. Sir Alfred wrote similarly.
The two letters crossed in the post. Nothing could have been
more regular. Next morning, that is to say on the morning of
Budget Day, Matheson phoned Sir Alfred offering further
underwriting, to wit another £1,000 at a higher premium,
fifteen guineas per cent. This Sir Alfred said he would take.

But some ten minutes later he called back 'apparently in a violent temper'. The burden of his complaint was that he had been induced to accept yesterday's line at a cut rate. He should have had fifteen guineas per cent on both and now 'he would stand for neither'. Matheson, in disgust and bewilderment, agreed to call both deals off.

*   *   *   *

No sooner had Sir Alfred thus curtly cleared his 'book' than he spread heavy bets, secretly, at short odds, on the very horse which, just before, he was so sure would lose! Whence came the hot tip which presumably inspired this *volte face*?

*   *   *   *

I had learnt that Butt and Bates shared one thing in common. They were both bosom friends of Mr. J. H. Thomas, M.P., then Colonial Secretary in Mr. Baldwin's government.

*   *   *   *

Little more than a week after Budget Day the Matheson statement and my analysis of the twenty-two apparently relevant policies were put into the Chancellor of the Exchequer's hands. On May 6th a Statutory Tribunal of Inquiry was appointed. Its chairman was Mr. Justice Porter.[1] The other members were K.C.s, Mr. Gavin Simonds[2] and Mr. Roland Oliver. This triumvirate, a very strong one, would whitewash nobody, high or low. The chief suspects, Thomas, Bates and Butt, filed through the witness-box, made their explanation, gave their denials and were disbelieved. Thomas

1. The late Lord Porter.
2. Subsequently Lord Chancellor.

O

had learned at a Cabinet meeting on April 9th that the Chancellor of the Exchequer intended to tax tea a little more heavily and to increase the standard rate of income tax by 3*d*. From April 10th to the 12th Bates and Thomas, living not far apart in Sussex, were continually together, playing golf and racing. On April 14th, the first business day after the Easter vacation, Bates took two significant steps. He gave instructions for the sale of some £50,000 worth of his gilt-edged securities, i.e. those most likely to fall if income tax should rise. And for the first time in his life he set in train insurances against the risk of such a rise. His excuses for using nominees in this connection did not satisfy the Tribunal. Nor could the Tribunal be persuaded that the 'Eves' policies—at least as to £2,500—were effected not for Bates (who had paid the premium!) but for one of Harold Eves' clients, a Mr. Waterton. Mr. Eves said that his brother, Mr. R. G. Eves, R.A., the portrait painter, had lent Waterton £750 and that by reason of this loan Waterton (described as 'impecunious') had the means of paying for the insurance. Mr. R. G. Eves, R.A., was called and questioned about this alleged use of his money. He was transparently truthful. But with the best will in the world he could give no help. It was clear that for the handling of his business affairs and similar sordid aspects of his non-artistic life he depended wholly upon Harold, who had unlimited authority to do with them just what he thought best. It became obvious that if there had been a 'leak' from Thomas there had also been subsidiary 'leaks' from Harold Eves to Waterton and from Waterton to others who had bought policies on the strength of his information. The particularly striking feature about certain of these casual punters was that somehow or other they understood income tax would go up by exactly 3*d*. There had been no 3*d*. fluctuation in that tax up or down since the 1914–18 War.

*   *   *   *

Sir Alfred Butt deposed that unlike Kosher-Bates he had at times in the past insured heavily against Budget risks. In 1934 he had laid out £12,000 in premiums and recovered £15,000 when income tax was reduced, making a pleasant capital gain of the difference. In 1935 he invested small sums in the Budget field and also (with a few hedging bets) was successful under policies regarding the date of the next election. Mr. Thomas was a sleeping partner in one of these ventures and picked up £632 as his share.

*　　　*　　　*　　　*

About noon on the vital Budget Day Butt had called to see Thomas at the Colonial Office. He failed to mention this when giving his pre-Tribunal statement to the Treasury solicitor. Thomas did not at first recall the visit at all. When reminded of it he said it was devoted solely to Sir Alfred's tip— Quashed—for the Derby and lasted no more than a minute and a half. Since Thomas had won a packet by backing this horse, the Tribunal thought it improbable that so fortunate an interview, in spite of its brevity, would have faded so quickly from his memory.

*　　　*　　　*　　　*

My clients had deliberately refrained from having any official representation before the court lest the public might be misled into thinking that underwriters were assuming the role of complainants whereas all they wished to do was pay up. The committee of Lloyd's, however, on a broad hint from the Tribunal that such representation would be convenient, instructed me to brief counsel for them. I had never before acted as solicitor for Lloyd's committee and was very happy to reach this new milestone in my career. The work directly imposed upon me by these instructions was negligible. But indirectly I was kept busy sifting the yarns, rumours and irrelevancies which poured into me from strangers all burning to topple Jimmie Thomas from his pedestal. The Tribunal's astute secretary, John Foster,[1] would discuss these matters with me in the corridor beyond the Bench—our seat being a sanitary dustbin. So far as he wished any action to be taken, I took it.

* * * *

After sitting for eight days and hearing the sworn testimony of sixty-one witnesses, the Tribunal found that there was an unauthorised disclosure by Mr. J. H. Thomas of information relating to the 1936 Budget and that use was made of it by both Mr. A. C. Kosher-Bates and Sir Alfred Butt for the purpose of their private gain.[2]

* * * *

While the evidence given by the insurance witnesses—particularly that of Matheson—was perhaps in itself conclusive I have always felt that Bates, Butt and Thomas were, in the main, convicted out of their own mouths. They were not charged with any offence whatever and could not therefore be 'convicted' of anything in a strict legal sense. Nevertheless, in view of the findings, Thomas and Butt, quite properly, no doubt, abandoned their political careers. In a practical sense they had been condemned—and they had no right of appeal. There are those who say that in this aspect Tribunal procedure is faulty and foreign to our normal practice. On the other hand, I have heard none say that the Budget Leakage Tribunal's findings were other than scrupulously fair.

* * * *

1. Now Sir John Foster, Q.C., M.P.
2. See *Budget Disclosure Inquiry*. Report of the Tribunal appointed under the Tribunals of Inquiry (Evidence) Act, 1921, 1936, Cmd. 5184.

In the summer of 1939 I ran into both the Eveses at the farm of a friend in Kent. R. G. Eves overwhelmed me with thanks for my 'kindness' to him during 'that *dreadful*' Budget affair'. When I mentioned my general interest in art he invited me to see his studio. There he demonstrated his skill by executing a charcoal sketch of my head and shoulders. At that time his idea, disclosed only to his brother, was to complete the portrait in oils and make me a present of it. Pressure of outstanding commissions, the intervention of World War II (in which he was official portraitist) and finally his death, prevented him from carrying out that amiable intention. But Harold, his executor, found the sketch and sent it to me in part fulfilment.

Twenty-Five

WORLD WAR TWO

BELONGING to the Law Society's Council, I learned how our profession is run and was taught to play my small part in running it. My colleagues and I had been chosen for our special experience in our own particular legal fields. My own contribution, over a perod of twenty-three years, leaned to the practical rather than to the academic side of the Council's work. When elected, I thought, as so many of the younger generation did, that the Council members cherished an almost impenetrable crust of tradition to protect lawyers from novel ideas. There was a crust of sorts, no doubt a valuable one, but it had already begun to weaken. And even as a newcomer, a suspected iconoclast, and a far-from-persuasive advocate, I found it could be pierced. My first triumph in this respect was scored when I asked that the notice 'BEWARE OF PICKPOCKETS' should be removed from the members' lavatory. And down it came! Voting was unanimous, and this in spite of the then Secretary's wail, 'But it has been up *for thirty years!*' Ancient usage was no longer enough to block sensible innovations. On the contrary, the Council welcomed them and during my first two decades with them were to introduce revolutionary changes, of great benefit to the general public and to solicitors alike. At the root of these moves was our new Secretary, Tommy Lund. He rose to that position in 1939, at a time when the Society sorely needed a man of his type. He had youth, vision, resource, natural administrative ability, and an insatiable appetite for work.[1] In the lull which prefaced World War II we did our best, with his aid, to contrive that the profession should be ready for the coming conflict. For this purpose, and for the first time in our history, we invited every solicitor on the Roll to answer (with a simple cross for 'Yes' or 'No') an exhaustive, it might even be thought impertinent, questionnaire. This concerned by the score such of his qualities, accomplishments and disabilities as might enable a hypothetically interested government to determine in which sphere of National Service he could, when the time came, be used to best advantage. The importance of this operation, as I saw it, lay not so much in its aim (the compilation of a catalogue showing, at a glance, what sort of solicitors we had in stock) but in the Council's readiness to adopt the Hollerith punched-card system to produce it. This was our first and most memorable leap into modernity.[2]

The Second World War produced many new legal problems and brought a few old ones into sharper focus. Defence Regulations proliferated. Gentlemen and ladies, of hitherto blameless lives, found themselves standing in magistrates' court docks, summoned for misusing petrol, for showing too much light in the black-out, for buying something without a coupon or for building something without a licence. We all lived under the shadow of sudden death, civilians in England no less than folk in the Armed Forces overseas. This meant that wills were made by the million. The estates of those who died were administered by the thousand. Lamentable numbers of people contracted a wartime immorality and insanely wrecked their marriages. Young husbands would inexplicably take up with drab wantons. Young wives would leave good homes to take up with down-at-heel foreign refugees or worse. Perhaps Dame Nature, fearing heavy casualty lists, was driving men and women to stockpile against the potential

1. Thomas G. Lund (now Secretary-General) succeeded Sir Edmund Cook as Secretary in 1939 and received the honour of knighthood in 1958.
2. The Law Society now run a large battery of punched-card equipment in their Legal Aid Department and contemplate installing computers.

loss. Presented with such sordid aspects of life we welcomed all the more the leaven of comic ones. How, for example, were we to satisfy a client, to whom the local police refused a written receipt for the pistol which he had, too belatedly, surrendered to them? My brother Walter's solution was amusing and effective. 'Why [he wrote] will you not give a formal acknowledgment regarding the *pair* of Colt revolvers delivered, by our client to your station, last Friday morning? . . .' This landed the expected reply: '. . . Your client surrendered only one Colt revolver and not a pair as you allege.". . .'

* * * *

This wartime work would have been most welcome but for the difficulty of handling it efficiently with our depleted staff. Arson, as an instrument of fraud, was rare. Merchandise of all kinds increased in value. In our rationed land it could be turned into cash very readily, if not always legitimately. Most of our adult population were serving, part time, in National Defence of some form or another, poking their noses and their hoses eagerly into the least suspicion of combustion. A good old-fashioned bit of fire-raising was, in such circumstances, so risky as to make the game, literally, not worth the candle. No! the clear-thinking business man had little encouragement to fire his premises before peace broke out. He did so, as a rule, only to destroy in a plausible way dangerous records of his black-market deals or of other illegal activities.

* * * *

But the war gave me at least one interesting fire investigation. I was asked by the staff solicitor for certain steel manufacturers to find out whether the conflagration which had recently destroyed his company's provincial plant was due to enemy action or to some other, and if so what, cause. In other words: who should pay for the loss, the government or the fire underwriters?

A week spent on the site, interviewing forty witnesses, gave me the answer. Top-secret sources established that no German plane reached within twenty miles of my client's premises on the night of their 'incident' either before, during or after the air-raid warning had been sounded. A warden who saw the glow of a fire in the sky, but could not place it on the ground from where he stood, set out to run it to earth, leaving word at his post that 'an incendiary might have dropped'. This message, mutilated as it passed along, ended in London as a definite assertion (indignantly rejected by the warden) that an enemy bomb had set light to my client's factory.

The fire had been very fierce. Of the main building only a steel skeleton remained, its pillars and joists twisted by heat. I noticed, particularly, one area in the roof beams where this distortion was abnormally severe. On the floor below it sat a large tank over a battery of gas-fed burners. Tin-plate, for export, must be given a coating of wax if it is not to rust in the warm and humid air it may meet abroad.

The coating process was conducted by three lads, A, B, and C. Huge cheeses of wax were loaded into the tank and were melted by heat from the burners underneath. The tin-plate sheets, dipped by hand into the hot liquid, gradually used this up and, since they were relatively cold, kept its temperature down to a safe level, i.e. one at which the liquid would not vaporise and ignite. Beyond dipping and stacking the plates and maintaining an adequate level of liquid wax, the ABC team had only two other duties: to turn on and light the gas when they arrived in the morning and to turn it off, both at the tank and at the main, before they left work in the evening.

By one of those chances which occasionally reward the investigator a member of the volunteer fire brigade called to the blaze was a hardware merchant who stocked gas-fittings. With an eye for such things he had at once noticed that both the main and tank taps were in the 'on' position and he had turned them off. With this testimony up my sleeve I saw A, B and C singly and took statements from each of them. And each assured me that one of the other two had shut off the gas, as usual, 'the last thing', before going home on the night of the fire. Unwittingly they confirmed that the gas had been left burning.

It was easy to picture the sequence of events. The wax, with no dipping of plates to keep down its temperature, had grown hotter and hotter until its heavy vapour, pouring down outside the walls of the tank, reached the naked gas jets and the whole mass had gone up like a giant torch. The enemy could claim no credit for this. The fire offices unhesitatingly agreed to foot the bill.

*   *   *   *

I recall only one other comparable case. I was asked to discover why the premises of a perfectly reputable shoe manufacturer continually went on fire. Some of my friends[1] from the Government Chemists' Department (of course in their own time) helped me, on the site, to eliminate such possible causes as faulty light and power cables, injudicious use of chemicals, spontaneous combustion with an oily base and mechanical overheating in the machine shop (where all the fires had started). A doctor, posing as my clerk, looked round the staff with me for any odd type who might be a pyromaniac. But none of us could guess how any of the fires had been caused. While I was gazing out of the window at the adjacent Town Hall (then brand-new) the works foreman said: 'When the old houses came down to make room for *that* we were overrun with rats. And it's not easy to get rid of 'em!'

Rats! I had not thought of rats! Could they have been the

1. Among them was L. C. Nickolls, later head of Scotland Yard's Forensic Laboratory. This must have been one of his earliest steps into detection.

fire-raisers? The factory's internal telephone system operated from a twelve-volt battery. Its wires (covered with a woven and waxed cotton insulation) ran beneath the machine shop's wooden floor. Experiment showed us that on tearing the insulation away with manicure clippers (which was as near as we could go to rats' teeth) we could obtain, from twelve volts, a good fat spark by 'shorting' the stripped wires—a spark sufficient to ignite the fluffed cotton. But would rats behave like the manicure clippers? And, if so, for what purpose? Messrs. Glaxo, with whom I enjoy a close contact, were good enough to study that question for me. They keep many small quadrupeds, including rats, for research purposes. A few feet of the telephone cable left with a brace of these rats in their cage overnight were represented in the morning by bare wire and a large heap of what had been coarse cotton thread but now resembled thistledown. Luxurious bedding for the rats' wedded life and the resulting progeny. Touched off with our twelve-volt spark this fluff proved not only inflammable; it was so finely divided as to be almost explosive.

The telephone cables at the factory were torn out and replaced by new ones running through lead piping. The rats were defeated. The fires ceased.

* * * *

When the war came in September 1939 I was fifty-three and soon became sergeant in the Local Home Guard. It seemed unlikely that I should ever be invited to serve my country in any more useful capacity. But I was. Lord Woolton, the Minister of Food, was director of an insurance company for which I had occasionally acted and knew of my experience as an investigator. He thought in the light of that experience I might be able to learn by what clandestine means the Black Market kept itself so amply supplied with good-quality meat. He invited me to look into this matter. I undertook the assignment on an honorary basis, and carried it through until near the war's end. I may properly say no more about it than this: the Black Market supplies consisted of carcasses stolen from the docks in wholesale quantities, that I used only a very few agents some of whom became on first-name terms with the leading gangsters (and would have died violently had fate given them away), that I kept Sir Henry French, G.B.E., K.C.B. (Secretary to the Ministry), acquainted with the situation from day to day so that he could plan such counter-measures as he considered expedient, and that, from first to last, my team suffered only one set-back. A very intelligent young lady from my own office undertook some delicate enquiries which entailed visits to certain night clubs where I knew that 'meat' was talked. Of necessity she required an escort and chose an American officer whom she had only recently met, a man ignorant of her true purpose. When these Clubland visits ended he married her and took her away to live deep in the heart of Texas.

In my scrap-album there is a clipping from the *Sunday Chronicle* for July 28th, 1940. It reports my appointment by the Prime Minister, Mr. Winston Churchill, as 'Chief Fifth Column Raider' on a committee of three (with Lord Swinton and Sir Joseph Ball) 'to investigate subversive activities in Britain'. In the House of Commons during the preceding week 'further information [about this committee] was refused in the Public Interest'. This means that, like the Ghost in *Hamlet*, I also 'am forbid to tell the secrets of my prison-house'. This is a pity. I could have told a side-splitting yarn, but at the risk of being disbelieved.

*   *   *   *

Happily no one would wish to censor the stories of my two outstanding World War II adventures. I put them on record as illustrating how very far from humdrum a lawyer's life may be.

Twenty-Six

THE TIN FISH

NEARLY all the diamònds cut and polished in Palestine during World War II were sent to America. They were posted (to a value of nearly $15,000,000 a year) as 'Registered Air Mail' and were insured against 'all risks' under Lloyd's policies. The underwriters on those policies suspected that heavy claims which they had continually to pay resulted from an organised system of larceny. They asked me to go to the Middle East to find out what was happening and to stop it.

I set out for the Middle East in the autumn of 1943 feeling very pleased with life. My mission was to my liking. And there was a novel thrill in sailing on a heavily manned trooper in convoy. There was a laugh in being promoted from the rank of sergeant in the Seal village Home Guard (where we were armed with primitive bottle-bombs—Molotov Cocktails) to that of wing commander (temporary and unpaid) so that I might justify my passage under R.A.F. Standing Orders on the Dutch ship *Marnix van Sint Aldegonde*, armed with Bofors guns to tell us there was still a war on. Last, but not least, my Lloyd's clients had given me an 'all risks' life policy for £50,000. The opulence of that figure tickled my vanity. Never before had anyone paid me so calculable a compliment. I meant in return to do all I could to stay alive.

Sharing with five other men what had once been a single cabin proved no hardship. We soon adapted ourselves to the confined space—and to one another. What a mixed party we were! A professor (now Master of an Oxford college), an architect, an insurance official, a French Capitaine de

Fregate, a Bagdadi judge and a City solicitor. Most of our other shipmates—3,000 or more—were Air Force men, with a sprinkling of nurses. By an odd chance there was also aboard one of my village friends, Eric Davies, a top-ranking Guy's surgeon, on his way to establish hospitals in Abadan. There was the quiet little Welshman in charge of an E.N.S.A. party, an illusionist who had invented a new method of cutting a lady in halves. There was his brother, a dead-pan ventriloquist, who could produce the faintly heard metallic voice of a non-existent person at the far end of an imaginary telephone line. We were a 'dry' ship, and he liked to speak into his cabin telephone (a dummy) to an imaginary steward who would be heard promising to bring along a bottle of Scotch when the coast was clear. The audience would be a few thirsty R.A.F. types who, completely deluded, would wait with tongues out for the liquor which never came.

As temporary-temporary officers we civilians did our best to fit into the ship's life. My surgeon friend and a few top-ranking Queen Alexandra nurses enjoyed themselves first in saving the life of a man down with a raging appendix and later in saving the No. 1 gunner's index finger (nearly severed by a falling ammunition-box lid). It was an important finger this. The No. 1 in civilian life was a professional pianist. For my part, on the invitation of the padre, it went into Orders that Wing Commander Crocker would stand ready each a.m. in the orderly room to proffer legal advice to any who might need it. It was with sorrow that we counted off the days and realised how soon our happy party must break up.

*   *   *   *

I was resting on my bunk when the signal bells rang for 'Action Stations'. Was this the real thing or just another drill? Almost at once our anti-aircraft guns began firing. This was no practice. We were being attacked from the air. There followed, immediately, an immense but muffled detonation;

not the deafening noise one would expect from a ton of T.N.T. letting off. It was like, and it was in fact, the punch of a gigantic underwater power—a torpedo. It lifted our vessel bodily and heaved her sideways. Our luggage slid around and from all quarters came the rumble and clatter and tinkle of loose gear. We grasped the bunk frames to keep our balance. Eternal hope suggested that perhaps we had suffered only a near miss, but, discouraging sign, the ship's list did not at once correct itself. And then the lights went out.

It was eerie, three decks down, in the dark, with engines stopped. The silence, following so much commotion, was oppressive. Our Standing Orders were to stay put, but the urge to learn the worst—or the best—was strong. My elastic conscience let me feel that, as second-in-command of rafts on 'C' deck, I had some special privileges or even responsibility in the matter. Taking a comforting torch, I peeped out into the corridor. Other torches by the score flickered in the gloom and emergency wall lamps gave a faint illumination.

I saw a ship's officer run into the cabin next mine. I followed him and found he was too hurriedly trying to fill a pocket flask from a pint rum bottle. My first sniff of alcohol for two weeks! Some of the precious fluid was spilling into the washbasin! I took over the dispensing while he held my light and was rewarded by a tot in a tooth-glass. He said we should begin disembarking very soon. I took this news back to my companions and we resigned ourselves to the possibility of some involuntary bathing.

A few minutes later the signal 'Boat Stations' came from the loudspeakers. We groped our way up to our assigned positions on deck. We had been practising the route daily with eyes shut in readiness for just such an emergency. The twilight was of a spooky amber tint due to the moon's beams filtering through a smoke-screen put up to hide us from the enemy. The first life-boats with the nurses and the E.N.S.A. ladies were lowered and made for our sister ship *Reuss* which was standing by. Then came the order 'Rafts overboard'. There was no sign of panic.

It is true that although the order 'Abandon ship!' had not been given, a few of my section went down the climbing mats prematurely. They missed the rafts and fell into the water. They were safe enough if they did not get crushed against the ship's side and if reliance could be placed upon the assurance we had received from the first officer that our life-jackets would keep us afloat for a fortnight. My firm belief was that I should escape not by raft but warm and dry in one of our lifeboats which were already shuttling between the *Reuss* and us. The *Marnix* did not appear to be sinking lower or listing more heavily. Carrying my flat leather business bag, I slipped down to our cabin for a last look around. The loneliness and murk and the slap and swell of the water below did not encourage me to linger. I snatched up handkerchiefs, shaving kit, pyjamas, a can of emergency rations, and, lastly (thinking they might come in handy), a fine pair of R.N. binoculars, the property of the Capitaine de Fregate who had been sent off in charge of the womenfolk.

Two hours later we were mustered on the saloon deck for roll-call preparatory to departure. The lounge, the scene of so many E.N.S.A. shows and of so much jollity, now looked dissolute, with chairs overturned and the piano sprawling drunkenly on its back. We were marched out on to the deck again and found our lifeboat ready. She seemed alarmingly far below, lurching and heaving in an oily swell. The descent was something of a feat and about equivalent to a climb from the top floor down to the garden of a three-storeyed house.

Some of my party missing a ladder rung fell awkwardly, but unhurt, into the arms of the waiting sailors. One of my own cabin companions, the professor, tumbled into the sea and looked as though he might be crushed among the milling rafts, but he was whipped out with nothing worse than the ducking and a few bruises. One cannot normally carry luggage on these occasions because to negotiate the climbing mat one needs the full use of both hands. But I was able to escape with my bag by tying its handle to the belt of my travelling coat. Thus laden I managed to reach the boat without even getting splashed and sat myself on a thwart to engage in what must be one of the slowest forms of loco-motion yet devised by man. This consists in the pulling, not of oars, but of levers to drive a propeller which judging from the rate of progress must have finger-length blades. Buoy-ancy in a lifeboat is, doubtless, a very desirable quality, but the motion of ours was intolerable. Most of us, not excluding some of the sailors, were soon half dead with seasickness. After three hours of this torture we were within hail of our rescue ship *Reuss*. Our bo'sun urged us to a final effort and the rowing levers were worked with renewed energy.

At this point a destroyer (*Croome* of the Hunt Class) glided up and a calm but greatly amplified 'voice', came from her loudspeaker. 'Do you hear me *Reuss*, do you hear me?' 'Yes,' we shouted in desperation. The 'voice', mildly reproachful, said coldly and very distinctly, 'I am not speaking to you!' and then, again addressing *Reuss*, was acknowledged and continued, one might say conversationally, 'I hear depth charges. There may be a submarine about. Will you please get under way immediately. I will protect you.' Our hearts sank into the depths as *Reuss*, obeying instructions, sailed away, leaving us with the Mediterranean, the moonlight and what was left of our smoke-screen all to ourselves. Our bo'sun summed up the situation in terse but unprintable language. In effect, he bade us rest and not to risk irremediable intestinal injury to no purpose.

As the destroyer steamed off, that calm and confident 'voice' floated across the water to inspire us with one of the finest prose passages I have ever heard, each word precisely bitten off: 'I shall return for *you* in thirty minutes!' And he did. Willing hands helped us aboard and after that tossing life-boat it was like going ashore. Dizzy and reeling with sickness I was lowered through a manhole to what I believe was the fo'c'sle. On the nobbly boltheads of its steel deck, wrapped in my soft old coat, with my business bag for pillow,

P

I was off, within two seconds, to one of the most perfect sleeps I have ever enjoyed in my life.

None of the officers or crew of that little battlecraft slept at all; they continued their rescue work until the ship was almost overwhelmed. Every inch of their own accommodation was given up to 'survivors'. All night and all next day we were plied with hot food, hot drinks and cigarettes. There was little one could say or do to return thanks. I did try a few words on a chief petty officer as the destroyer ran alongside the quay at Philippeville, Algeria. He thrust an orange into my hand and looked threatening. The 'voice', the destroyer's young commander, stood at the gangplank to see us go. My cabin mates and I contrived to be the last to leave. We told him at speed, before he could protest, how grateful everyone was for the kindness they had received and in Lloyd's best tradition (and much to his surprise) presented him with the fine pair of R.N. binoculars which I had 'lifted' from the *Marnix*!

*   *   *   *

Coincidence is a curious phenomenon. Most of us meet it fairly often in our daily lives and when we do we say 'How odd!' But if some wretched fellow in the dock pleads (perhaps truthfully) under a cloud of circumstantial evidence that he is innocent and merely the victim of coincidence everyone laughs him to scorn.

The reserve battalion with whom we spent our first night ashore were living on a war footing; they had no facilities for entertaining civilian survivors. We did not expect the Ritz. We paraded in single file with the 'other ranks' next morning to draw breakfast. None of us was more philosophical than the professor. After his ducking of the day before his clothes had dried on him. He stood among us looking like a wet hen, albeit a man of distinction. He was recognised by a young Guardee captain who froze in his tracks and came rigidly to attention with a salute such as a field marshal might expect from a Sandhurst cadet. 'Do you remember me, sir! Evans, sir!' (giving his name and college). Polite professorial attempt to capture some recollection of this full-blown soldier who had once been no more than an insignificant mite in the university cheese. 'Back in a moment, sir!' And sure enough he was. Our section of the parade was about turned and sat down to a civilised meal in the officers' mess. This was coincidence No. 1.

Alexander Selkirk on his desert island could have felt no more cut off from the world than I and my fellow survivors did in Philippeville from which the enemy had only just been driven. The war still had two years to run. We were *les bouches inutiles*. Only the forces counted. It was the task of nobody to set us on our road again. Our chance of reaching Egypt before the war's end looked slim.

Racking my brains for strings to pull I recalled that a solicitor friend of mine had become O.C. of an army department known as 'Hirings and Claims'. There was a branch of that department in Philippeville. I called there with my architect cabin-companion Webster, and asked how the brigadier might be reached. The captain who received us regretted that the brigadier was in Italy and 'out of touch'. Our hopes dwindled. Then the captain asked me: 'Are you not William Charles Crocker of Lloyd's?' Here was coincidence No. 2. This captain had been given command of the battery of artillery which Lloyd's had raised in 1939. Once, when he visited Lloyd's in that connection, I had been pointed out to him as the Fire Gang Buster. He listened sympathetically when I said how sure I was that the brigadier, had he been available, would have found an aeroplane to take us to Cairo. 'The man to wangle that for you,' he said, 'is my C.O. at Constantine, Colonel Curtis.' 'Not *Ronnie* Curtis, by any chance?' asked Webster. 'Yes,' replied the captain, 'do you know him?' 'He's my partner,' said Webster. That was coincidence No. 3. And that was how our party, within forty-eight hours, got into the air and made the first leg of our trip East—as far as Tunis. There we were stuck!

The Tunis airport was in American hands. There was no regular air service to Cairo and no likelihood of thumbing a ride even from the free-and-easy U.S.A. pilots. In this fix we went to the local R.A.F. liaison officer, Squadron Leader Pearce. Although he eyed me with mild amusement, there was no doubt of his willingness to help. After a lot of telephoning we were taken to an American Air Force V.I.P. who gave us air passes across which was scrawled in scarlet ink: 'MUST GO'. When I thanked Squadron Leader Pearce he introduced himself with a grin as the junior partner of the solicitor who had for a good twenty years acted as my agent in Nottingham. So thanks to coincidence No. 4 our party within twenty-four hours made the last leg of the trip East and reached Cairo.

Twenty-Seven

DIAMONDS IN THE DESERT

MY INVESTIGATIONS in Palestine showed that the non-arrival of registered diamond packages posted in Jerusalem (and ultimately paid for by Lloyd's) had been due to theft at the Jerusalem end. It was fairly easy to pin-point the leak and so soon as this was plugged by a slight change of postal routine the losses ceased.

But among the diamond losses which fell on underwriters a heavy one had arisen when, according to a top-secret certificate from the Jerusalem Postmaster General, a consignment was destroyed by an accident to the aeroplane carrying it.

My clients, mildly curious to know when, where and how that accident had happened, invited me while in the Middle East to make a few enquiries about it 'without going to a lot of trouble'!

In Cairo I learned unofficially that the mail-carrying plane, the subject of the Postmaster General's certificate, had crashed in the desert about four miles from Khartoum. Air Force and British Overseas Airways personnel and Sudanese soldiery, on the spot almost immediately, had taken charge. In spite of the terrific heat of the flaming wreckage they had recovered the bodies of the twenty men who were aboard and had salvaged from the vicinity of the craft a quarter of a ton of mail. Such of it as was decipherable dribbled back to the senders *via* the various post offices concerned. Only part of one package of our diamonds, however, got back to Jerusalem. The remaining gems (some 23,000 in all) were generally thought to have adhered somewhere among the multitude of sticky fingers between the Blue Nile and the Jordan.

This ungenerous view did not seem to tune in with some of the known facts. Nearly 1,500 £1 notes, gathered from a wide area around the wreck, had been passed to the local R.A.F. and through them had reached Cairo safely. This alone would have warned me not to accept the 'sticky fingers' idea without proper enquiry.

*   *   *   *

In Cairo the B.O.A.C. engineers who had studied the accident on the spot told me that the forces developed by the plane hitting earth at terrific speed were unimaginable. Sheet steel used in its construction was torn to ribbons. Stout mail-bag canvas disintegrated as though it had been muslin.

Diamonds for mailing are made up into flat paper packets which resemble Seidlitz powders. Covered with extra paper wrappings or put into tough cardboard boxes they go into ordinary registered envelopes. All these envelopes travel in a small sealed 'registered' canvas sack which in turn goes into a mail-sack of ordinary size.

*   *   *   *

A paper bag of marbles will burst if dropped a few feet. Substitute canvas for the paper and the bag will survive such a fall intact. Increase the drop sufficiently and even the canvas will infallibly burst. Could I assume that my diamonds had been thrown far enough and hard enough to cut through the several layers of paper and cardboard and canvas which confined them and so to escape? My friendly B.O.A.C. expert, instead of laughing, accepted this as quite within the bounds of possibility. Any theory which allowed for the missing diamonds being still in the Sudan desert attracted me strongly. However far-fetched this one was, it seemed reasonably clear that since diamonds are well-nigh indestructible, there were, in fact, only two possibilities: either the gems had been stolen (which I refused to believe) or they were still resting in the sand.

I decided to fly down the Nile from Cairo for a personal survey of the *locus in quo*. The young B.O.A.C. station manager at Khartoum, Mr. Ogilvie, was used to dealing with all sorts of odd situations and passengers. A polite man, if ever there was one, he smiled hardly at all when I asked to be driven to the scene of the six months' old accident for the purpose of recovering any diamonds which might yet be lying there. He reddened a little when I asked him to provide me with a shovel and rake, and a haversack (which he assumed was to carry the catch!).

*   *   *   *

Khartoum sits at the edge of a hard-packed and immense sandy tract on the surface of which a motor vehicle can run almost without leaving a wheel mark. To the newcomer any one part of this terrain looks like any other part. At the end of an hour's driving the place we wanted, four miles out, still eluded us. The district, as one would expect, is not thickly populated and it was by the merest chance that we met an elderly native to whom we turned for help. He had no English. Neither Ogilvie nor his aide Lloyd (who was with us) had adequate Arabic. I resorted to pantomime and did sketches of a crashed aeroplane with crumpled wings. With a long 'Ah!' of understanding the native climbed into our car and had led us for some miles before an Arabic-speaking army officer, encountered in a Jeep, put a few questions for us. He learned that our guide thought it was our wish to see a flying boat alight on the water and was accordingly steering us to the B.O.A.C. 'landing' area on the Blue Nile. Our interpreter put the guide right and within ten minutes we were examining the unpromising rumpled circle of earth—twelve yards across—for which we had been looking. The carcass of the

aeroplane had long since been removed and all that remained
to mark the accident was a pencil-sized scrap or so of metal,
an odd piece of paper here and there, and a few handfuls of
rag or cotton waste, vestiges of what had once been sturdy
mail-bags. Ogilvie, who had already given up more time than
he could well spare from his duties, left Lloyd and me to our
own devices and, promising to come back for us in an hour,
drove off to Khartoum smiling.

'What do we do now?' asked Lloyd.

I explained my notion that if diamonds were there they
would glitter if the sand above them were stroked away.
Lloyd, although patently embarrassed and sceptical, joined
me in scraping and scanning as though we might, in truth, be
standing over all the wealth of Sheba's queen. Alas! My
glitter theory proved a failure. The sand was heavy with
quartz particles and everything glittered. We were not a very
happy pair. At the end of thirty-five minutes Lloyd's boredom was hidden with difficulty. So would mine have been but
for the novelty of the situation. The desert shimmered under
a grilling sun, a distant lake was ringed and dotted with
waving palm trees. In the middle distance a Sudanese pony
patrol rode curiously by, no doubt wondering what madness
impelled a young British officer and a big man in London
clothes to play like children in the wastes so far from town.
We went on with our sand-stroking, but the glare taxed my
eyes and I rested them for a while on the hazy horizon.

'How far off is that lake?' I asked.

Lloyd straightened his back and replied patiently: 'There
is no lake, there are no palms. That is a mirage,' and perhaps
added *sotto voce*, 'like your diamonds.'

Any faith he had in me went when my 'glitter' idea blew
up. Reaching a stage of ennui in which I was ready to pick up
anything other than dirt, I idly collected what I thought was
a bit of green beer-bottle glass. I dusted it off, looked again
and saw it was a good-sized square-cut emerald, but I kept
an outward calm, and showed Lloyd my find without
comment. Making a brave effort to believe the unbelievable,

he asked me, 'What is it?' I told him. His attitude changed completely. All his doubts vanished. He resumed work with a will. A moment later he took something from the ground, examined it and passed it to me with a diffident 'I suppose this wouldn't be anything would it, sir?' It was a small ruby. Then, by merely stroking away the surface of the dry earth, we uncovered ruby after ruby. In half an hour we had found fifty.

*   *   *   *

Ogilvie, returning with the car to rescue us at lunchtime, asked politely, 'Any luck, sir?' The chance of a leg-pull was too good to miss. Glumly I replied, 'No, we've searched most assiduously ever since you left us and we've seen nothing that even begins to look like a diamond [pause]. All we can find is emeralds and rubies.' 'You're joking, sir!' he said. I handed him our collection of gems in a matchbox. Gulping down his astonishment he enthusiastically joined the treasure-hunt. Within a minute he dropped into my hand a little split pea which I took to be a blob of melted paint from the plane's fuselage. In almost the words which Lloyd had used about the first ruby, he asked, 'This isn't anything, sir, is it?' I dusted it, looked at it again and said, 'This, Ogilvie, is a cabuchon emerald. What I want is *diamonds!*' By this time we were a really gay team, laughing, excited and determined to extract from this hidden hoard at least one of the diamonds I now knew *must* be there. Finally I found it myself by the tedious process of concentrating on a square foot of soil pinching it up millimetre by millimetre and examining everything which was larger than a grain of soil and glittered.

*   *   *   *

On reaching my hotel with a haversack full of sand I confirmed the richness of the 'lode' by washing a few ounces of it in a saucer under a gentle stream from my bedroom tap until all the soluble matter had been carried away. In the small residue of clean hard sand which remained I found a few more diamonds and several rubies. It seemed probable, therefore, that the site from which the sample came was, in mining parlance, 'rich pay-dirt'.

My chief concern now was to bring the whole of that 'dirt' into Khartoum for safe custody and scientific sifting. The Provincial Governor, to whom I appealed, blessed my project and appointed to carry it out his municipal engineer, whose name was Watson! Two days later the mound, brought away in 1,600 linen sacks, was under lock and key. During the months which followed, 'my dear Watson' washed and sifted and re-sifted it. In the final count it yielded nearly all my clients' diamonds, thirty-two emeralds and 1,000 carats of Burmese rubies. In spite of world-wide publicity the owners of the emeralds and rubies were never traced. The Sudan Government in my case rejected the time-honoured legal principle 'findings is keepings'. On the other hand, Lloyd's treated me with such princely generosity (they gave me 25 per cent of the net salvage recovery) that I felt it within my means to buy back from that government my good fat square-cut emerald and a few dozen of the rubies. These gems, with some of the Lloyd's diamonds, adorn the saddle-cloth and neck-band of a disdainful Sudanese camel in gold and platinum which I designed as a present for my wife.

Twenty-Eight

AMY JOHNSON

AMY JOHNSON, daughter of a wealthy fish broker in Hull, grand-daughter of a former mayor of that city, made up her mind to live independently of the family purse. She began by selling ribbons in a London store, but sought a post with wider scope and asked advice from Vernon Wood who had known her since childhood. At that time he was facing a crisis. His secretary—Vi Roberts—had given long notice to leave on the excuse (in his view an idle one) that she wished to get married. Amy, who could type and write shorthand, came as a gift from heaven. After three months' training under Vi, Amy took over and did V.S.W.'s work with great efficiency.

But it soon was seen that she had a bee in her bonnet. She was crazy about aviation. At a small club she took flying lessons. Not content with that, she plunged into the practical side of aero engineering. To find extra money for these activities (as we learned much later) she toiled from dawn before, and until midnight after, her office hours. The truth of all this came out when she was asked why she always looked exhausted and why her hands were so rough and grimed with oil. She then confessed that it was not her ambition to be a lawyer. It was to own a small plane—a de Havilland 'Moth'—and in it to be the first woman to fly solo from England to Australia. Papa Johnson's first reaction to this was that he wanted no part in helping his daughter to break her neck. But in the end, persuaded by V.S.W., he put up the necessary funds. The plane was bought and christened

'Jason'. This name did not, as many have thought, invite comparison between Amy's forthcoming voyage and that of Jason in search of the Golden Fleece. It was chosen as a delicate compliment to a generous father, 'Jason' being his firm's telegraphic address.

* * * *

Amy's triumphs and achievements as a pioneer aviatrice belong to history.[1] During World War II she was a member of Air Transport Auxiliary, a corps of 'ferry pilots' who flew planes from the factory to the Forces and vice versa. On January 5th, 1941, she had to take an aircraft from Blackpool, Lancashire, to Kidlington, Oxfordshire, which is some sixty-nine miles north-west of London. A blanket of fog gave good excuse, even good reason, for postponing the flight. But Amy said, 'I'll crack through and go over the top.' At 3.30 on that murky afternoon, in the Thames Estuary, when a choppy sea was running and visibility was cut down by a heavy drizzle, some of those on board H.M.S. *Haslemere* saw a parachutist descending from the clouds. A little later a plane dived into the waves and broke up. Several of the witnesses thought they subsequently saw two leather-helmeted airmen in the water. From the nearer of these came a cry, 'Hurry, please.' It was the voice of a woman, beyond doubt that of Amy Johnson. The second was silent, perhaps unconscious and on the point of drowning. Lieutenant-Commander Fletcher, R.N., O.C. *Haslemere*, dived overboard fully clothed to rescue this other victim. Amy drifted under the heaving stern of the *Haslemere* and disappeared. Her

1. Amy Johnson, C.B.E., B.A. (Econ.), was Associate Royal Aeronautical Society, Hon. Fellow Society of Engineers, Hon. Member Guild of Air Pilots, Elected Member Women's Engineering Society, Gold Medallist Society of Engineers 1931, Gold Medallist Royal Aero Club 1936, first woman to obtain ground engineer's licence, first woman to fly solo England–Australia (1930). She established two record flights, England–Cape Town and return, and three records London–Cape–London flight (1936). Joined Air Transport Auxiliary 1940—killed on this service January 5th, 1941.

Amy Johnson

The sketch by R. G.
Eves, R.A., of Sir
William Charles
Crocker (see p. 213)

The *Marie Celeste* as
she was found,
abandoned, from a
wood engraving by
Rudolph Ruzicka
(see Chapter 30)

body was never found. Lieutenant-Commander Fletcher, according to his crew, 'reached the second pilot, supported him for a short time and then began to swim back alone'. But the water was icy. He collapsed and died from cold and exposure.

*   *   *   *

From this story grew the rumour, painful to all who knew Amy's high sense of duty and honour, that she met her end while trying to smuggle an alien out of the country. The Johnson family asked me to find out what had really happened, firstly to scotch that false rumour and secondly so that we might have the facts on which the Probate Court would give us leave to presume Amy's death and to administer her estate.

*   *   *   *

There was unimpeachable evidence that when Amy left Blackpool she carried no passenger. Experts testified that the prevailing fog, very low, dense and widespread, would have prevented her from seeing the ground from any point on or near her way south. The irresistible conclusion was that, forced to fly blind and searching unsuccessfully for a clear patch through which a landmark might be picked up, she ran out of petrol. One may also assume that in this perilous situation Amy's concern was for the plane's fate with little for her own. She fully recognised the dangers inherent in her job. So far as intelligent planning would allow she eliminated them. Those which were left she faced with that cold flame of courage which conquers fear. Losing height or about to do so she had no choice but to bale out. Her personal luggage, as always on these delivery trips, was light. She had a canvas hold-all and a port-landing bag for pyjamas and toilet articles. There was nothing else to be salvaged. She kicked them overboard and jumped, hoping, of course, that luck might give her a soft field to fall in.

*   *   *   *

When Amy's plane hit the water one of its wings broke off and floated away. By one of those coincidences too far-fetched for fiction, this wing, identified by its markings, was picked up by a passing vessel whose master was an old friend of Amy's father. And a whaler lowered from another Navy ship, H.M.S. *Berkeley*, picked up the 'airman' to whose rescue Lieutenant-Commander Fletcher had gone. For over a year this tragic 'airman' lay in a corner of my City room. 'He' was Amy's round-topped and nearly airtight leather port-landing bag which in its close resemblance to a flying helmet misled all who saw it low in the water and took the life of a very gallant officer.

*   *   *   *

The affidavit in which I set out the scope and results of my researches persuaded the Probate Court to grant the 'presumption of death' we needed. But under war-time conditions when newsprint was scarce the story received only limited publicity. The truth as I have now told it may perhaps convince those who vaguely remember 'something about some alien or other' that Amy Johnson did not lose her life, wholly out of character while on an amorous and illegal adventure, but gave it in doing what she had always done— her duty.

Twenty-Nine

PIONEERING IN CRIME

THIS story starts on **March 2nd, 1937,** when a young man was taken on by Cable and Wireless Ltd. as a surgeon for one of their cable ships then about to sail. The company felt they were in luck to find at the last moment a man so well suited for the job, one in which there is small hope of using medical or surgical skill and where there is nothing to break the boredom of being isolated for months at anchor above a damaged cable. The years went by, marked only by the growing file of ship's health reports mailed home by the doctor in the ordinary course of routine. A Chinese carpenter had died and been buried at sea; a toe had been amputated after an accident. Apart from these events the doctor had nothing to tell beyond a tale of the ships' monotonous well-being.

After serving for six and a half years he was put ashore at Rio de Janeiro with duodenal ulcers. There he developed mental symptoms, but of so slight a character that he was allowed out from the clinic where he was receiving treatment to visit the city for a game of billiards or to make a little pocket money by teaching English. Under a kindly provision of our law the cost of his care and maintenance fell upon his employers, the ship-owners, and through them upon their marine underwriters. At this time (1948–9) it was difficult for anyone, without influence, to get a passage from South America to the United Kingdom. For a mental case it seemed well-nigh impossible. Steamship lines, able to pick and choose among desirables to fill their passenger space, were hardly likely to assume responsibility for carrying even the mildest of lunatics. Dr. Thomas (for that was the name by which he was known) might have been flown from Rio to board one of the Cable and Wireless ships homeward bound. But the patient vehemently refused to leave Rio for any destination whatever, least of all for England. He was more than content to stay where he was in a delightful climate, eating and sleeping and amusing himself to his entire satisfaction—gratis.

*   *   *   *

I was called in to help. Twelve years had gone by since Thomas's engagement and no one could say who he was or which of the sixteen Dr. William Thomases listed in the *Medical Directory* he had pretended to be when seeking the post. He was certainly none of them. His story of having formerly served as *locum-tenens* and as a ship's doctor was true. There had been nothing in his application for employment to create suspicion. But it now seemed clear that he was an impostor with an unknown background. When questioned about his past or his family he would fall dumb. When yarning to his fellow officers on board and later among his Rio chums he had spoken freely of his connections at home, of a sister married to a prosperous Glasgow pastry cook, of a famous veterinary professor with whose family he was on terms of close friendship, of his long-dead father, an erstwhile port officer from Kingston, Jamaica.

In the belief that these claims might be the streaks of truth with which a romancer often interlards his fictions I checked them all. The Glasgow police were co-operative. They interviewed every confectioner in their bailiwick without picking up the slightest clue. Enquiries in Jamaica ruled out the possibility of our 'Dr. Thomas' ever having had a parent there in any sphere of government service. What inspired either the Kingston or the Glasgow inventions I never knew. I had more success touching the tale of the veterinary professor. That gentleman was dead. His will had been proved by a solicitor of my acquaintance, who assured me that neither Thomas nor anyone else could be on terms of friendship with the deceased's immediate family. There was no such family.

Yet in Thomas's conversations the professor cropped up as surely as King Charles's head in Uncle Dick's Memorial. Why this obsession? Had Thomas ever been connected in any way with the Royal Veterinary College? I had managed to obtain a copy of his passport photograph. With its aid the college caretaker identified Thomas as a young man who long ago had called upon him occasionally, representing the Edenbridge concern from which the college bought live rabbits for laboratory use. At the rabbit farm I learned only this: Thomas had come to them in answer to an advertisement, had worked well and finally vanished, leaving no trace behind him. In all probability his stories with the Scottish and Jamaican settings were similarly unsubstantial.

*   *   *   *

In my client's files was a carbon copy of a letter in which Thomas was being told of a complaint made about his non-payment of a commission due to his 'medical agency'. When I had identified the agency concerned (then defunct) and traced one of its former owners I was disappointed to learn that of its records those which survived enemy action had been sent for salvage. Was it possible, I asked, that some interest would still remain in the papers relating to a man for whom a job had been found and who had not paid the agency's commission? It was possible. In the half-dozen documents which had escaped both bombing and pulping was an application form which 'Dr. William Wyllie Thomas' had completed and on the strength of which he had obtained the Cable and Wireless post. Thomas was, in fact, a rogue who had obtained that appointment by assuming the name and professional qualifications of a respectable practitioner

Q

whose signature he had forged for the purposes of his imposture.

*　　*　　*　　*

It was now easy to see why Thomas preferred the amenities of Rio de Janeiro to the fate he might expect to meet in England. So long as he could maintain the role of a sick mariner marooned abroad, so long would his employers, *via* the Consul, continue to pay for his keep. My sole duty was to stop that continuing outlay. If I could do this and at the same time bring the rascal home in custody so much the greater satisfaction. We swore out a warrant for the arrest of the pseudo 'William Wyllie' Thomas for forging the signature of the true one. The Director of Public Prosecutions was then asked to institute extradition proceedings. but his department knew that the extradition treaty formerly existing between our country and Brazil had been abrogated in 1913 (a fact not recorded in the usual reference books) and Thomas could not be extradited. I was stymied again.

*　　*　　*　　*

I had once rendered some professional service to a group of corporations owning, among other things, a line of steamships trading with South American ports. I took lunch with their chief secretary and told him the unfinished 'Dr. Thomas Story'. He was not only interested; he used his influence to such purpose that I was able to offer Thomas what seemed the unattainable—a passage home from Rio. The patient reacted violently. Sooner than embark on any ship he would, he declared, 'die fighting'. This was all I needed. The Foreign Office agreed that since Thomas had refused repatriation he was obviously no longer detained abroad as a sick seaman and that the liability of Cable and Wireless to pay for his keep had now ceased.

Although I thus achieved exactly what I had been asked to achieve I accepted my fees and marked my file 'dead' with regret, since the villain of the piece was still at large.

*   *   *   *

Two years later I was brought back into the affair by an old friend from an adjuster's firm in Paris. Post-war work for the Allies on the Continent had lifted him on to the staff of the Foreign Office in London. Inheriting the Thomas dossier and seeing my name in it he phoned me, off the record, to say that this man was still being maintained at government expense (no one quite knew why) and to ask me what could be done about it? We toyed with the idea that should Thomas become destitute the Brazilians would probably be not only willing but anxious to be rid of him as an undesirable alien. I do not pretend to know what steps, if any, were taken along those lines. It is, however, a fact that shortly afterwards Thomas was deported to Bermuda. Thence he was brought home by our Navy *en route* for prosecution.

It happened improbably Thomas's case was the first to come before a new Old Bailey judge, the late Mr. Commissioner Bass. Can it ever have happened before that a judge has been called upon to break his duck *qua* judge by the trial of a prisoner who *qua* prisoner was also in a real sense breaking his duck and making criminal history? Hundreds of men have gone to gaol for practising as doctors without being qualified. No one had ever been convicted of coupling with that offence the impersonation of an existing medico. Although the charge against Thomas was forgery, the gravamen of it was that the crime enabled him with no qualifications as a doctor to pass for one, to sign death certificates, to perform operations and to live at the expense of Cable and Wireless for thirteen years. Thomas's luck still held. He pleaded guilty, but enjoying the merciful treatment which it is said, of course playfully, a new judge must hand out to his first 'customer', he did not go to gaol at all. He agreed to submit himself to medical treatment and was *put on probation.* In other words he walked out into the City air a free man.

*   *   *   *

Coincidence had not quite finished with this case. Often while my enquiries were drawing their disheartening blanks I had discussed the matter, especially in its medical aspects, with one of my personal friends, a physician. He became registrar of a well-known London hospital. Into that establishment, eighteen months after his exit from the Old Bailey, Thomas was admitted suffering from acute asthma. And there shortly afterwards a heart attack killed him. He had refused to give any account of his family or to reveal his true name. He was buried, as he had lived, under his alias.

Thirty

MARIE CELESTE:

AN EXERCISE IN DETECTION

MARINE insurance losses rarely came my way. But chance led me to investigate one solely for amusement and I think it not out of place to tell the story here in this my penultimate chapter. As a preface I record that my maternal grandfather one night 'saw' a ghost, a woman in white, floating eerily through a village churchyard. He was terror-stricken. His mouth dried up, his hair stood on end. But he had great courage. He forced his trembling legs to carry him towards the spectre. It proved to be a big black cow with bold white markings. If by chance the cow had turned black end on to him and moved away behind the monuments this ghost story would have gone to swell the other established records of ghostly lore.

I relate this incident to show how a mystery may easily arise, and persist because the facts relevant to it are misread or misreported, or both. The case with which I am concerned —that of the *Marie Celeste*—is, I think, one of the best examples of how a simple story may retreat further and further from reality as the years roll on.

The commonly accepted version runs as follows: Long ago the *Dei Gratia*, crossing the Atlantic, encountered the *Marie Celeste* and flew signals which were unanswered. The master of the *Dei Gratia* decided to investigate. His men found (so the story goes) a strange state of affairs. The ship, un-damaged, had all sails set and not a rope or spar out of place. There were all the signs of peaceful occupation: work in the sewing machine, a cat asleep, a hot meal on the cabin table with cups of tea still warm and more food in the galley on the still-warm stove. Her boats were undisturbed and yet the whole ship's company had vanished! It is hard to understand now, more than ninety years after the event, how the world came to accept that distortion of the facts.[1]

The true story may be put quite shortly. The single-deck brigantine *Amazon* was built at Spencer's Island, Nova Scotia, in 1861 and registered as British. She subsequently went ashore on the United States coast. In 1868 she was sold as a wreck to an American who made extensive repairs and put her on the American Register under the new name of *Mary Celeste*. She was sold again and a few years later was torn down to her copper, rebuilt, and made a double-decker.

On November 7th, 1872, she sailed from New York for Genoa with a cargo of alcohol. Benjamin S. Briggs, a God-fearing New Englander, was her master and part owner. His wife and baby daughter, Sophia, were passengers. The first and second mates, and the crew of five, were all experienced men of good character. On December 4th, 1872, the *Dei Gratia*, bound from New York for the Mediterranean with petroleum, David R. Moorhouse, master, being then 600 miles from Portugal, sighted *Mary Celeste* headed westward under very short canvas, 'yawing some' and apparently in distress. Bringing up alongside and obtaining no response to a hail, Captain Moorhouse sent his mate across in a boat with a couple of men to see what was wrong.

What they found is in marked contrast to the story of popular belief. Instead of the legendary ship in full sail with not a spar or rope awry, they saw a bedraggled vessel with only a jib and foretopstaysail set, the main staysail hauled

1. The facts were garnered over years of patient research by a distinguished American marine underwriter, the late Charles Edey Fay. His book embodying them is published by the Atlantic Mutual Insurance Company under the title *Mary Celeste, the Odyssey of an Abandoned Ship*. In this he examined the growth of the legend and the many theories advanced for the abandonment. But he was concerned only with the facts. He did not offer any guesses. He kindly gave me a copy of his book and I gratefully acknowledge that it is the source to which, for the purposes of this story, I have looked for practically all the historical data.

down and lying loose, the lower fore-topsail hanging by the corners, the rigging in bad order and the upper fore-topsail and foresail gone—apparently blown away from the yards. There was water between decks, three and a half feet in the hold, most of it presumably shipped through the open fore-hatch and some down a hole by the galley hearth. The deck house was full to the coaming. In the sodden cabin was nothing resembling a meal, warm or otherwise. The galley stove, stone cold, had been washed out of place. There was no cat. The entire ship's company, apparently impelled by some dire apprehension, snatching up only the scantiest necessities, such as chronometer, sextant and provisions, had obviously rowed away from the *Mary Celeste* in the missing ship's boat. That these poor souls were subsequently drowned is a foregone conclusion.

The real mystery lay in the cause of that panic departure. The likeliest cause with such a cargo as alcohol was the threat of fire or explosion. No trace of either was seen when the vessel, brought into Gibraltar by her salvors, was examined by John Austin, the Crown Surveyor. Neither he nor other experts could offer any reason for the abandonment. Nor has any plausible explanation ever been offered by anybody since. Many people have deduced theories from the wrongly accepted facts. Thanks to their efforts the *Mary Celeste* mystery has become the *Marie Celeste* myth. The earliest of these myth-spinners was an elderly eccentric, F. Solly Flood. As Attorney General for Gibraltar he took a leading part in the local court proceedings when the witnesses were examined and the claims of the *Dei Gratia*, owners and crew, as salvors were assessed. His theory was that the *Mary Celeste*'s crew got at the cargo and, in a drunken frenzy, slew Captain and Mrs. Briggs and their infant daughter. There was nothing to support this. The sailors were of blameless character. None of the casks had been broached. On a decorative sword, a curio, which came from Briggs' cabin were some dark patches. Flood believed them to be blood-stains. Chemical analysis proved them to be merely citrate of iron. But Flood clung to his own theory and suppressed the analyst's certificate.

Two members of the *Mary Celeste*'s crew came from Utersum, a village on the Prussian island of Föhr. When the leader of that village wrote the American Consul in Gibraltar for news of them Flood reported he was 'almost convinced' the letter 'was dictated by or on behalf of some of the crew who had left the vessel conscious of having been guilty of a great crime and desirous to learn whether they could safely emerge from concealment', and claim the things which they had left behind them when escaping 'on board some vessel bound for North or South America or the West Indies'.

The Gibraltar survey of the *Mary Celeste* disclosed that on either side of the bow under the cathead and two or three feet above the water-line a narrow strip of about one and three-quarter inches wide and three-eighths of an inch deep and six or seven feet long had been removed recently 'apparently with a sharp cutting instrument' from the edge of an outer plank. The surveyor, although he had no doubt that the cuts had been made deliberately 'and not other-wise', could not account for this strange carpentry. But Mr. Flood could. The crew, he surmised, after killing Captain and Mrs. Briggs, the baby and the chief mate—'then damaged the bows of the Vessel with the view of giving it the appear-ance of having struck on rocks or suffered from a collision so as to induce the Master of any vessel which might pick them up if they saw her at some distance to think her not worth attempting to save'. As against this a Captain Shufeldt of the U.S. Navy, writing to the American Consul, said: 'The damage about the bows of the Brig appears to me to amount to nothing more than splinters made in the bending of the planks—which were afterwards forced off by the action of the sea, without hurting the ship nor by any possible chance, the result of any intention to do so.'

Twelve years later the American Consul at Gibraltar wrote of Flood, who was claiming from the *Mary Celeste*'s owners fees to which he had no right: 'He had always been considered an individual of very vivid imagination and to have survived to some extent at least the judicious application of his mental faculties.'

* * * *

The *Mary Celeste* story might have faded from public memory but for the novelist Arthur Conan Doyle. Under the title *J. Kabakuk Jephson's Statement*, he wrote, anonymously, in the *Cornhill Magazine* for January 1884, an account of the tragedy in the words of a supposed survivor, Jephson himself.

Although he adopted the error made by *Lloyd's List* and called the *Mary Celeste* the *Marie Celeste*, thus fixing this more euphonious name firmly to the legend, he gave the name of the salving ship correctly as *Dei Gratia*. He set forth Jephson's statement without any hint to his readers that it was fiction.

The narrator, voyaging on the *Marie Celeste* for his health, tells of a villainous quadroon, Septimus Goring, who took passage at the last moment with a 'little darkie servant'. Two of the white crew failed to report for duty. Their places were taken by two Negroes, who with Goring's connivance stood handy on the quay. Things grew more and more sinister as the voyage proceeded. The captain's wife and child vanished. The captain died: apparently a suicide. In fact Goring, a homicidal maniac, out to kill all whites, had murdered the three of them. He diverted the *Marie Celeste* to a spot 'near the unexplored country which skirts the Great Sahara'. There the ship's company, with Jephson the only white member left, went ashore and met an isolated tribe of which Goring had planned to become the chief.

The tribe's idol was a sculptured deity lacking one ear. It chanced that an aged Negress some years before had given the missing ear to Jephson as a potent charm. He habitually carried it around with him as one might carry a holed coin, for luck. The restoration of this sacred fragment to the tribe

R

not only saved Jephson's life at the hands of the savages but earned from them a veneration so deep as to threaten Goring's own claim to the tribal throne. In fear of this rivalry Goring furthered the escape of Jephson, who lived to tell his story years later through the mouth of Conan Doyle.

It seems surprising that this yarn was taken anywhere as anything but fiction. Yet the American Consul in Gibraltar reported it to his home government so that they might 'ascertain whether there be the least suspicion of truth in any portion of what is stated'.

* * * *

Conan Doyle's lead was followed by other writers. Most of them thought any solution must explain the ship under full sail, the boats at davits, the half-eaten meal and some at least of the other traditional but fictitious elements. One story was of a monstrous octopus rising from the deep and exploring with its tentacles the innermost recesses of the ship to extract and eat her company one by one! Others were that yellow fever exterminated all hands, that Riff pirates (not known to operate in those waters) carried them into captivity, that while becalmed they had been press-ganged to fill vacancies in the crew of another ship. Lastly it was mooted that the abandonment was staged as an insurance fraud. Marine insurance swindlers over-insure and scuttle. The *Mary Celeste* and her cargo and freight were covered for reasonable commercial figures. She was worth to the owners more in being than as a claim on underwriters.

It is almost common form that when a vessel out of sight of any other is inexplicably lost a 'survivor' turns up, years later, with his own account of what happened. Under scrutiny these accounts always prove to be untrue.

Twenty-three years after the S.S. *Waratah* had been sunk without trace John Noble announced that although not aboard her when she left Durban he was transferred to her later from the *Telemachus* in mid-ocean to act as chief stoker.

In fact the *Telemachus* and the *Waratah* at that time were some thousands of miles apart. Having reached the shore when the *Waratah* capsized, he speeded to Cape Town, where he and his story were derided. So he took ship on the *Themistocles* (which was not built until two years later) and spoke no more of his escape until it may be supposed age had strengthened his imagination at the expense of his memory.

The *Mary Celeste* produced among other 'survivors', one named Abel Fosdyk. His story appeared in the *Strand Magazine* for November 1913. As the *Mary Celeste*'s cook and steward he tells of the terrible weather which the ship encountered. Under constant strain and almost without sleep for a month, Captain Briggs suffers a nervous breakdown. And a further trial awaits him. While at the wheel on one of the calm days which follow the storm he is horrified to see his adored baby standing balanced well out on the bowsprit 'without holding on to anything'. Fosdyk snatches her to safety, but Briggs, almost demented, slaps her savagely. And then by way of amends for this harshness he has the carpenter 'fit up a little barricade by the bowsprit which should be safe for the child to sit on in fine weather'. This structure hoisted on the bows is known as 'baby's quarter-deck'. Sophia sits on it and croons little songs. Or as though on watch she struts up and down and calls out, 'Ship on the port bow!' There comes a day of flat calm. The captain, now obviously out of his mind, insists on showing that he can swim round the ship fully clothed in five minutes. Two of the crew, to comfort the distressed Mrs. Briggs, swim with him. Two more join them just for the fun of it. All the rest of the ship's company—including Mrs. Briggs and Sophia—crowd on to 'baby's quarter-deck' to watch the swimmers. Under their weight it gives way, they fall into the sea and all but Fosdyk are drowned. *The Strand* in a footnote quotes the Gibraltar survey report. 'It appears that both bows of the derelict had been recently cut by a sharp instrument', and asks: 'Can these marks have been left by the stays used to support the platform?' Abel survives by drifting ashore on 'baby's quarter-deck', which is providentially seaworthy.

The yarn abounds in absurdities. If the author, whoever he was, had seen the Gibraltar court record he would have known that the *Mary Celeste* sailed not as he puts it in 'the early autumn' but on November 7th. Nor would he have made her voyage up to the abandonment (actually eighteen days) last a couple of months. Above all, he would have known that Baby Sophia was far too young to fill the role he gives her. She had only just turned two. The shades of Baron Munchausen and Louis de Rougemont might well hail Abel Fosdÿk as a brother artist in mendacity.

Oliver Deveau, the mate of the *Dei Gratia*, who with the help of only two other men sailed the derelict *Mary Celeste* 600 miles to safety, gave evidence before the Gibraltar Admiralty Court. He said (as everyone confirmed): 'There was no appearance of damage by fire nor any appearance of fire or smoke in any part of the ship.' He added: 'The only explanation of the abandonment which I can give is that there was a panic from the belief that the vessel had more water in her than she had as afterwards proved.' But Captain Briggs knew that the barrels of alcohol which filled his hold to capacity would leave little space for anything else. Three and a half feet of sea-water swilling round those barrels would have meant very little to him, certainly not enough to cause alarm. In fact, Deveau, using only one pump, had the hold dry in a few hours. No; it must have been some more deadly threat which impelled Captain Briggs to put off with his wife and child and the crew in the ship's boat rather than to remain aboard. If he did this in the forenoon of November 25th, 1872 (as may be assumed from the last log entry— noting a landfall at 8 a.m.), the weather conditions then prevailing probably helped him to make his decision.

According to meteorological records the sea was then comparatively calm. That the cabin skylight had been left open tends to confirm this. That the sailors left their personal belongings, even their tobacco pipes, behind shows the haste of their departure. The navigating instruments were missing, no doubt taken by Briggs lest he should be unable to regain his ship. If he had no hope of saving the *Mary Celeste* he would have carried away her log and the ship's papers. This he did not do. The conditions noted by the salvors when they boarded the vessel favour the view that the main-peak halyard, a stout rope 300 feet long, being instantly available, had been used as a tow-line. Riding in their boat at the end of this Captain Briggs and his party could have felt reasonably safe while awaiting developments. Alas! after the calm in which the small boat (sixteen to twenty feet long with only nine to twelve inches of free-board) first lay off there came a sudden wind of gale force. Exactly what happened then must always remain a matter of conjecture. The salvors found the main-peak halyard 'broke and gone'. If this rope was the tow-line it is likely that when the *Mary Celeste* plunged forward the line, in spite of its strength, gave under the sudden strain. Or the bend coupling the line to the boat's painter may have come apart. The boat may have been drawn under the waves before the tow-line parted or it may have been overwhelmed afterwards—no one can say. That ultimately the boat and her passengers went down seems to be beyond dispute. No trace of it was ever found. Dismissing all the mythical solutions in which the *Mary Celeste* mystery has wrapped itself, one still faces the real mystery. 'What led to the abandonment?' All reputable investigators have leaned to the idea that what drove all hands to take to the boat in the open was an explosion in the hold and the fear of another and more destructive one to follow. Against this theory, however, it has been pointed out that the most searching examinations which were made, first by the marine surveyor and an expert diver while the vessel was at Gibraltar, and later by others when the cargo was discharged at Genoa, failed to reveal the slightest signs of any such happenings.

*　　*　　*　　*

The *Mary Celeste*'s cargo, alcohol in 1,700 barrels, was highly volatile. Exposed to varying temperatures and the ship's motion it inevitably 'leaked' or vaporised during the voyage. The loss in this way of a quantity—the equivalent of nine barrels between New York and Genoa—was accepted by the consignees as normal.

A mixture of air and the vapour of alcohol, such as the *Mary Celeste* carried (specific gravity 0·815), is explosive when the alcohol vapour represents not less than 3 per cent and not more than 14 per cent by weight. Beyond those limits at either end the mixture will not fire. If one spills alcohol on the floor of a room one may get just above it a fairly deep layer of explosive mixture, and above that again a layer so weak in vapour as to be safe. If the dangerous layer be ignited the force of its explosion will depend upon the volume of the charge and upon the proportions in which that charge is mixed. Towards the upper and lower limits of explosibility, where the mixture is on the verge of having too much or too little alcohol vapour, the explosion may be quite mild. But a mixture well within those limits may release immense power, enough to send a ship sky-high. Captain Briggs was, of course, alive to this and to the need for opening hatches occasionally to give full ventilation. If heavy weather had prevented him from doing so he may well have grown acutely apprehensive. There was, had he known it, good cause for such uneasiness. In fact he was navigating a potential bomb.

Above the hold was the galley where the ship's cooking was done. Connecting the galley with the hold was the aperture which surveyor Austin found 'in the deck near the hearth'. This he and his fellow inspectors regarded as no more than one of the routes by which sea-water, invading the galley, had drained away. Its resemblance to the touch-hole of a cannon escaped notice. It was, however, highly probable that alcohol vapour creeping up through it would sooner or later be lit by the flames or a cinder from the stove and flash back to the lethal cargo below. In my view this is what happened. The resulting detonation was sufficiently alarming to persuade Captain Briggs that worse was to come. That he should ride astern in the ship's boat at a safe distance either for the further explosion or until ventilation through the hatch should make it safe for him to return was logical and prudent.

*　　*　　*　　*

The planks forming the hull of the *Mary Celeste* did not overlap. They were laid smoothly edge to edge. The outer fibres of the planks, which were bent to take the curve of the bows, would be under continuous strain. Normally those fibres, if the timber was sound and had been skilfully worked, would be tough enough to stand that strain without splintering off. But they would, of course, splinter if they should be strained further and too far. They would then present externally the appearance which Captain Shufeldt so confidently and rightly saw as 'splinters made in the bending of the planks'. I do not doubt that the agency which developed those splinters around which so much mystery has arisen was an eccentric explosion in the hold. It happened to deliver its main punch well forward and three feet above the water-line where the fibres of the bowed planks, already under stress, could not absorb such a powerful blow without cracking.

*　　*　　*　　*

How is it that the Gibraltar team failed to link the splintered bows with an explosion in the hold? The answer is a simple one. The first petroleum well in U.S.A. was drilled in 1859, yet even before 1872 ships carrying that spirit had been known to blow up. Such casualties involved no mystery. Eye-witnesses survived to describe them. The resulting marks of burning and other havoc were plain for all to see. With those events in mind the examiners of the *Mary Celeste* concluded that since her hold showed no such marks, no explosion could have taken place there.

There is, however, a difference between an explosion of petroleum and an explosion of alcohol. When a petroleum-air mixture explodes it generates carbon and leaves ample signs around in the form of soot. Alcohol contains oxygen and burns with a non-luminous flame. Its explosion rarely leaves the smoky signs of burning for which the *Mary Celeste* inspectors sought in vain. Who could blame them? They reached their verdict upon 'circumstantial' evidence so clear that it has stood unchallenged for ninety years. Many an accused has been hanged on circumstantial evidence no stronger.

Thirty-One

CURTAIN

MY WIFE and I were never apart except during the wars or when business abroad forced short and most unwelcome separations upon us. On May 20th, 1953, after only a few weeks' illness, her heart failed and she died peacefully in her sleep. This left me dumb with sorrow, loneliness and self-pity.

*   *   *   *

My good friend the late Major Edmund Howard, to whom I was Hunt Secretary during the old Drag days, mercifully offered me a voyage round the world as his guest. Shortly after my wife's death I was elected President of the Law Society. Custom decreed that the society's provincial meeting must begin with a lengthy presidential address. Working at this oratorical chore on shipboard, seeing new places and new people, gave me just the anodyne I needed. I returned to face the future in good heart.

*   *   *   *

Scarborough, the scene of the provincial meeting that year, saw a novel experiment. For the first time in legal history we staged a Business Machinery Exhibition. Impressive quantities of time- and labour-saving devices were bought by our members upon whom the general public and the gratified exhibitors had hitherto looked as old-timers impervious to new ideas.

Apart from that one innovation my presidential life trod the usual path, mainly smooth but with rough patches here and there. To speak with the voice of 18,000 colleagues is a flattering duty. It is, alas, also a fattening one, since much of the speaking is done at feasts laid on by learned and hospitable societies scattered throughout our land. And I like good food.

Of the routine duties, presiding in Council, sitting in on our own multifarious sub-committees or on those of bodies with whom we shared common interests, serving on or receiving deputations, acting as whipping boy when things went wrong and offended the mighty, few were dreary, most were lively and all had to be met with an even temper.

I talked a lot about institutions who by wide advertising (legitimate 'touting') oust the family solicitor and secure appointments as executors and trustees; I wished the Law Society to run an advertising campaign emphasising that a client can die in peace when he knows that his affairs will pass into the hands of his old and trusted solicitor and not into those of a corporation running remote and robot-like on a percentage basis. And I pleaded that we might add to our staff a trained public-relations officer who would present to the world solicitors in their true image as good friends, wise counsellors and courteous adversaries. If these two bees buzzed in my bonnet to no immediate effect they did no harm.[1]

There is solace for the President in Carey Street, a name which rings uneasily in the ears of most of us. It means the Bankruptcy Court. But at the solvent end of Carey Street stands No. 60, a perfectly preserved early eighteenth-century mansion. There amid period pieces, waited upon hand and foot by a married couple (the Thomases, to whom a long line of Presidents owe so much), the reigning President lives in

1. Mr. Herbert M. Lloyd, solicitor and member of the Society of Public Relations Officers was appointed in 1957. His successor, Mr. Forsyth Ballantyne, similarly qualified, heads a well-staffed department with the backing of substantial finance.

state. And there protocol directs that he shall entertain, at easy-going lunches, newly appointed judges and other notables recently lifted to high office. Moreover, at his own cost in these unique surroundings he is privileged to lunch groups of his own particular friends. And when at times after a fourteen-hour day the presidential limousine has dropped me at No. 60 (perhaps to the sound of Big Ben striking midnight) what a comfort it was to be received on the doorstep by a sympathetic Thomas ready to do duty as valet (or, if the wilting presidential form suggested it, as butler) and to throw back the snowy sheets of that venerable but so inviting four-poster bed! In that pleasant milieu I felt one regret: it was that my father was no longer alive to look with me from No. 60's bedroom along Star Yard, across which, as a mischievous junior clerk, he had tossed lumps of coal from his window on to a resounding tin roof opposite solely for the purpose of startling passers-by.

My twelve months as President sped away as though they had been twelve weeks. They returned a splendid echo: the honour of knighthood conferred upon me by Her Majesty the Queen on January 1st, 1955.

*   *   *   *

This I know is the point at which these my legal memoirs should end. But I cannot resist the temptation to write, by way of epilogue, the tale of just one more case; a case not in itself of great moment but one which of all my cases had the happiest sequel. It arose in 1925 and concerned disputed values on a big burglary claim in California. I was acting for Lloyd's. The assured's Los Angeles lawyer, Frederick W. Williamson, saw me in London and we negotiated an amicable compromise. This meeting led to a close friendship between our two families. Fred and his wife Ruth would visit us when on holiday in Europe. My wife and I would visit them in their Californian home at San Marino where we ultimately entered the charmed circle occupied by Fred's and Ruth's relatives and convives. When during the early days of World War II Fred died from a sudden heart attack we in England grieved as we would have grieved for the loss of a brother. But in no sense did this calamity loosen the ties he had made. Nor did our home, Crockers', at Seal Chart, Kent, cease to be a regular port of call for our Californian friends 'doing Europe'.

*   *   *   *

When I stepped down from the presidential chair I was glad enough to be back in active practice again and found plenty to do. The last day of 1954 saw me in a B.O.A.C. plane *en route* for Australia *via* New York. This particular journey, made for the committee of Lloyd's and against time, gave me only one night's sleep on the ground, in a motel near San Francisco's airport. I took the opportunity of phoning Ruth with New Year's greetings. In response I received a cordial invitation to spend a few days with her coterie in San Marino on my way back. I promised to treat myself to an acceptance should my Australian mission go well. It did go well. I did so treat myself and found especial joy in meeting so many old friends again on their home ground. My next visit to California was made in November 1956 when Ruth and I were married.

*   *   *   *

I am very much alive to the fact that I have always been rewarded far beyond my deserts.

Index

ABBOTT, Barker Robert (T. E. Crocker's clerk), 23–6
'Agents' in personal injuries claims cases, 74
Alexander, Herbert, and the Histon case, 32–4
Alfred Alton, Ltd., and the fire frauds, 130, 132–4
Allan, Detective-Inspector, and the fire frauds, 156
Alverstone, Lord (Lord Chief Justice), and the Histon trial, 34
'Ambulance-chasing' organisations, 92
Anarchist Club (Jubilee Street, Whitechapel), 36, 45, 47
Anarchist groups in London's East End, 35 ff.
Antecedents, parentage, early life of author, 13 ff.
Army days (World War I), 87–8
Art Publishers (Accrington) Ltd., and the fire frauds, 142 ff.
Atkinson, Sir Edward (Director of Public Prosecutions), 154

BALL, J. Loughborough (insurance claims adjuster), 122, 127, 132, 141 158, 168, 169; sentenced, 170; claims miscarriage of justice, 176–7
Ball, Sir Joseph, 220
Baxter, J. W. (veterinary surgeon), and insurance cases, 66–7
'Beck': see Beckley, Florence G.
Beckley, Florence G. ('Beck'), 29, 63, 76, 87, 88, 89, 171–3
Bentley, Police Sergeant (Houndsditch murder victim), 38
Bergolz, Felix, and the Poland Street fire insurance fraud, 116, 135, 158; sentenced, 170
Birkett, Norman, and the fire frauds, 167, 168, 170
Black Market investigations (in World War II), 219–20
Blackmail: see 'Mr. A.' case
'Bob': see Whiting, Robert
Borley Rectory fire fraud case, 199–205
Bowman, Bernard, and the fire frauds, 130, 132, 158; sentenced, 170

Brezinski, Fred, and Willy Clarkson's will, 190, 192, 193
Bryant, Police Sergeant, and the Houndsditch murders, 38
Buckle, Colonel Cuthbert, and the Barley Rectory fire frauds, 203, 205
Budget leakage case, 206–13
Burglary, legal definition of, 58
Burt, Chief Inspector Leonard, and W. C. Hobbs, 194–6
Bussell, Francis R. (of Lloyd's), 57–9, 68, 87
Butt, Sir Alfred, and the budget leak, 208–12 passim
Byrne, Lawrence J. (later Mr. Justice), 154 n.

CAMPBELL, William Charles (of Lloyd's; author's cousin-in-law), 56–7, 59–61, 87
'Cappa': see Capsoni, Camillo
Capsoni, Camillo ('Cappa'), and the fire frauds, 116, 126 ff., 146–52, 167, 177
Capsoni, Mrs. (wife of Camillo Capsoni), 125–9, 136, 147, 149–50, 167
Cassels, James D. (defence counsel, Fox murder case), 110
Central Criminal Court: see Old Bailey
Central Criminal Court Brotherhood, 25
Choate (police officer; Houndsditch murder victim), 38–9
Christopher Brothers and the fire frauds, 119, 120, 137–8
Churchill, Winston, and the battle of Sidney Street, 41; appoints author for 'subversive activities' investigations, 220
Clarkson, Willy, King Edward VII and, 179; his fraudulent fire claim, and the forged will, 178 ff.; death, 188
Clements, A. J. (litigation clerk), 86, 88
Cockney rhyming slang, 16
Collins, Michael (Irish Free State leader), 99, 100
Cook, Joseph Augustus (accountant), 141, 142, 160–1
Cope, Victor Ewart, and the fire frauds, 138, 139, 158; sentenced, 170

Cornhill Insurance Co. and the Sidney Fox murder case, 103, 104
Cornock, and the fire frauds, 113 ff., 167
Costers, 16–17
'Cramming' for law examinations, 29–30
Crocker, Archibald (brother of author), 20, 21–2, 28–9, 30, 62
Crocker, Jack (author's uncle), 63
Crocker, Mrs. Thomas (author's mother), 14, 17, 63
Crocker, Thomas Edward (author's father), 14 ff., 62
Crocker, Tom (author's grandfather), 13–14
Crocker, Walter (author's younger brother), 63, 76–8, 89, 100, 101, 216

DANCEY, A. H., and the budget leak, 206–7
Darling, Mr. Justice, 67, 72
Dearden, Dr. Harold: his praise for Florence Beckley, 172
'Death and spare parts' policies ('K' policies), 78–9
Detective work, recipe for success in, 65
Diamonds: author's search for, after loss from crashed plane, 221–34
Director of Public Prosecutions, functions of, 154
Disguises and impersonations in detective work, 179–80
Dummett, R. E. (Bow Street magistrate), 155, 159–60

EDWARD VII, King, and Willy Clarkson, 179
'E.L.' work: see employers' liability claims
Emmens, W. J. (staff investigator), 91, 92, 104, 105
Employers' liability claims, 73; in World War I, 80–1
Eves, Harold, and the budget leak, 210, 213
Eves, R. G. (portrait painter), 210, 213

FILM PRODUCER'S INSURANCE POLICY, ingenious re-wording of, 69
Fire insurance frauds, 84, 94–6, 113–205
Fleeson, Marcus (claims adjuster), and the fire frauds, 173–4
Fox (Sidney Fox) murder case, 102–12
'Fritz' (Gardstein's aide) and the Houndsditch murders, 39, 40, 41, 45, 46

'GARDSTEIN' and the Houndsditch murders, 36 ff. passim
German battleships' hit-and-run raids (1914), 81
Gershon, Mrs. Betty (landlady of Sidney Street 'besieged' house), 40
Gibson and Weldon (law coaches), 29

Gilbert, Harold, and the fire frauds, 137
Glen, Richard & Co. (silk merchants), and the fire frauds, 136–7
Goodrich, Harry (staff investigator), and the Fox murder case, 104, 105, 106
Gould, Harry (salvage buyer), and the fire frauds, 120, 129, 130, 140, 153, 164, 167; sentenced, 170; and Loughborough Ball, 176–7
Gregson, Captain William, and the Borley Rectory fire fraud, 200, 203–4
Gurrin, G. F. (handwriting expert), 198
'G. Y.': see Yandell, George

HAMBROOK, Chief Inspector Walter, and the Fox murder case, 107
Handley-Page, Frederick, 86
Hari-Singh (Maharajah of Kashmir): see 'Mr. A.' case
Harris, David (brother of Leopold Harris), 127–8, 144, 158; sentenced, 170
Harris, Ernest Albert (clerk to T. E. Crocker), 17–18, 20–1
Harris, Leopold ('The Prince'), and the fire frauds, 95–6, 120, 122, 123, 127 ff. passim; sentenced, 170; helps author with fraud investigations from prison, 172 ff.; see also 'Prince, the'
Harris & Co. (assessors) and the fire frauds, 75, 94; 156: see also Harris, Leopold
Hartley Cooper & Co. (of Lloyd's), 56–7, 60
Hastings, Sir Patrick, 191
Hawkins, R. E. (claims inspector Ocean Accident ·Corporation), and the Fox murder case, 104
Haycock, C. J. (Margate Chief Constable), and the Fox murder case, 106, 107
Heath, Cuthbert E. (inaugurator of Lloyd's non-marine market), 60
Herivel, William (silk trader), and the fire frauds, 123, 131, 136, 141, 158; sentenced, 170
Histon, Honora (Histon case victim), 32–4
Histon murder case, 32–4
Hobbs, William Cooper, 92–3, 183 ff.; sentenced, 198
Houndsditch murders, the, 35–48
Howard, Major Edmund, author's world trip with, 257
Humphreys, Mr. Justice, 171, 176

INSURANCE BUSINESS, beginnings of, 49 ff.
Insurance frauds, 65–7, 70: see also fire insurance frauds
Insurance policies, new phraseology for, 69

JARVIS, Louis, and the fire frauds, 125, 127, 128, 158, 169; sentenced, 170, 177

Johnson, Amy: vindication of the circumstances of her last flight, 235–8

'Josef' (Gardstein's aide) and the Houndsditch murders, 39, 41, 46

Juries and Motor insurance claims, 72–3

'KIDNEY, the' (Lloyd's employee), 50

'Knock for knock' tactics (vehicle insurance), 73

Kosher-Bates, A. C., and the budget leak, 207–12 passim

Kyffin, J. B., and Municipal Insurance Ltd., 68–9

LAW FINAL, author postpones his, owing to business pressures, 62

Law Reform (Contributory Negligence Act, 1945), 82 n.

Law Society, Author elected to council, 214 ff.; and becomes President, 257

Levi, Joe, and the Houndsditch murders, 42, 46

Lloyd George, David, and compensation for war injuries, 82

Lloyd's, history of, 49–52; beginnings of non-marine business, 55 ff.

Loe, 'Sammy' (managing clerk), 90, 94

London United Male and Female Costermongers and Street Sellers Benefit and Protection Society, 15–16

Loss adjusters (insurance officials), function of, 70–1, 73

MACCULLUM BROTHERS (personal injury claims agents), 74–5

Mackie, Edward (solicitor), 86–90 passim

Mansfield, W. W. (handwriting expert), 198

Marie Celeste mystery; the theories and the circumstantial evidence, 245–56

Marks, Bernard, and the fire frauds, 141, 158; sentenced, 170

Marshall, Keith (underwriter), and the 'K' policies, 78–9

Marshall, 'Timmie' (underwriter), and the Riots and Civil Commotion policies (Ireland), 97–8

Martin, Police Constable, and the Houndsditch murders, 38

'Marx' (Gardstein's aide) and the Houndsditch murders, 46

Matheson, Jimmie (of Lloyds), 208, 209, 212

Mathews, George Simpkins, and the fire-raisers, 113 ff., 155, 167

Matthews Wrightson & Co. (of Lloyd's), 61

Metro Radio Ltd., and the fire frauds, 138, 140

Miles, Captain Brynmar (Chief of London Salvage Corps), and the fire frauds, 173–6

Mnemonics as author's aide-memoire in law studies, 29–30

Motor car insurance cases, 52–5, 65 ff., 71–3

Motoring, early days of, 64–5

'Mr. A.' case (blackmail), 185–7

Municipal Mutual Insurance Ltd., 68–9

Murder cases, 32–48, 102–12

NAME-PLATE, author's design for a, 63.

National Omnibus Company, 91

Neighbour, Harry (staff investigator), and the fire frauds, 118, 156, 157

Niemeyer, Otto, and insurance claims over the Irish 'Troubles', 100

Nops, Sir Wilfred ('Clerk' of the Central Criminal Court), 163–4

OCEAN ACCIDENT CORPORATION, and the Fox murder case, 104

O'Connor, Edmond, and Willy Clarkson's will, 189–97 passim; sentenced, 198

O'Connor, General Rory, and the Irish rebellion (1922), 99

Office organisation in the 19th century, 19–22

Old Bailey, the (Central Criminal Court), history of, 162–3; first murder trial in new building, 34; longest trial ever held in, 170

Oliver, Roland (barrister), 153–4, 167, 173

Otter-Barry, W. W. (general manager, Sun office), and the fire frauds, 117–18

Owen, Messrs. William (assessors), 137

PARMOOR, Lord, and the Irish 'Troubles' insurance claims, 99–100

Partnership with provincial solicitors, 76

Penney, William (claims investigator), 145–6

'Peter the Painter', 36, 42, 44–5, 46–8

Piatkow, Peter (alias Schtern): see 'Peter the Painter'

Pilenas, Casimir, and 'Peter the Painter', 45–8

Pilenas, Peter: see 'Peter the Painter'

Piper, Police Constable, and the Houndsditch murders, 38

'Pooling' tactics (vehicle insurance), 73

Price, Harry, and the Borley Rectory 'hauntings', 199–205

Priest, Harry Christopher, and the fire frauds, 113 ff., 135, 137, 156, 158; sentenced, 170

'Prince, the' (alias of Leopold Harris), 115, 116: see also Harris, Leopold

Psychical research and 'hauntings', 199–205 passim

Publicity, author's dislike of, 111–12
Punch, author's first press notice appears in, 67

'R. & C.C.' POLICIES: *see* 'Riots and Civil Commotion'
Richard Glen & Co. (silk merchants) and the fire frauds, 136–7
Riley, Alan, 119–23
Riley, Leonard (Priest's partner), and the fire frauds, 123, 137, 144, 145, 158; sentenced, 170
'Riots and Civil Commotion' policies, and the 'Troubles' in Ireland, 96–101
'R. O.': *see* Oliver, Roland
Roberts, Violet (employee), 78, 81, 87
Robins, Davies & Co. (assessors), 120, 122
Robinson, Teddy (W. C. Hobbs' blackmail victim), 184
Rowlatt, Mr. Justice, and the Fox murder case, 107, 109
Roylance, Robert Walker (of Lloyd's), 117–18

SAMUELS, Herbert D. (barrister), 154 *n*
'Sausage Machine', the (author's office system), 80–1
Scanlan, Dr., and the Houndsditch murders, 39–40
'Sidney Street, the Battle of', 40–4
Sinton, John (Newcastle-upon-Tyne solicitor), author's limited partnership with, 76
Solicitors, qualities needed for success, 80; call-up position of in World War I, 83
Spilsbury, Sir Bernard, and the Fox murder case, 107; and Willy Clarkson's death, 188
'Spy Mania' in World War I, 83
Stewart, Walter (barrister), and the Histon trial, 34
Street-traders' fraudulent insurance claims, 65
Strongman (police officer) and the Houndsditch murders, 38
Swinton, Lord, 220

TAPSELL, Police Sergeant, and W. C. Hobbs, 194–5
'Tariff offices' (insurance), 67
Thomas, J. H., and the budget leakage case, 209–12
'Thomas, Dr. William', impersonation case, 239–56
Thompson, Tommy (telephonist-receptionist), 152–6

Thorpe, Sergeant (later Superintendent) Arthur (head of Fraud Squad), 157
Toplis and Harding, Messrs. (assessors), 81, 137
Trassjonski, Sara (Russian anarchist immigrant), and the Houndsditch murders, 36, 39, 44
Tucker (police officer; Houndsditch murders victim), 38

UMBERTO I, King of Italy, assassination of, 18
Underwriting (Lloyd's), origins of, 49, 50

VASSILEVA, Nina (Russian anarchist immigrant), and the Houndsditch murders, 35–44 *passim*

'WAR RISKS POLICIES' (insurance; World War I), 84
Westwood, Walter E., and the fire frauds, 141, 158; sentenced, 170
Whitecombe, A. J. (of Lloyd's), 53–4, 55–6, 67
Whiting, Robert C. (employee; later partner), 78, 86, 89, 147–8, 149
William Owen, Messrs. (assessors), 137
'W. J.': *see* Emmens, W. J.
Wolfe, Ernest, and the fire frauds, 137, 158; sentenced, 170
Wolfe, Simon, and the fire frauds, 135, 137, 157, 158, 175; sentenced, 170
Wood, Vernon Spencer (Manchester solicitors), limited partnership and amalgamation with, 76, 101, 102
Woodhams (police officer), and the Houndsditch murders, 38
Workmen's Compensation Act, 82
World War I, effects on author's insurance cases business, 80–1; conscription introduced, 82; 'spy mania', 83; call-up and Army days, 86–8; postwar reunion dinner, 89
World War II, effects on legal business, 215–17; in the Home Guard, 219; adventures on way to Middle East detective assignment, 221 ff.: *see also* Black Market
Worship Street Police Court and T. E. Crocker's practice, 23–6

YANDELL, Chief Inspector (later Superintendent) George, 155, 156, 170, 173